# MORE
# TESTING
# TIMES

# BY MIKE BROOKE

*A Bucket of Sunshine: Life on a Cold War Canberra Squadron*

*Follow Me Through: The Ups and Downs of a RAF Flying Instructor*

*Trials and Errors: Experimental UK Test Flying in the 1970s*

*More Testing Times: Test Flying in the 1980s and '90s*

# MORE TESTING TIMES

## TEST FLYING IN THE 1980s AND '90s

MIKE BROOKE

The
History
Press

*For Linda*

*Cover illustrations. Front:* The author, flying Buccaneer XW 987, refuelling Dave Southwood's Jaguar FGR 1A fitted with an over-wing AIM-9 Sidewinder missile, during support for Operation Granby. (A&AEE (OGL)) *Back:* A&AEE Harvard IIB KF 183 over Stonehenge. (Peter March)

First published 2017

The History Press
The Mill, Brimscombe Port
Stroud, Gloucestershire, GL5 2QG
www.thehistorypress.co.uk

British Library Cataloguing in Publication Data.
A catalogue record for this book is available from the British Library.

ISBN 978 0 7509 6985 7

Typesetting and origination by The History Press
Printed and bound by CPI Group (UK) Ltd

# CONTENTS

# A DEDICATION

To Air Commodore David L. Bywater FRAeS FIMgt RAF (Ret.)

In planning this series of books I had hoped to ask the test pilot for whom I had worked during three tours of duty, Air Cdre David Bywater, to pen the foreword to this volume. Very sadly, especially for his family and everyone that knew him, David passed away on 24 September 2015, aged 78. I was honoured to be asked by his wife Shelagh to help officiate at his funeral and memorial service.

David Llewellyn Bywater was born on 16 July 1937 and was educated at the Liverpool Institute High School for Boys, where he was a keen rugby player and an excellent swimmer. He joined the Combined Cadet Force, won a flying scholarship and qualified for a private pilot's licence in the Miles Magister. He was awarded a scholarship to the RAF College Cranwell in April 1955 and graduated in 1958.

David was posted to RAF Gaydon to fly the Handley Page Victor Mark 1 with XV Squadron, which then moved to RAF Cottesmore. This was a busy time for these early V-Force squadrons, as the nuclear deterrent role was developing at a rapid rate to keep up with the growing Soviet threat. David showed his piloting and technical skills from the start and helped develop the scramble start procedures that were demonstrated at the Farnborough Air Show in 1959 and 1960. Meanwhile, he completed the Intermediate Captain's Course to qualify to fly in the left-hand seat.

Air Cdre David Bywater in test pilot mode.
(Courtesy of Shelagh Bywater)

In the spring of 1961, he returned to RAF Gaydon as a Victor captain and, over the next two and a half years, he and his crew flew more than 700 hours, gained the top Bomber Command rating of 'Select Star' and achieved a very creditable second place in a bombing and navigation competition against crews from all the RAF's V-Force squadrons.

In 1963 David was selected to attend the 1964 Empire Test Pilots' School (ETPS) course at Farnborough. From the course he was posted to B Squadron at A&AEE Boscombe Down, where he became re-acquainted with the Victor. He also flew the Vulcan for the first time and was able to compare the two V-bombers while flying release-to-service trials for the Terrain Following Radar.

After attending the RAF Staff College at Andover in 1969, David was posted to HQ RAF Germany as an Operational Plans Staff Officer. One of his major tasks was to plan the introduction of the Jaguar as a strike aircraft and the construction of hardened aircraft shelters on RAF bases in West Germany. In 1974 he returned to the UK to take up the post of Officer Commanding (OC) Flying at the Royal Aircraft Establishment, Farnborough, where – apart from managing all aspects of experimental flying – he was heavily involved with planning and managing the flying display for the Farnborough Air Show. After a staff tour at the Ministry of Defence (MOD), in 1981 David was promoted to group captain and returned to Boscombe Down as Superintendent of Flying. This was a busy time, particularly during the build-up to operations for the Falklands War, when emergency clearances were required for some unusual combinations of systems, weapons and aircraft. In 1985 David moved on to the RAF Staff College, Bracknell, as a group director, where he helped many young officers expand their knowledge and improve their career prospects. It was no surprise that his final RAF appointment would be to return to Boscombe Down as the Commandant, on promotion to air commodore. He retired from the RAF in 1992 after what can only be described as an extremely successful RAF career.

David's second, civilian, career began when he joined Marshall Aerospace of Cambridge as Airport and Flight Operations Director. Over the next ten years, he was responsible for major improvements to the airport, including the construction of a new ATC tower, installation of a radar instrument landing system and a modernised airfield lighting system. He also maintained his commercial pilot's licence together with a flying instructor's qualification and continued to fly company aircraft. He amassed a further 1,000 hours' flying time on a variety of civil and military aircraft types, bringing his total hours to more than 4,000 on 155 aircraft types; only such an enthusiastic test pilot could have achieved that.

David was a Fellow of the Royal Aeronautical Society, Fellow of the Institute of Management, Liveryman of the Guild of Air Pilots and Navigators, Vice President of the Aircraft Owners and Pilots Association and of the Royal International Air Tattoo, Honorary Member of both the Airport Operators Association and the Cambridge University Air Squadron, a member of the Society of Experimental Test Pilots and of The Air League, past Chairman of the XV Squadron Association, committee member of the No. 104 Cambridge Squadron of the Air Training Corps and Director of the RAF Charitable Trust. That very impressive list summarises David's major contribution and dedication to so many aspects of British aviation.

David Bywater was meticulous in all he did, whether it was planning and flying a sortie, managing major updates of operational facilities or checking on tides and currents when sailing, which was another of his passions. He was highly respected and admired by all who worked with him or were involved with him socially. He is survived by his wife Shelagh, whom he married in June 1960.

I first met the then Wg Cdr David Bywater, very briefly, while on a visit to Boscombe Down shortly before I joined the course at the Empire Test Pilots' School (ETPS) in 1975. When I graduated at the end of that year I went to the Royal Aircraft Establishment at Farnborough where he was OC Flying. During that tour I discovered what a first-class senior officer he was; he always had time for us junior guys and was ever ready to socialise with us, as was his wife, Shelagh.

Two years after the end of my tour at Farnborough I was posted to ETPS at Boscombe Down and the now group captain, David Bywater, was the Superintendent of Flying. We had both gone up a rank, but he was still a man who would listen and consider before deciding on action: qualities of a true test pilot. During that tour both David and Shelagh went out of their way to help, encourage and support my children and I when my marriage failed.

David finished his RAF career in a truly fitting appointment for a test pilot of his experience and quality as the Commandant at the Aeroplane and Armament Experimental Establishment at Boscombe Down – by then familiar territory for both of us. Yet again, and deservedly so, he had stayed two ranks above me and once more his measured wisdom and unflappable character made him an excellent leader and manager. Most of all, the solidity of his marriage and family life gave him a stable base. He was and still is an inspiration to me. I am very grateful to Shelagh, and David's family, for agreeing to me making this dedication; and to his brother-in-law, Air Cdre Norman Bonnar for helping me with its compilation.

# ACKNOWLEDGEMENTS

I cannot overemphasise the part played by my wife and soul mate Linda in getting this book to a state fit to publish. She has, now for the fourth time, been wonderfully supportive in reading, correcting, suggesting and criticising my writing. I cannot thank her enough.

Thanks are also due to many other erstwhile colleagues and helpers without whom this tome would not be so well illustrated or contain the right 'facts'; in particular Roger 'Dodge' Bailey, Peter 'Toggie' James and Rogers Smith for refreshing my flagging memory banks. To ex-RAE colleagues Tony Karavis, Phil Catling and Graham Rood for helping with illustrations; the latter two are very involved with the Farnborough Air Sciences Trust (FAST), which can be found at www.airsciences.org.uk. My thanks also to Tim Prince, of Royal International Air Tattoo fame, for connecting me with professional photographer Peter March, who has very kindly provided many of the photographs. Lastly my gratitude extends to all the wonderful, anonymous souls who put lots of relevant info on the internet!

My very sincere thanks also go to my good buddy and fellow test pilot Tom Morgenfeld for writing the foreword to this book. I have known Tom since we shared the experience of the ETPS course in 1975, where I know he particularly enjoyed flying the Canberra T4; we have remained good friends ever since. Tom went on from ETPS to become a test pilot for the US Navy and the USAF, the latter on still-classified projects. After retiring from Naval Aviation he worked for many years for Lockheed at their famous 'Skunk Works'. Tom flew the first flight of the second YF-22 prototype (pre-cursor to the F22 Raptor), many test flights in the F-117 Nighthawk stealth fighter, and he finished his career by flying the first flight of the F-35 Joint Strike Fighter, now known as the Lightning II. Tom is a past President of the Society of Experimental Test Pilots and finished his naval career as a captain in the US Naval Reserve. He once baulked at the media's use of the description 'legendary', but that is typical of the modest guy he is – I think the word applies in full.

Last, but by no means least on my list of folk to thank, is the team at The History Press without whom I might have had to publish this myself! Especially my commissioning editor, Amy Rigg, and her colleagues Chrissy McMorris and Andrew Latimer.

# FOREWORD

The email was short and straight to the point, just like the author himself. (Sorry Brookie, no pun intended … really!) It read, 'I'm getting close to finishing the writing of my latest book – *More Testing Times* – that covers the time of my RAF career from 1984–94, which included two flight-testing tours, and then continues to the very end of my flying in 2004. I would very much like it if you could write the Foreword.' Never being one to turn down a friend, especially one as close as Mike Brooke, I gave him a cheery, 'Wilco!'

Immediately thereafter it began to dawn on me that I had absolutely no idea of how to approach this humbling and important task! So, for all you literary folks out there, please accept my apology if this fails to meet your expected standards. For those more intent on getting to the meat of this fine book, I say, 'Good for you, this is all the Foreword you probably need.' Get on with your reading! For those somewhere in between, I'm reminded of the great Louis 'Satchmo' Armstrong's reply when asked how he came up with his music: 'I just blows what I feels.' If you have the time, please give me a second to toot what I feel about Mike and this excellent book.

I first met the cherubic Mike Brooke in January 1975, the day after we moved to England for test pilot training at ETPS. Instantly we became friends and have remained so ever since. Mike's effervescent personality, aviation savvy and piloting skills were appreciated as a rare gift by all, but it was his innate leadership that propelled him to become the de facto leader of our class. In addition to enduring the normal student struggles, Mike was the glue that held our diverse group together so closely, both professionally and socially. His spur-of-the-moment caricatures were loved by all. Indeed, his 'Diary and Line Book' recounting our course's tumultuous year, complete with those caricatures, photos, quotes and even movement orders, is worthy of independent publication in itself. It clearly illustrates what a vital asset Mike was to the entire class.

As his career progressed, Mike continued to use his gifts in ever more important postings. His uncanny intimacy with aeroplanes, coupled with his uncompromising sense of integrity made him a most successful test pilot. His easy-going yet strong leadership style made him a most successful officer. That he was named a Fellow of the Society of Experimental Test Pilots alone puts him at the top of the heap.

Here I must give you an idea about his character. I have one big debt that I owe in part to Mike, of which he may not even be aware. Simply through his example as a committed Christian, he encouraged me to rekindle my faith. For that I will be eternally (literally!) grateful.

Mike's fascinating aviation career has spanned everything from being a teenage Cold War warrior to being a world-class test pilot, and back to being an inspiration to young hopefuls on an Air Experience Flight. His résumé of aircraft flown reads like the index to *Jane's All the World's Aircraft*. Besides operational flying and testing, he's done everything from instructing to performing flight demonstrations to humanitarian flying. So go ahead, brew yourself a cuppa and settle in to read about the career of one of the finest gents ever to don RAF flight gear. I know you'll enjoy it.

Tom Morgenfeld
May 2016

# PROLOGUE

It's really dark outside the cockpit. As black as the ace of spades. In fact it's pretty dark in here too; just a soft greenish glow from the flight instruments illuminates my flying-suit legs and gloved hands. There are two of us, crammed cosily together, side by side, as our much-modified Hunter T7 skims along at 250ft above the undulating night-time English countryside at a speed of 420 knots (close to 500mph).

I can only see the ground ahead and around me because I have the latest generation of night-vision goggles attached to my helmet. I also have a large head-up display (HUD) right in front of me showing a moving image of the ground ahead in monochrome greens, overlaid by all the flight information that I need to fly the aircraft safely and efficiently.

I can manoeuvre over the hills and into the valleys, turn to change direction while maintaining the low altitude and get a clear sense of my speed and height as the scenery flashes by below us. It's not as easy as doing it by day, but it's not far off. The adrenalin helps keep the concentration level up and the navigation system keeps us on track towards our target.

It is April 1987 and it is ten years since I was doing this last, in the very same aircraft, Hunter T7 WV 383, of the same unit: the Experimental Flying Squadron at the Royal Aircraft Establishment (RAE) at Farnborough, Hampshire, in southern England. Ten years back we were just starting to experiment with what are known as electro-optical aids, to allow fast-jet military aircraft to fly covertly towards their targets, below radar, at night. Then we had a low-light television (LLTV) camera mounted in the Hunter's nose and a small TV screen set into the right-hand pilot's instrument panel. Comparatively speaking, it was all pretty crude; but it worked to a degree. We occasionally frightened ourselves but nobody died!

The problem with LLTV was that it needed some external light to enable it to present its images to the pilot. That minimum light level was defined as clear starlight – a night of overcast skies was no good. We had started, as in all test flying, cautiously and progressively, gradually lowering the heights and increasing the speeds, but when I left the RAE in 1978 there were still several problems to be solved before one could say that low-level high-speed night navigation and attack was feasible in all light levels.

In those intervening years, while I had been testing radar systems, teaching pilots the art and science of test flying and being guided into the realms of senior management and leadership, things had progressed. But now I was back at the sharp end of experimental flight-testing at Farnborough. However, I was no longer doing much of the flight-testing myself. My appointment as OC Flying meant that I was overseeing the flight-test programmes, as well as managing the increasingly scarce resources that allowed the Experimental Flying Squadron to achieve the results required by our rapidly modernising air force.

So how had I got here? By 1987 I had fully expected to be still doing 'penance' on a ground tour, behind a desk with little prospect of getting back into the esoteric and fascinating world of flight-testing. This book will take the story on from the point where I was first told, 'Brookie, you're grounded, but it will be good for your career.' Words that were new to me on both counts!

# PART 1
# PREPARATION

# 1 1984

As 1984 took over from its temporal predecessor the world was still locked in the throes of the war that had become known as 'Cold'. The two main protagonists of that war, the USA and the USSR, would carry out nuclear weapons tests throughout the year. Even France and China would join in with their own experimental explosions. Two right-wing politicians, Ronald Reagan and Margaret Thatcher, were working in concert to confront any expansionist ambitions of the Russian Bear. Both the USA and the USSR had active space programmes – the Space Shuttle and Soyuz projects respectively – and the USA was embarking on a missile-based self-protection scheme that would become known as 'Star Wars'. Another missile-based programme had matured sufficiently for them to be deployed to sites in Europe – the cruise missile. In 1984 the world was still an unsafe place and Europe was still the potential front line.

Twenty year earlier I had been despatched to that front line, where NATO forces were ranged against the forces of the Warsaw Pact. I was based in West Germany, flying the Canberra twin-jet bomber in the low-level strike/attack role; 'interdiction', we called it. We had nuclear weapons; we called them 'Buckets of Sunshine'. During the two decades that had passed since those days, the fundamental East–West stand-off had not changed. Many summits and treaties had come and gone but, like my parents' generation in 1939, we had no idea that the Cold War had only another five years to run.

The year 1984 had an ominous overtone for my age group thanks to the disturbing book written by George Orwell, published in 1949. His dark novel *Nineteen Eighty-Four* told a very sinister tale of a dystopian world after a nuclear war, set in a devastated land called 'Airstrip One', once known as Great Britain. Reading the book, as well as viewing the film and TV versions in the 1950s, had given people of my vintage an uneasiness about the arrival of that year, despite the fact that nuclear war had not yet happened and that democracy and not dictatorship still existed in our sceptred isle.

In January 1984 I had been serving in the RAF for twenty-two years, employed throughout that span as a pilot in a variety of roles and places. In all that time I had spent less than six months not flying – 'grounded' – while I recovered from a medical problem. But in late 1983 those in charge of stopping aircrew from having fun had found me out and earmarked me to be sent to the Advanced Staff Course at the RAF Staff College. That meant I was going to be prepared for senior leadership and management. Of course, at this point I had no idea what the future might bring.

My recent private life had become somewhat turbulent. My marriage of seventeen years had been dissolved and I had spent my last year on the staff of ETPS as a single parent. However, the silver lining was that during 1983 I had met, fallen in love with and proposed to a lovely lady called Linda. Our marriage was set for spring 1984. The only slightly darker cloud on my horizon in that year was that I would turn 40 years of age in April. This was a milestone that seemed have arrived far too quickly.

But 1984 would turn out to be much better than I could have imagined. As planned, I married Linda in March and we moved that very day into a brand-new, three-storey town house in central Oxford, which had sufficient room for our four children and us. As our relationship had blossomed during the previous year we had both felt drawn back to our childhood Christianity and we had started attending a local church regularly. We were, through the family of that church – St Ebbe's, Oxford – reintroduced to Jesus Christ. Over the first year of our marriage our faith grew and matured and has been a central part of our lives ever since.

In 1984 the RAF Staff College was located in an enclosed green oasis in the brick-clad environs of suburban Bracknell, in the Royal County of Berkshire. There I would spend almost a year as a student again, living in the Officers' Mess, and commuting to and from Oxford at the weekends. I was supposed to learn how to become a useful and knowledgeable member of the middle and senior leadership cadre of the RAF. There would be no flying and the only airborne activity I would see would be the airliners going in and out of London Heathrow airport, only a handful of miles to the east.

The Advanced Staff Course turned out not to be as dire as I had at first imagined. There were about ninety of us students from a couple of dozen nations. We were split first into three groups and then into syndicates of seven or eight. There were going to be three terms and we would therefore have three tutors, known at Bracknell as DS (Directing Staff). My first DS was Wg Cdr Ian Dick. Ian was a past leader of the RAF Aerobatic Team, the Red Arrows, and I had briefly flown with him as his instructor when he arrived at the Central Flying School to fly the Chipmunk, ahead of him taking command of a university air squadron. This route had been curtailed when he was diverted to take charge of the 'Arrows'.[1]

The staff course had a multitude of paper exercises, a great deal of writing, plenty of listening to distinguished speakers, lots of socialising and two periods when we mixed with the students and staff from the army and navy staff colleges for joint exercises.

There was also a European tour, which included a visit to Berlin. There we were able, in uniform, to visit East Berlin. Although it is difficult to imagine now, more than thirty years later, as a one-time 'Cold War Warrior' I had a palpable frisson of excitement, mixed with trepidation, as we passed through the Berlin Wall at Checkpoint Charlie on our way to a Soviet military museum inside East Berlin. The contrast with the western half of the city was immediately obvious. The roads were rougher and, apart from the smoky little cars called Trabants, traffic was lighter. The citizens' tenement living quarters were tall, grey and awfully drab. There was also a very noticeable lack of advertising hoardings, adding to the bleakness.

When we reached the museum we came face to face with Warsaw Pact soldiery. The enlisted men's uniform looked as dowdy as the rest of the place; the material was rough and they were what any decent guards regiment sergeant major would call 'a right shower'! I was so taken with looking at these chaps, many of whom were but spotty youths, that I missed seeing a sign that said '*Niet Fotografy*'. Hence about halfway through our visit I was hailed by one of the aforementioned khaki-clad young men who told me, in Russian, that I was breaking the rules. I didn't hear the mention of Lubyanka or the Gulag, but he did rip my camera from my grasp, open the back and pull the film out. Of course at this stage I had no idea why and began to get a bit indignant. This was not a good move. More spotty soldiers arrived, but one of my compatriots said that there had been a sign at the entrance banning photography, so I backed both *off* and *down*. I even tried a smile and lots of 'Sorry – sorry – didn't see the sign'. This seemed to placate the reds and I was left to put my camera back together. I know I brought it on myself but I had lots of other quite legitimate snaps on that film!

We also visited the Berlin Air Safety Control Centre. There, military officers from all four occupying powers – the UK, USA, France and the USSR –

---

1.  The full story is related in my book *Follow Me Through* (The History Press, 2013).

worked together to regulate all air traffic coming into Berlin. Aircraft coming to Berlin from the west used three established air corridors so that they could overfly East Germany safely. It was another glimpse into the effects of the Cold War. Something that I, twenty years earlier, sitting at a couple of minutes' readiness with a live nuclear weapon, had no concept of. The Russian officer we met seemed rather jolly, although I suspect that he could not be easily backed into a corner.

When we got back into our coaches and set off to return to democracy I noticed a road sign that indicated this was the route to Prague and the distance was about 350km. That really brought home to me that we truly were inside the Warsaw Pact bloc. The thought that East Berliners could drive to Prague in about three hours was, in 1984, amazing to me; that is if they had a car or were even allowed to!

If I'd thought that the contrast between East and West was vivid on arrival in the East, it was even more apparent as we travelled back into the West. It was as if someone had been decorating the place while we were away. The liveliness and colour, openness and commercialisation shouted the good life to one and all. That must have really upset the East German President, Erich Honecker, and his cronies. One thing we learnt that really did distress the East German *apparatchiks* was the effect of the sun shining on the Fernsehturm TV tower. The tallest structure in Germany, the tower was built in the late 1960s by the communist German Democratic Republic under the then President, Walter Ulbricht. It was meant to be a symbol of the GDR's strength. Two-thirds of the way up the 365m needle there is a globe of glass and steel – a restaurant and observation deck. The top half of the globe, which was modelled on the first man-made satellite, the Soviet *Sputnik*, is made of stainless steel tiles. Whenever the sun shines on this burnished orb a large, bright cross can be seen from all over the city. Berliners nicknamed the luminous cross the '*Rache des Papstes*', in English the 'Pope's Revenge'.

In 1984 we were still less than forty years from the end of the Second World War, whose outcome had led to this island of democracy in a sea of communism. There were some hesitant signs of the Cold War thawing, through the Strategic Arms Reduction Treaty (START), but the rhetoric flying back and forth across the Iron Curtain was still pretty vehement at times.

There were other visits but none made the impression on me that this one did. In other locations, we learned at first hand about much of the command-and-control systems within NATO, even visiting its headquarters in Belgium. Of course, all these visits had a social side that served to educate us even more:

from mussels and chips with Belgian beer in Brussels to breakfasting and dining with the Royal Navy in the Painted Hall at Greenwich, designed by Christopher Wren. As we looked in awe at the ceiling inside this magnificent edifice, which rivalled that of the Sistine Chapel, one of our dark blue compatriots said, 'If the answer is 133, what is the question?' Nobody came up with a decent guess. Later we learnt that it was the number of breasts on view (one of the nubiles had only one uncovered!).

Another great day out – for what educational purpose I am not sure – was to Epsom for the Derby. We had our own tent in the centre of the racecourse with refreshments arranged by the Officers' Mess at Bracknell; Linda dressed for the occasion and looked stunning – more Ascot than Epsom! Indeed, while we were walking around the fairground that is a feature of Derby Day, a lady at one stall said to her, ''Ere my love, you do look good, but yer at the wrong racecourse, ain'tcha?' Not only did we win a little money but part way through the afternoon the Staff College's Deputy Commandant, Air Cdre Joe Hardcastle, approached us and took us to a quiet corner where he told me that I was to be awarded the Air Force Cross in the forthcoming Queen's Birthday Honours List. More champagne was needed!

So the year went slowly by: reading, researching, listening, writing, talking, playing all sorts of sports, mixing with other armed services, other nationalities and, whenever the possibility arose, making mischief for the staff. There was also lots of eating and drinking, sometimes formal but more often informal, and usually with international flavours. Like most courses, you get out of it what you put in. My rule for such events has been to always act the student. Don't moan, it's a waste of time as nothing will change, at least not while you are there, and turn up when and where you are told to. Most of all, take advantage of the time out from responsibilities – they'll soon come back in abundance once you have graduated and been posted to your new 'career-enhancing' job.

November brought a very special day. It was the same day as the Queen and Prince Philip's wedding anniversary that Linda and I attended the investiture at Buckingham Palace so that HMQ could pin a shiny new Air Force Cross on to my best uniform. So we got aboard my yellow Triumph Stag and drove into central London, down the Mall, up to and, after showing our invitation cards, through the wrought-iron gates into Buckingham Palace. We were directed to park in the central courtyard and then made our way to the entrance that we had seen so often on TV. Once through we were fairly unceremoniously split up. I was directed to a long corridor where there was gathered a large number of people representing a good cross section of the British population.

There I met up with one of my fellow course members, Colin Thirlwall, who was also to receive the Air Force Cross. A very well-dressed gentleman was patrolling the corridor with a sheaf of papers in his hand. His duty was to arrange the throng into some semblance of the right sequence. Colin and I soon learnt that we would come well down the pecking order.

When that was done we received the briefing as to procedure. At this point a minion took our RAF hats. *I'm glad I didn't invest in a new one*, I thought.

'Don't worry you'll get them back before you leave,' the minion assured us. *I would hope so; I'm sure that HMQ is not into nicking officers' headgear!*

The investitures took place in the ballroom and the next corridor we entered gave direct access. Much 'shushing' went on up ahead, which must have meant that things were now under way. We then shuffled spasmodically down the corridor with not much to amuse us, other than some rather grand pieces of artwork hanging on the walls. Eventually the corridor made a sharp right turn and over the heads of the folk ahead I could see the doors to the vast space of the ballroom.

I now had to remember the briefing. When the recipient ahead moves forward to receive their honour or award I had to move to the edge of the stage and wait. Another minion there would then give me the nod to walk smartly forward until I was abeam Her Majesty. Then a left turn and step forward until I was within pinning distance. Got it!

Before I knew it I was on my way. I was terrified that my leather-soled shoes (Oxford pattern, RAF officers for the use of) would slip on the well-polished ballroom floor. So, perhaps a little gingerly, I made my way into place. There I was greeted by a smiling monarch with a gentle handshake. She asked me a couple of apposite questions; she obviously had been well briefed but also had an impeccable memory. She then fixed the medal in place, offered her hand in congratulation and gently pushed me back to give the hint that I could go. Three steps backwards, right turn, marching off to be met at the opposite door by yet another minion who quickly unclipped my gong and put it in a box.

Linda was in the ballroom watching, but I never got the chance to look for her. Now we had to wait until the whole thing was over, so Colin and I loitered in yet another corridor for our spouses to appear. Soon we were reunited with them and our hats and made our way out into the courtyard where a huge amount of milling about and photography was going on. We declined the no doubt extortionate professional snapper; Linda was quite an accomplished photographer and that would be good enough for me. Of course, from that day on people would ask me the question, 'What did you get that medal for?' I don't really have an answer. If there was a citation I had not seen it, so I could only guess that it was for eight years' continuous service as a test pilot in Her Majesty's Royal Air Force. I had done some high-risk stuff, as well as some classified things, and had not broken any aeroplanes on the way.[2] It was a tremendous honour to receive the AFC and a wonderful experience to do so from the hand of a reigning monarch.

At about that time my posting notice arrived. I was going to some job in the Ministry of Defence Main Building in Whitehall, London. The job had several initials and a couple of numbers. However, before I could find out what it was, it changed! Two days later I was told that I was now posted to something called the Strike Command Briefing Team at High Wycombe, north-west of London. The location suited me much better as, at less than 30 miles from my home in Oxford, it was easily commutable by car. But the clue in the name did not give much feeling for the job. Briefing whom and on what?

So 1984 ended on a great note – George Orwell had got it very wrong! I had married a wonderful lady, I had rediscovered my Christian faith, I had received a prestigious award and it looked like I had a good job coming, albeit on the ground. Most importantly, I was looking forward and not back. Life really had begun (again) at 40! But what did the future hold?

---

2.   The Air Force Cross is one of the highest awards in flying and was then officially awarded for 'an act or acts of valor, courage or devotion to duty whilst flying, though not in active operations against the enemy'. It has since been changed to a peacetime award for a single act of outstanding courage and skill while flying.

# 2 THE BRIEFING TEAM

Yet again I started an RAF appointment just one week before Christmas! On 17 December 1984 I reported to RAF High Wycombe, the headquarters of the RAF's highest-level operational formation, Strike Command, to discover just what I was in for over the next three years. After completing all the usual reams of personnel paperwork I was directed to a large brick building, constructed as a hollow square and known as 'B Block'; ominous echoes of incarceration crossed my mind. There on the top floor I followed instructions to the three rooms occupied by the Command Briefing Team (CBT). I first met the boss, a very young-looking wing commander called Phil Sturley, then I was introduced to Peter, the man I was replacing; he was leaving on promotion to take over the reins of No. 51 Squadron.

The next introduction was to my office companion and co-worker, John Thomas, who was a squadron leader in the RAF's administrative branch. John was a Geordie[1] and I would soon learn that his Tyneside humour would keep our spirits up when the going got tough. The final member of the team was a female RAF corporal called Jan, who gave lots of sterling support and supplied tea and biccies to order, as well as all the stationery.

It took most of the week to discover what I would have to do as the junior GD[2] member of the CBT. Most of the time John and I would be producing written briefs for the Commander-in-Chief (C-in-C) or his deputy covering a range of topics. The most often required would be for changes of command at RAF Strike Command stations (air bases). Then there were briefs to be prepared for visiting VIPs who would be received by the C-in-C or his deputy. Sometimes we would have to produce briefs for the chief's visits to other locations, especially commercial or military ones. Phil Sturley's prime duty was to give audio-visual presentations to visitors, tailored to their areas of interest. I was Phil's deputy for this task, and covered his leave or sickness.

---

1. For those readers not familiar with this nomenclature, 'Geordie' means someone from the north-east of England, usually the environs of Newcastle-upon-Tyne.
2. GD means General Duties and indicates a member of the aircrew and operations branch of the RAF.

Finally, I would occasionally have to produce short briefings for the C-in-C using the in-house TV system; the whole HQ could watch these – so no pressure then!

As if that wasn't enough, John filled me in on one more thing that the boss had not mentioned. During the regular, but thankfully not too frequent, war simulation exercises it would be our job to prepare and give TV or written briefs on the latest situations as supplied by the intelligence folks. John said that he would do the written stuff if I went on TV! A fair deal that I accepted with alacrity.

So I went off for my Christmas leave with all this rattling around in my head. I had by then discovered something about the command structure within the HQ, although I still had to meet most of the principals. The C-in-C was Air Chief Marshal Sir David Craig, a tall, dark-haired, distinguished officer, and his deputy was Air Marshal Sir Joe Gilbert. The man I would have contact with in the C-in-C's office was his personal staff officer (PSO), Gp Capt Peter Squire, a pilot who had led his Harrier squadron with distinction during the Falklands War. He was also a previous commanding officer of the CBT, so he knew all the wrinkles and the excuses! We worked in the Plans Division and were collocated with all the various elements of that discipline on the top floor. The man in charge of planning was Air Cdre Mike Stear: an officer with a rugby forward's build, an outwardly stern demeanour and, as I would soon learn, a relentless work ethic.

These important figures aside, I soon learnt that the most important people to keep on-side were the lovely ladies of the typing pool, this still being the era before desktop PCs. They were all gathered in one large room on the opposite side of the hollow square, one floor down, and we often had visual and aural contact through open windows across that space. It seemed, at times, to be John's favourite pastime!

As 1985 progressed I got used to the sometimes frenetic pace of work, the requirements for briefs often mounting up faster than the two of us could churn them out. Gathering the information was a major part of our lives and we could often be seen buzzing round these particular corridors of power at high speed with papers under our arms. If any of the staff officers spotted us coming doors would slam, phones picked up or early lunches suddenly taken. They knew that we'd be interrupting them and nobody likes interruptions! But I soon worked out cunning ways to trap the unwary, like walking quickly past the target office door and then making a U-turn and catching the poor occupant as he relaxed. There were a good few people on the staff that I already knew: a couple of ex-fellow course members from Staff College and a handful of guys I'd met on previous tours.

Perhaps the most interesting, but also most demanding, work was doing TV briefings. The staff in the TV studio, which was based in the old Bomber Command underground bunker, were extremely helpful. I learned how to make my own autocues, using strips of paper stuck together with sticky tape. Occasionally this simple device would let me down by the tape unsticking, so I always had a script to hand. I also learnt the TV presenter's trick of moving one's head but still scanning the words on the autocue. This stopped the goldfish effect of the rigid head and moving eyes variety! I combed all sorts of military publications and the HQ's photographic library for suitable illustrations, which could be projected full screen or 'over the shoulder'. All in all, the TV studio was a well-run professional outfit – at least until I got in there. It was primarily used for a daily morning briefing, with one wing commander staff member employed to do that job. There was a sound feed from the C-in-C's office so that he could ask questions. Thankfully he rarely did. I was only an occasional user of the TV system, but still had to prepare all the material and have at least one rehearsal before transmission. This was not something that I had ever expected to be doing.

An unexpected benefit of this, and the occasional audio-visual presentations I gave to visitors, was that the C-in-C knew me by sight. RAF High Wycombe had a splendid rule for the staff of all ranks that allowed us, nay told us, to walk around the station hatless or, as we Yorkshire folk have it, 'baht t'at'. This made life much easier as we did not have to be giving or returning salutes every five paces. However, I was out and about one day, on a quest for material for yet another written brief, when I spotted a tall, distinguished, dark-haired officer walking towards me. It was the Commander-in-Chief.

As we passed (I think he was on the way to the station barber's shop) the resistance I had to apply to my right arm to stop it shooting up was immense; I swapped my clipboard to my right hand to prevent it saluting.

'Good morning sir,' I said with a smile.

'Good morning, Mike,' he replied returning the smile. It was a bit of a shock for such a lofty ranking officer to address me by my first name, but I realised that it was soon after my first TV appearance. So my performance could not have been too bad – and even very senior officers feel that they know people they have seen on TV!

The headquarters was not just that of the RAF's prime operational formation, but also the headquarters of the UK's military aviation contribution to NATO; hence it was also known in NATO-speak as HQ UKAIR. So Sir David Craig also held the NATO title CINCUKAIR, and many of his subordinates were similarly 'double-hatted'. That had the knock-on effect of making it important for all of us in the CBT to ensure that we understood all the implications of the NATO element and so would reflect the correct emphasis and terminology in our briefings, especially to visitors from allied nations.

In July 1985 RAF High Wycombe held its Summer Ball in the Officers' Mess. One of our neighbours in Oxford was a single USAF pilot based at RAF Upper Heyford. We invited this dashing young officer to escort Linda's daughter, Melanie, to the ball – with the proviso that he drove us all there in his handsome, growling, black Chevrolet Corvette.

After we had arrived at the Mess and had started our initial exploration of the various diversions for the evening, our chauffeur was walking around in his USAF mess kit with Melanie on his arm, in an open-mouthed state of wonderment. As we headed for the seafood bar, the traditional starting point of any Summer Ball, I spotted the C-in-C, his deputy and their wives coming towards us. Sir David spotted me and said, 'Good evening, Mike. Splendid isn't it?'

I, of course, agreed with him as his party passed by.

'Gee, is that CINCUKAIR?' said our American companion with awe. 'And he knows your name?' I remained modestly silent.

Not many weeks after I had arrived and was just about getting to grips with the job, Phil Sturley invited me into his office. He enquired as to how I was finding it.

'Well, it is quite demanding and, at the same time, fascinating to be working in the headquarters, but not stuck with one specialised field like most other people.'

He agreed with my analysis and then said, 'Well, Mike, I've got management to agree that this appointment is on a par with a personal staff officer's job in terms of workload and responsibility. That means that your three-year tour here will be cut to two – good news, eh?' I readily agreed; one year less to wait for a possible return to flying was certainly good news.

Although it was demanding on time and talent, the job was a fascinating way to find out, at first hand, about all the wide-ranging activities undertaken by the RAF's Primary Command, still in its Cold War posture. Indeed the major work going on within the very secure grounds of the HQ was the construction of a new, advanced and nuclear strike-proof underground bunker – yet another thing to learn about. The visitors that came to the HQ were many and varied. On one occasion the head of the People's Army of the Chinese Republic, another time the French chief of the Armée de l'Air and then, later, NATO's outgoing Supreme Allied Commander in Europe (SACEUR). Then there were visits from politicians, captains of industry, the press and foreign defence attachés. All of these had to have tailored briefings. Every outgoing Strike Command station commander came for his end-of-tour debrief with the C-in-C and a written brief had to be prepared, including any future plans for the station. Our friends that shared the same corridor used to be particularly helpful in this. If we could rope them in, it was all go!

While I was at home, taking a spot of leave tacked on to the Easter weekend, the phone rang.

'Hello.'

'Good morning, Mike, it's the boss. I've got some news for you that I thought I you should hear straight away.'

'Good news or bad news?' I asked.

'Well, there's good news, good news and good news,' he replied, somewhat enigmatically.

'Well you'd better give me the good news then!' I said, mystified by this triple good fortune.

'First, you will be leaving us in August – that's more than a year earlier than expected. Second, you are going to be promoted to wing commander and, third, you will take over as OC Flying Wing at the Royal Aircraft Establishment Farnborough.'

I could hardly believe my ears – all that and now less than six months more writing and presenting to do. I could already sense that the summer would pass slowly because of my impatience to get back to flying.

One of the first thoughts that crossed my mind was that, as OC Flying at Farnborough, I would get to fly the SE.5a First World War fighter that was jointly owned and operated by the RAE and the Shuttleworth Collection of historic and vintage aircraft. This was something I had wanted to do ever since I sat in it on the ground during my first tour there in the late 1970s. But, of course, there was so much more in store. I couldn't wait!

# 3 AIRBORNE AGAIN

During my time at the RAF Staff College and HQ Strike Command I had not remained totally tied to the ground. I had gone along to No. 6 Air Experience Flight (AEF) at RAF Abingdon,[1] not far from our home in Oxford, and got myself 'on the books' as a staff pilot flying, yet again, the dear little de Havilland Chipmunk. In that part-time capacity I gave the air cadets twenty-minute flights to try to instil in them an appreciation or even a love for aviation. Perhaps it was a lofty ambition, but many of them seemed to enjoy the experience; just a few spent most of the time shouting into a sick bag! My attendance at Abingdon was mostly at weekends, although I was able to take an occasional afternoon off and 'slip the surly bonds of earth'.[2]

Then in June 1985 an old friend and colleague from Radar Research Squadron days, now retired RAF navigator Peter Middlebrook, contacted me to see whether I would be willing to go with him to view and test fly a Piper Cub that he was hoping to buy. I readily accepted and the following weekend we and our ladies travelled to a small airstrip in Suffolk to look over the high-winged 1940s American flying machine. It was a pretty little thing and appropriately registered G-OCUB! I had flown a Cub before on a few occasions and, after Peter had flown with the vendor, I took to the air with my wife; this was the first time we had flown together. Everything seemed to work as advertised, not that there was a lot that could go wrong with such a simple aeroplane. It handled like it should and flew in trim. The only small problem was that, being a hot summer's day, the windows on each side of the tandem seats had been removed and that gave Linda a feeling of extreme insecurity, especially when we banked to turn. Then she remembered how much effort had been applied to get her into the front seat in the first place, so she relaxed a bit. Well, at least until I asked her if she could see the airstrip as I pretended that I had no idea where we were!

---

1. In the 1980s the RAF's Air Experience Flights were in twelve locations all over the UK. Their function was to give air cadets flying experience and they were manned by volunteer serving and ex-service pilots.
2. A phrase from the poem 'High Flight' by RCAF pilot John Gillespie Magee, which he wrote in 1941 not long before he was killed in a mid-air collision. He was 19 years old.

The upshot of all this was that Peter bought the Cub and we flew it back to Oxford Kidlington airport, where he had arranged to keep it. Over the next two months I began to teach him to fly it. The *quid pro quo* was that I could use it any time I wanted to – I just had to put the petrol in. So the summer weekends during my very short tour at High Wycombe still contained an element of aviation, albeit in light aircraft.

However, all that was invisible to the Royal Air Force. As far as they were concerned I hadn't flown a 'real' aeroplane for at least eighteen months. So I had to attend a fast-jet refresher course, flying the BAe Hawk trainer at RAF Brawdy in south-west Wales. And that was fine by me.

Brawdy airfield was on the far-west Welsh coast, not far from the cathedral city of St David's, the patron saint of Wales. Brawdy's major claim to fame was its 'forty-knot fog', caused when the moist air blown in from the southern Irish Sea was thrust up and over the cliffs just off the end of the main runway. In the right, or should that be the wrong, conditions, the increase in height of just a few hundred feet was sufficient for the moisture in the air to condense and form a cloud that lay on the ground – in meteorological terms, advection fog. In good weather Brawdy's coastal location gave its squadrons easy access to a nearby weapons range, the UK Low Flying System and lots of airspace for manoeuvring over the sea. The course that I was to join used the Hawk to get us ex-'ground-pounders' back up to speed. The Hawk had first flown in August 1974 and entered RAF service two years later. It replaced the Folland Gnat and in 1979 was then adopted by the RAF Aerobatic Team – the Red Arrows.

I had flown the Hawk during 1983 at Boscombe Down so it wasn't entirely new to me. The Hawk is a delight to fly, with excellent stability and control characteristics, especially during rolls; you can easily stop a maximum rate roll precisely, with no perceptible 'wobble'. The maximum speed performance of the Hawk is a little down on the Gnat and its company predecessor the Hunter, but its economy of operation is much better than both. The biggest improvement was in the 'office'. The cockpit was well designed with everything in the right place and the field of view was first class. It was one of the few aircraft I had flown in which I didn't have to raise the seat to its highest position; I have very short back.[3]

---

3.  See Chapter 4 of *A Bucket of Sunshine*, by this author (The History Press, 2012).

I arrived at RAF Brawdy at the beginning of September 1985, after what felt like a very long drive from Oxford, and took up residence in a well-worn room in the rather utilitarian Officers' Mess. After the usual week of preparation, with ground school and simulator rides, I was deemed knowledgeable enough to start flying again. However, my first two flights were in a Jet Provost – the JP that I had trained on twenty-two years earlier! There were two or three of these at Brawdy, specifically for training forward air controllers; to this end they were finished in a camouflage paint job. But it still didn't make the little JP any more aggressive! As it turned out, one of the JP pilots was an ex-Canberra student of mine, Flt Lt Dave McIntyre, and he had picked up the job of taking a JP to the Battle of Britain Air Display at RAF Abingdon for the weekend.

As Abingdon was just a stone's throw from home, I asked if I could go with him and be his batman for the day. He readily agreed; and that was nothing to do with me now wearing my wing commander's rank tapes! Linda met us in the static aircraft park and we spent the day at the air show before spending the rest of the weekend together. What bliss, and I didn't have to drive to the far end of Wales on Sunday night.

My flying in the Hawk started a couple of days after I returned to Brawdy. After two dual sorties I was sent off on my own. It was a sheer delight to be back in a manoeuvrable jet, doing aerobatics and just enjoying the freedom of the skies. When I got back my instructor, Flt Lt Burkby, said to me, 'You enjoy your flying, don't you, sir?'

I readily agreed but silently wondered how he knew.

He soon let on. 'I watched your take-off from the tower,' he said, somewhat enigmatically. I said nothing but I supposed that my usual Canberra and Buccaneer style of 'get the gear up quickly and hold it low' was perhaps a little out of the ordinary for the 'students'.

The course progressed and included a few days at Linton-on-Ouse in Yorkshire to escape the 'forty-knot fog'. I was also allowed to drop bombs (little ones) and shoot bullets, as well as fly some one-on-one and two-on-two air–air combat sorties.

It all came to an end too soon, exactly one month since I had arrived; I had flown a total of twenty hours in as many days. I had thoroughly enjoyed myself and felt up to speed, so I got back into my car and drove back to Oxford with a huge smile.

I was only there for the weekend because on the Monday I had to drive in a different direction to report to RAF Shawbury for my helicopter course. The last time I had been there, in 1979, I had learned to become a pilot of those airborne threshing machines, flying the venerable Westland Whirlwind. Now, six years later, the 'Whirlybirds' had been consigned to scrap or museums and were replaced with a little sports car of a helicopter – the Gazelle.

I had been very fortunate in my earlier flying career to have been in a post where I could fly fixed-wing and rotary-wing aircraft during the same tour of duty.[4] As I would again be commanding flight-test units with both classes of aircraft, I had persuaded the powers that be that it was essential I flew helicopters in my new post, and they had readily agreed. However, they had only given me three weeks to complete the eighteen-hour syllabus. So no pressure then!

Flying helicopters is similar but different to flying aeroplanes. I liken the difference to that between motorcycles and motorcars. The helicopter, like a motorcycle, requires more attention to balance and is essentially 'flying' even on the ground once the blades are turning. The 'stick' looks like the one found in an aeroplane and it does still raise and lower the nose. But the other control, the collective lever, is unique to rotorcraft and that essentially controls the vertical movement of the machine. In conjunction with use of the stick, it also controls forward speed. So quite a different skill set is needed. And that's even before you learn to hover.

My instructor was Flt Lt Geoff Connelly, a man who would later become a distinguished helicopter test pilot himself. His patience was tested at first as the Gazelle is a skittish little beast and it took me some time to adapt. The control forces and amounts needed to manoeuvre and control the Gazelle were much less than those in the Whirlwind and Wessex, the two types I had flown previously. But I found my feet (and hands) in this delightful helicopter and came to enjoy its handling characteristics. I soon forgot my previously learned, rather heavy-handed, techniques, and the view from the bubble cockpit was so much better! Under Geoff's gentle ministrations I went solo after five sorties and then my confidence caught up with his ambition for me. We did all the usual stuff: landing on sloping ground and in confined areas,

---

4. See Part 3 of *Trials and Errors* (The History Press, 2015).

flying backwards and sideways, engine-off landings from all sorts of starting conditions, navigation, instrument flying and even some flying in the dark. I left Shawbury looking forward greatly to flying the Gazelle again, once I had settled into my new job at Farnborough.

Officially I had a third refresher course to do and this would involve the longest journey, thankfully not by car but by train. That was to attend a short Jaguar refresher course with No. 226 Operational Conversion Unit (OCU) at RAF Lossiemouth, in northern Scotland. I arrived there at the beginning of November 1985; I had last been with No. 226 OCU five years previously when I converted to the Jaguar in preparation for my tour as a tutor at the Empire Test Pilots' School. As usual, OCU life started with classroom lessons and simulator trips. But after a week a big exercise was called and it was suggested that I return home so that I wouldn't be in the way. Just as I was about to leave, the OCU boss called me in and explained that someone somewhere had not 'joined up the dots'. He said that he had not received approval from his ivory towers for my flying and his bosses were telling him to pass me back to the Ministry of Defence Procurement Executive (MODPE) to get them to sort it out. A couple of phone calls later the man at MODPE HQ told me that he had arranged for my Jaguar refresher flying to take place at Farnborough, during my take-over period.

So that was that; with just a couple of simulator rides to my credit I took the long train journey back to Oxford. My preparation for command was over. My next move would be back to the hallowed and historic environs of the Royal Aircraft Establishment at Farnborough.

# PART 2
# FARNBOROUGH

PART 2

FARNBOROUGH

# 4 TAKING UP THE REINS

I arrived back at the main gates of RAE Farnborough in late November 1985; I was actually on temporary duty as my in-post date was not until 13 December and I was only here to complete the flying part of my Jaguar refresher course. But before I could even drive to my destination at the Experimental Flying Squadron (EFS) I had to stop to get a temporary pass.

'You'll get a permanent one when you've completed all this paperwork and we've taken your photograph,' said the person behind the desk, handing me a couple of trees' worth of buff forms.

At EFS I met up with Flt Lt Mervyn Evans, as well as many of the squadron personnel, few of whom I knew. Over the next few days Mervyn put me through my paces during two dual sorties in Jaguar T2 ZB 615. I then flew it twice on my own and after those four flights I felt quite at home back in the Anglo-French Jaguar. It was nearly five years since I had last flown this rather complex operational fighter/bomber and trainer. But, as so often when one has flown a jet for more than a handful of hours, the familiarity with the cockpit layout, the aircraft's handling characteristics and the inevitable foibles of its design soon come back. The Jaguar is a sharp-pointed aeroplane that can slip through the air easily at high speed and low level; it is supersonic at high altitude and can climb rapidly if the afterburners are used all the way up. It also has some oddities from its French parentage: for instance, the fuel amount is measured in litres, not in pounds, as in most British aircraft. Similarly all weights are in kilograms and a lot of the instruments have a chic continental look to them! The main things to relearn were the operation of the inertial platform-based navigation and attack system, the use and management of the HUD and flying the jet with one engine 'failed'. The latter is affected by the fact that at the lower speeds used for approach and landing the drag tended to be more than the remaining single Rolls-Royce Adour engine could cope with; a judicious use of afterburner was sometimes required. The final thing that I needed reminding of was just how much vibration and buffet there was when flying around the landing pattern. This short refamiliarisation was also a bit of a homecoming to Farnborough after seven years away.

By early December I was ready to start the takeover of my new job so I proceeded to the control tower, where the OC Flying's office was located.

There was a very handy car park outside the tower with a nominated space, presently occupied by the car of my immediate predecessor. He was Wg Cdr Richard 'Rich' Rhodes, who, as a squadron leader, had been my boss during my previous tour at Farnborough. I parked, entered through the double glass doors into the minimalist and well-worn art deco interior and up the broad stairs to the first floor. I remembered it all very well, mainly from a few summonses by its then senior occupants a decade beforehand. However, back then climbing those stairs had usually meant some sort of one-sided conversation with 'he who must be obeyed'!

I stopped at the first floor and entered Rich's office, through his PA's space, to find him sitting at a large desk with his usual beaming smile. Coffee was procured via the group captain's PA, a very friendly and chatty lady in her thirties called Heather. Once equipped with refreshment Rich and I chatted over times past and present. He was in the process of leaving the RAF to take up gainful employment with Flight Refuelling, an aviation company within the Cobham Group based at Bournemouth airport. He told me that he was looking forward to the new challenges that this would bring. By now he had introduced me to the man who he assured me really knew what was going on and who would keep me both up to speed and on the straight and narrow. He was the OC Flying's PA, a retired RAF squadron leader called Roger Cooper. I would get to know, like, admire and rely on Roger over the coming three years.

Across the corridor was the office of the Commanding Officer Experimental Flying (COEF), presently occupied by a senior RAF test pilot called David Scouller. He had been the OC of the fighter test squadron at Boscombe Down when I had been a tutor at ETPS. I had not come across him much personally, but his reputation as a stickler for correct procedure and observance of rank was well known. After introductions, Rich and I retired to what would become my office and set about the process of the transfer of command, which would take about a week.

Over the days leading up to the date at which I would assume the mantle, 13 December, I read a large number of official documents, met an even larger number of the appropriate people, both civilian and military, and considered at length what my *modus operandi* should be. I decided to follow the philosophy I had used for my first spell in command in the late 1970s: watch, listen and learn; don't change anything for three months unless something affecting safety crops up; get to know all the folk who 'worked' for me; and try to lead from the front.

It was the run up to Yuletide and each department and section at Farnborough seemed to be holding their office Christmas parties; it also appeared that I had been invited to all of them – an impossible task to fulfil! But I got along to as many as I could, turning down festive drinks as I was now commuting daily the 50 or so miles to and from Oxford. However, sausage rolls, mince pies and other seasonal snacks were gladly accepted! This way I met or reacquainted myself with many of the civilian staff and scientists, always known affectionately as 'boffins'; I also learned informally about many of their pet projects. And I gently acquired some inside information as to how they felt the test squadron supported them.

One day, having already met the 'flying doctors' of the RAF Institute of Aviation Medicine (IAM), I was asked if I would like to go flying with one of their number on a trial of a new oxygen system. I accepted with alacrity, dusted off my flying kit and joined Commander McPhate in the cockpit of the IAM Hunter T7, XL 563. During my previous incarnation at Farnborough I had spent many hours, not all of them comfortable, in this very aircraft being subjected to a variety of usually physically demanding aeromedical trials. Thus it was that my first test flight in my new appointment was back in the role of guinea pig. But it was great to be back in one of my favourite aeroplanes and the trial was not too taxing either. It was to test a new type of oxygen system for the Harrier. Instead of pressurised bottles of oxygen being installed, oxygen would be generated on board the aircraft using air taken from the engine compressor. It seemed to work, although I was told that my breathing was occasionally too shallow to signal the system to blow oxygen into my mask!

Christmas was soon upon us, as was the traditional shut down of the establishment for about a week to cover the Christmas and New Year public holidays. So I would be driving back from Oxford to really get my teeth into the job on the first Monday of 1986.

# 5 DEFINING THE JOB

One of first things you have to do on taking up a new appointment is get a clear picture of what you are supposed to be doing each day. Sometimes there are terms of reference or a written job description, but my experience of the RAF of the late twentieth century was that they were a rarity. You had to find out from your predecessor what he or she had done and then you were on your own. Of course there was always a sharp-eyed superior who would put you straight if and when you got it wrong; you just had to be a fast learner!

The job of OC Flying at Farnborough was what the military call a Command Appointment, which just means that you are in charge of something and/ or somebody. Having served previously at Farnborough, I was broadly aware of the tasks of OC Flying. I would be responsible to the group captain (my direct boss and COEF) for the conduct and safety of all flying activities at Farnborough. I would have command of all the flying units, as well as having operational control and oversight of the airfield fire service and any works and maintenance activities on the airfield. Although the civilian air traffic control (ATC) service was under the aegis of a civil servant Senior Air Traffic Control Officer (SATCO), we were duty-bound to work cooperatively. So, in effect, the appointment was like that of a normal RAF squadron commander and an OC Operations Wing rolled into one. I would also be the COEF's deputy. It was a lot to grasp.

To service all the research programmes the aircraft fleet at Farnborough was fairly large and varied. The fast jets were the three special-build Buccaneers for weapons trials, a two-seat Jaguar, a pair of two-seat Hunters, a two-seat Harrier and another Buccaneer for electro-optical equipment development. For rotary-wing trials there were various helicopters, including a Lynx, a Puma, two Sea Kings and a Gazelle. The radio- and navigation-related experiments took place on board a BAC 1-11, a DH Comet 4 and an Andover. Last but by no means least, the Air Transport Flight had three Cessna PA-31 Navajo Chieftains and a venerable Douglas DC-3 Dakota.

To fly and support the operations of these aircraft there were the Flying Department's military aircrew and civilian and military operations support staff. These key personnel were from a wide variety of backgrounds and all were experienced in their fields. There were about a dozen fixed-wing and rotary-wing test pilots, all graduates of military schools in the UK, USA or France. For the operation of the transport and larger trials aircraft, there were appropriately experienced and often mature pilots, air engineers and navigators. The Experimental Flying Squadron had its own operations centre, with several supporting civilian and service personnel. The Technical Department provided highly qualified and skilled civilian people to service the aircraft fleet, as well as to complete the diverse specialised installations of experimental equipment and systems.

In a command appointment you carry the can for all that is under your purview. As I settled into this post I decided on my tried and trusted approach. First, spend three months observing how things run. Second, get my feet out from under the desk by doing what I call 'MBWA' (management by walking about) – spending as much time as possible out of the office, visiting all the people under my command and getting to know them and find out what they were doing. Once I'd done that I would get a feel for who was happy and who was not, and why they were not.

During one of my early MBWA sessions I visited the Fire Section, at that time located in the famous Black Sheds, adjacent to Cody's Tree. The Black Sheds were two of the very earliest aircraft hangars at Farnborough – the centre of operations during the First World War for the preparation, testing and despatch of military aircraft to the Western Front. The sheds were virtually in line with the main runway and a few hundred metres from the beginning of it. Cody's Tree, located just west of the sheds, was where, in the first decade of the twentieth century, 'Colonel' Sam Cody used to tether his flying machines. He had a hefty spring balance set into the rope and used it to measure the thrust of his aircraft by running them up to full power. The tree was obviously strong enough, as it was still there; although it must be said that the thrust horsepower it had to restrain was hardly over-whelming! By the late 1980s the tree was no longer in its natural state. Various liquids had been injected into it to preserve it for posterity. It was but a shadow of its former self. Nevertheless, it was an almost sacred object, and rightly so.

Having admired the tree, albeit in its artificial, preserved state – akin to a wax figure at Madame Tussaud's – I moved into the Fire Section to make the acquaintance of the Fire Chief and his trusty troops. As an aviator whose greatest fear was to be trapped in a burning aircraft, I have always seen firemen as heroes; of course, like many heroes, they are just ordinary chaps doing an important job. The firemen at Farnborough were civilian members of the MOD fire service. I would soon learn a good few things about them, the first of which was that the best mug of tea to be found anywhere on the airfield was served in the Fire Section. This fact soon drove the timing of my occasional visits! The second was that if you want to buy a second-hand car look first at a fireman's; they have frequent periods of inactivity and lots of water and hosepipes to hand. Firemen will often be seen tinkering and titivating their means of personal transport. On the whole they are a good and dedicated bunch. However, I would later get peripherally involved in disputes over manning levels and shift patterns, usually brought about by diktats on cuts to defence spending handed down from Thatcher's Conservative government in power at the time.

On one occasion I did have to pass on the group captain's displeasure to the Fire Chief. It was when a fire engine rushed at high speed past the office window with its blue lights flashing. Within a few microseconds my intercom from the group captain's office came noisily alive.

'Where's the fire?' my master's voice demanded.

'Sorry, sir, I don't know,' I replied.

'Well find out!'

So I rang the Fire Section and asked what the emergency was. This only elicited a baffled response, which left me no wiser. I asked to speak to the watch supervisor. His explanation was more prosaic. 'They were just on their way to the canteen,' he said.

'Well, please tell them to use the road and not the airfield in future – and no flashing lights! We're all wondering where the crash was.'

It didn't happen again.

There was the usual wide variety of flight trials work going on at Farnborough – much as it had been during my previous time there. Perhaps the most high-profile work was that involved with the use of electro-optical (EO) sensors to allow all types of military aircraft to fly safely at low altitudes at night. There were also trials of advanced navigation equipment, improved long-range communications systems, anti-submarine sensors, parachutes for safe low-level personnel drops, advanced display systems, laser and infrared countermeasures and a variety of aeromedical flight trials, mainly aimed at increasing the ability of pilots to sustain high G-values in combat.

My job would be to approve the protocols for many of these trials, or filter them for approval by higher authority in the office next door. This meant meticulously checking the procedures submitted by the trials officers and, when necessary, getting clarification or amendments until they were acceptable for passing to the test aircrew.

The latter were, at least in my mind, our greatest asset. Without good-quality, well-trained, experienced and responsible folk in the cockpits and on the flight decks all the facilities and desired experimental programmes in the world are nothing. With many unique platforms, usually equipped with one-off experimental or developmental systems, we could not afford to lose a single aircraft. Although, as I knew by now, much test flying is routine and sometimes even boring, there is a need for in-depth preparation and there is no place at all for overconfidence or complacency. There were a few of the older aircrew that I knew, some very well from previous tours of duty, but most were younger, more recent graduates from test pilots' schools or the navigator's equivalent, known as specialist navigators, or 'Spec N'. They were all people that deserved the best service I could give them by way of making sure that they could get on with their work without having to be bothered by external distractions.

An additional presence at Farnborough was that of the Meteorological Research Flight (always referred to, for obvious reasons, as MRF), whose HQ was located in a shady grove of trees to the north of the airfield. This unit was not part of the MODPE fleet. The MRF operated a specially modified C-130, known as the Mark W2, which had many extra probes and on-board facilities for its esoteric climatic work. The most notable of these was a 6m-long horizontal mast sticking out of the nose. So that folk didn't bump into it, it was painted red and white like a barber's pole. Because of this nasal appendage the MRF Hercules was known throughout the world as 'Dumbo'. The RAF provided and supported this aircraft and the Met Office tasked them. My responsibilities lay solely with the safe conduct of their flying in and around Farnborough, as well as being in the reporting chain for the aircrew's annual confidential reports.

I started my tour hoping to become as involved as time would allow in the test flying; after all there was plenty on offer. However, there was one more flying activity that was my responsibility, albeit shared with my boss: flying and displaying a First World War SE.5a fighter that was part owned by the RAE. But more on that later.

# 6 FLYING THE FERRIES

I was, of course, eager to get more directly involved in some of the current flight-test programmes on the aircraft in which I had recent flying practice. At this stage they were the Hunter, Jaguar and Hawk; however, only the first two were then part of the RAE air fleet. But my first regular flying hours were going to accrue from an airborne activity that was automatically allied to my appointment: flying the establishment's small fleet of communications aeroplanes, colloquially known to all and sundry as 'The Ferries'.

Since I had last flown with the Air Transport Flight (ATF), in 1978, their three 1940s vintage de Havilland Devons had been replaced with something a little more up to date. Four Piper PA-31 Navajo Chieftains had been purchased for the Procurement Executive fleet – three for Farnborough and one for Boscombe Down, who had a lesser requirement. The former were finished in an attractive version of the red, white and blue 'raspberry ripple' colour scheme. For reasons I never did discover, the Boscombe Down machine remained in a dull buff finish.

In 1962, under the project name 'Inca', at the behest of company founder William T. Piper, his aircraft company began the development of a twin-engine, corporate and commuter transport aeroplane designed to carry six to eight passengers: the PA-31. After its first flight on 30 September 1964 it was officially announced to the world. It was a low-wing monoplane with a conventional tail, powered by two Lycoming TIO-540-A turbocharged engines housed in so-called 'tiger shark' cowlings, a feature shared with two other Piper twin-engined types. As testing progressed, two extra cabin windows were added to each side of the fuselage and the engines moved further forward. The PA-31, now named 'Navajo' after a Native American tribe (a Piper practice), was not certified by the Federal Aviation Administration until 24 February 1966, and deliveries began the following year.

Over the following six years the Navajo was developed even further, including an increase in engine power. In what became known as the Navajo B there was air conditioning, increased baggage space (achieved by the addition of storage lockers in the rear part of the extended engine nacelles), a third door next to the cabin entry doors to facilitate the loading of baggage, and an optional separate door for the pilot to enter the cockpit.

In September 1972 Piper unveiled the PA-31-350 Navajo Chieftain, a stretched version of the Navajo B, with more powerful engines and counter-rotating propellers to prevent critical engine-handling problems. The fuselage was lengthened by 2ft, allowing for up to ten seats in total. Variants of the Lycoming TIO-540, developing 350hp, were fitted to the Chieftain and the maximum take-off weight was increased to 7,000lb. However, the Chieftain's introduction to service was delayed by a flood in Piper's factory at Lock

Haven, Pennsylvania, caused by Hurricane Agnes, and deliveries did not commence until 1973.

In my previous appointment at Farnborough, ten years earlier, I had been just another test pilot among many. Getting to fly as a so-called 'guest artist' with the ATF was down to waiting for a slot to become available, as well as plying OC ATF with sufficient ale at happy hour.[1] Now my loftier position gained me a slot by right, so I would only have to find enough time to present myself for training.

Having obtained a copy of the Aircraft Operating Manual and Checklist, I made it my evening reading for a few days. On 24 January 1986 I presented myself to Sqn Ldr Fred Hambly, the ATF training and categorisation pilot, to take to the air in the Chieftain.

Over the next six working days I was guided by Fred's gentle ministrations through the conversion syllabus. We did all the usual handling exercises, including lots of flying around with one engine going and the other idling, stalling in all possible configurations, and lots of take-offs and landings. Then it was on to instrument flying and the use of all the navigation kit (much more extensive than that of the Devon) until Fred was satisfied that I could go off on my own – well, with one of the ATF navigators to keep an eye on me.

After a couple of supervised ferry flights, including one with the ATF boss, Sqn Ldr Peter Cullum, I was declared rated and categorised and therefore fit to take passengers to and from their destinations, as directed by the weekly schedules. Those destinations could include any of the four main RAE outstations. These were the research and developmental airfield and wind tunnel site at Thurleigh, near Bedford, to which we flew three times daily; then there were the airfields at Llanbedr and Aberporth in west Wales, both of which supported the activities in the large air weapons range in Cardigan Bay. Up north, in south-west Scotland, the destination was the RAE airfield at West Freugh, which supported the air-to-ground weapons ranges in Luce Bay. The latter was a delightful all-day run with a good Scottish lunch included. Other routine destinations were Boscombe Down, Cranfield and Gloucester Staverton.

---

1.  See *Trials and Errors* by this author (The History Press, 2015).

Whilst the CO ran ATF, a lady called Jane Pelling was an important lynchpin in the organisation. She occupied an office next to a small waiting room for passengers on the ground floor of the control tower. It was Jane who took the bookings for flights and then passed this information to the aircrew. She was a tower of strength in making sure that our sometimes forgetful civil servants turned up on time and on the right day. Jane was a wonderful character and had a catalogue of fascinating tales to tell. She was a personal friend of a childhood hero of mine – Michael Bentine. He had been a Second World War RAF fighter pilot, but then got involved in radio and TV entertainment after the war. As a child I used to watch his rather zany puppet shows on our tiny black and white TV. He also became a founder member of an even zanier radio programme, *The Goon Show* – another personal favourite of my teenage years. Through Jane I met Michael at one of the Farnborough air shows, when he was her guest.

The PA-31 Navajo Chieftain was ideal for the job and mostly a delight to fly. The only drawback I found was not achieving nice, consistently smooth landings. This was because of a spring that had been installed in the longitudinal control system to improve the apparent longitudinal static stability at low speeds. This was a common 'fix' in aircraft of the type and you just had to live with it. Hence the only thing I missed about the Devon was its delightful handling characteristics in pitch, which meant that smooth landings were often easily achievable. That's very important when you have a handful of passengers sitting very close behind you!

The cockpit facilities on board the Chieftain were a leap ahead of the Devon. There was radar for picking out heavy rain or storm centres, and it showed coastlines and high ground. This system was colloquially known as 'cloud and clonk'. Another nice feature was the autopilot. I used this as much as possible – why work when you can supervise? There was also an electronic synchroniser for the propellers. This stopped the annoying, monotonous beat when the prop revolutions were not exactly matched. In the Devon you had to fiddle with the rpm levers to get the props synchronised, and it never seemed to last long before you had to do it again – very tiresome on a long trip. And the trips were now not quite so long, as the Chieftain's economical cruising speed of around 180 knots was a good 40 knots faster than the Devon. It also had a range of well over 850 nautical miles – not that we needed to go that far on a regular basis.

Piper's brilliant idea to equip the Chieftain with engines that went round the opposite way to each other meant that there was no tendency for the aeroplane to wander off to one side of the runway during take-off. It also meant that the loss of one engine would be felt equally; in technical terms there would be no difference in the minimum control speed depending on which engine had failed. On take-off, in common with many twin-engined aircraft I had flown, the aircraft became airborne below the minimum control speed. As such, the practice was not to raise the undercarriage before that speed was attained; if an engine failed, the drill was to throttle back and land ahead. Helpfully, a blue line was painted on the airspeed indicator at 105 knots (the 'safety speed'), above which the aircraft should be able to fly away safely after an engine failure, so the wheels could then come up.

The Chieftain had a healthy rate of climb, normally about 1,200ft per minute, but unless the weather was poor and we were going to transit in or above cloud, much of our route flying was done at heights between 2,000 and 4,000ft. Once levelled out I used to engage the autopilot, synchronise the props and stick my right hand out towards my companion, the navigator occupying the co-pilot's seat, in expectation that he would furnish my upturned palm with a mint.

As I had found in my previous incarnation at Farnborough, coming into work early and flying the first ferry of the day, to Bedford and back, was a great way to kick the day into life. I could be back in the office by 9 a.m., ready to attack the in-tray and the telephone calls. By the end of my three-year tour I had flown nearly 200 hours in the Chieftain; much of this time was routine but, nonetheless, very enjoyable!

# 7 'SEA KING' FURTHER EMPLOYMENT

Early in my tour I initiated a weekly Shareholders Meeting. This was held in my office at 4 p.m. on Fridays and was attended by the flight commanders of the experimental test squadron (or their nominated stand-ins), OC Met Research Flight (MRF) and OC Air Transport Flight. The day and timing was deliberately chosen to encourage everyone to be concise, as I decreed that we should be finished by 5 p.m., when the Officers' Mess Bar opened for happy hour! The meeting was meant to be a very informal get-together to review the past week, get updates on the current airborne trials programmes and consider the known demands of the week ahead vis-à-vis our resources, especially aircraft and aircrew.

I asked the flight commanders that should they see a gap in their ability to man any trials, either long or short term, they were to apprise me as soon as they could. I could then contact my opposite number at RAE Bedford to see whether there was any spare capacity there or, as an experienced experimental test pilot, offer my services or that of the group captain. I told them I would leave it to their judgement as to whether the balance of my gaining and keeping flying currency on the aircraft type in question would be worth it.

The first to take up this offer was Sqn Ldr Hugh Northie, who commanded the rotary-wing flight of the test squadron. Hugh was a tall man, upright and very military in appearance, enhanced by his trim moustache. Although RAF to the core he fitted the picture of a cavalry officer perfectly: one could imagine seeing him walking around the place with a riding crop and a Labrador dog bolted to his right leg! Notwithstanding this first impression, Hugh was a likeable and competent officer and an excellent helicopter test pilot. He appeared in my office and saluted smartly, and I invited him to sit and asked Roger to organise coffee for us both.

'How can I help, Hugh?' I enquired.

'Well, sir, I'm a bit short of bodies to operate our Sea Kings.'

There were two, and sometimes three, of these large helicopters operational at either Farnborough or Bedford at any one time. Each needed two men in the cockpit, preferably both pilots qualified on type. However, we could operate with other aircrew acting as second pilot, so long as they had been given a short course on the operation of the engines. The most critical case, requiring more than one pair of hands, was an engine failure, when the overhead engine speed control levers needed adjustment, while the operating pilot had both his hands occupied with the flying controls.

'Well, I'm current on the Gazelle, Hugh, and I've flown the Wessex, but the Sea King would be new to me,' I replied, with an expectant hope of what was about to come. And come it did.

'Do you think that you could get a Sea King conversion course organised, sir? I see a longish-term need for your help if you could.'

Trying not to beam too much, I responded, 'I'll see what HQ says and let you know.'

I wasted no time in putting a call through to our man in town, retired test pilot Wg Cdr Bill Sewell. I also told Gp Capt Scouller what the situation was and that I might be away for a month or so. After an appropriate senior officer's pause for thought he acquiesced.

Bill called me back after a couple of days. 'I've got you a place on a special course at the Royal Naval Air Station [RNAS] at Culdrose in Cornwall with No. 706 Naval Air Squadron. I'll send you the posting notice in the mail, but they want you there, ready to go, at 0830 hours on Monday, 17 February.'

As it was now mid January and I was about to convert to the Chieftain, I put this info on the back burner. However, I was surprised about one aspect: that I was going to be trained by the 'dark blue'. I knew that the RAF's Sea King Training Unit (RAFSKTU – but known as the CRABTU by the matelots!)[1] was also based at RNAS Culdrose. As a 'light blue' pilot I had expected to go there. However, I wasn't going to stir the waters – it would only confuse things. Nevertheless, there was a slight disappointment because my very good friend and my navigator from our first tour, Geoff Trott, was on the RAFSKTU staff.[2]

Time passed, the posting notice arrived, I arranged a rail warrant to Penzance and I contacted Geoff. We arranged that he would meet me off the Sunday afternoon train, I'd stay overnight with him and he would drive me into the base the next morning. Meanwhile, on the Thursday and Friday before I travelled, I refreshed my rotary wings in the Gazelle and Hugh gave me an introduction to the Sea King.

At 8 a.m. on Monday, 17 February 1986, Geoff dropped me and my luggage at the main gate of the Culdrose Air Station, officially known as HMS *Seahawk* (despite the fact that it wasn't a ship). I checked in at the guardroom, was furnished with a pass and pointed at the Officers' Mess, called The Wardroom. After trudging there I was booked in and allocated a room (sorry, a cabin). That turned out to be down several very long corridors and up two flights of stairs.

---

1. Naval personnel always refer to RAF personnel as 'Crabs' – it's something to do with being land based and walking sideways.
2. See *A Bucket of Sunshine* by this author (The History Press, 2012).

When I had divested myself of the surplus baggage, changed into uniform and grabbed all my flying kit, I found my way back to the hangar where I would work for the next month or so. On arrival in the squadron offices it was heartening to discover that I was actually expected and that all the elements of my conversion to the Westland Sea King were in place.

Inevitably, the first of these elements was a series of lectures on the Sea King's technical systems, which were fairly extensive. I soon learnt that I was not expected to be allowed anywhere near the real thing for at least a week. However, after a full day on a voyage of discovery into the bowels of the beast, I was told that I would start simulator flying from the following day. The first week unfolded in that pattern, classroom lessons, practical study and an hour and a half practising all the checks and learning to handle the aircraft in the 'sim'.

By the end of the week some of it was actually sinking in and staying there. I had also got used to the naval way of doing things, especially in the wardroom. One surprise came to me on my first morning. At about 7 a.m. there was a rap on my cabin door. It opened before I could respond and there was a cheery, 'Good morning, sir!', then in walked two small, female naval persons with the biggest teapot I had ever seen. The one whose turn it was not to be weightlifting reached out for the white mug on my bedside table, while the other poured the amber nectar into it. They didn't ask whether I wanted milk or sugar and I soon found out why. The tea in the pot had already been adequately laced with those condiments. By the time I'd realised this, the two little ladies were gone. However, the tea got me going and I soon started to look forward to this morning visitation.

By the following Monday I had been allocated an instructor, one very youthful-looking Lt Alan Duthie; the sudden realisation that I was getting older hit home. He and I took to the air for the first time on Tuesday, 25 February, so beginning an intensive and steep learning curve for me to become proficient enough to go solo within a week or so. The simulator time had paid off, in that I didn't test Alan's patience too much as he watched me carry out the pre-flight checks, start the engines and then wind up the rotor blades. More Fleet Air Arm (FAA) terminology was involved in all this. The helicopter was referred to as a 'cab' and one didn't start the engines – one 'flashed them up'. So once my instructor was confident that I could do all that on my own he would instruct me to 'Go out and flash up the cab'.

The next two weeks also 'flashed' by. Alan patiently built up my skills in all aspects of flying the Sea King, which, at a weight of around 10 tons, was much larger than any helicopter I had flown before. He demonstrated the rotary-wing equivalent to the fixed-wing aircraft's stall, when the lift is reduced by the airflow separating from the wing at low speeds and high angles of attack. The rotary-wing version is called 'vortex ring', and Alan then boldly got me to put the machine into that condition and recover it. There was lots of shaking, rocking and rolling, and a lot of height was required to get the aircraft back into safe, forward flight. The dangerous trap of flying too slowly with a high rate of descent was well illustrated by this rather disturbing exercise. The vortex ring phenomenon is caused by the downward movement of the helicopter causing an up-flow of air near the centre of the rotor disc; this reduces the overall amount of air being pushed down through the rotor blades, which gives lift. The recirculating airflow spreads out along the blades resulting in a further loss of lift and an increasingly rapid descent. Adding power just makes it worse. The only thing to do is to reduce power and move the stick forward to gain forward flight and escape from the vortex. All this means a considerable loss of height, so getting into this state near the ground, even 1,000ft above it, in the Sea King means an inevitable uncontrolled arrival on *terra firma*. In the front seats of the Sea King the pilots are very much the first people on the scene of the accident!

Once past this exciting milestone more handling exercises followed, including lots of practice engine failures, flying around with only one of the Rolls-Royce Gnome engines operating, landings on sloping ground, flying into restricted areas – with a rotor diameter of 62ft, this was a very different kettle of fish to the diminutive Gazelle – and even simulated take-offs on water. I also flew one sortie in the dark. This venture was only my second night sortie in a rotary-winged aircraft so I found it fascinating. The mix of instrument and visual flying required to manoeuvre safely in the dark, with less horizon reference, was much the same as with fixed-wing aeroplanes. The Sea King's cockpit was well lit with very few dark corners, and the modern instrumentation helped. But as ever in the dark, watching out for other helicopters' lights against the stationary lights on the ground was a constant challenge.

One interesting technicality about the Sea King was the ability it had to fold its rotor blades, so that it could be stored below decks or in a hangar. I was taught how to fold and unfold the blades as the course progressed. One engine had to be running to provide the hydraulic power and, after the appropriate hand signals had been exchanged with the ground crew, one had to slowly rotate the rotor head, controlling it with the overhead rotor brake lever, until the appropriately marked blade was in the correct position. Then the brake was fully applied and the 'blade fold' switch operated. If you had got it right the blades magically moved back on each side until they were out of view and the cycle was complete. Oddly, it was entirely possible to get the whole thing 180 degrees out and fold the blades ahead of the helicopter. Amusing but not much good for storing it in the hangar!

Following my final handling trip, whose outcome proved my competence and allowed me to be despatched home with the appropriate accreditation in my logbook, I was offered a bonus trip: a 'dunking' sortie. This didn't involve sitting in the crew room with coffee and biscuits, but rather flying out over the sea and learning how this part of the Royal Navy does its day job – listening for and locating submarines using SONAR[3]. The latter is in a submersible unit that is lowered into the water on a long cable, while the Sea King and its crew hover at 40ft. The specialist SONAR operator down the back listens for the telltale sound of a submarine going about its nefarious business. Once located the fleet's submarine hunters can be updated with the sub's position and track.

Once I'd flashed up the cab and got airborne we headed out into a sea area reserved for just this sort of exercise. There wouldn't be any big black boats under the water today – this would be just for me to experience and practise the procedures required to get the whole shooting match operational.

My mentor was Lt Wells and we had Leading Aircrewman Hewitson down the back to operate the cable gear and SONAR. Once we were in the operational area, Lt Wells took control and gave me a full demonstration of the flight pattern to be flown. This included the selection and operation of the autopilot, including its programme that took us automatically down to 40ft above the water and then reduced speed until we were stationary. It was quite unnerving how accurate the machine was. All we had to do was keep our hands very close to the flying controls just in case of the very rare event of the autopilot dropping offline. Having lowered the SONAR unit into the water, we then stayed in the hover for a few minutes; operationally the hover could last much longer.

---

3. The acronym SONAR comes from the descriptive phrase 'sound navigation and ranging'. The equipment deployed in the Sea King was the AN/AQS-13.

After the SONAR unit had been reeled in and stowed I was invited to disconnect 'George'[4] and fly away back to the start conditions of height and speed. Once there, it was my turn to do the whole thing, tightly supervised of course. I tried desperately to remember the exact sequence of events and, with a little help from my mentor, we finally ended up back at 40ft with our listening device submerged once more below us. It was at this point that a strong visual illusion hit me. The powerful downwash of air being forced through the rotor blades was making a circular pattern of waves radiating out all around us. Of course, the only bit of that expanding circle I could see was in front of us and, as I monitored the instruments, my peripheral vision was assaulted by the very strong feeling that we were moving backwards. One glance at the hovermeter soon confirmed that we were absolutely stationary, but the illusion remained. Like all the other illusory effects that assault pilots from time to time, I just had to try to ignore it and believe the instruments.

We did several more patterns, even doing it manually without George's help, and also practised an engine failure in the hover. That was challenging as the proximity of the water meant that I had to react correctly and quickly to avoid any embarrassing contact with the wet stuff. Then it was time to go home for tea and biscuits. I was exhausted and had a new and even higher respect for the guys that do this for a living – especially in the dark.

So that was the end of my training. Now I had to go back to Farnborough and offer my newfound skill set to the squadron – when they needed it. Of course that would be when they'd run out of truly professional helicopter pilots!

Back at base there were two Sea Kings: a Mark 1 (XV 371) and a Mark 4 (ZB 507). XV 371 was the second prototype and had been transported by sea in the late 1960s from Sikorsky Helicopters in the USA to Southampton and then by road to Westland Helicopters' factory at Yeovil in south-west England. There it and its sister ship, XV370, had been modified to become the first UK Sea Kings. When one strapped in there was a reminder of this heritage under one's feet. The rudder pedals had Sikorsky's logo on them and not Westland's 'Flying W' that adorned all subsequent airframes.

---

4.   George is the universal name given to autopilots.

A trap for the unwary was that the Mark 1, like the Mark 5 that I had learnt on, had a retractable undercarriage, but the Mark 4 did not. So if one had flown a series of trials or training sorties on the Mark 4 and then moved to the Mark 1, more than usual attention had to be paid to ensure that there were wheels to land on before that last lowering of the collective lever. One young test pilot from Bedford fell into this trap one day and we received a message that our Mark 1, which was on loan, had a flatter bottom that it should have! The said young man soon appeared at Farnborough in his best uniform with a sheepish expression and passed a few minutes with the group captain. Before he went in I told him that he needn't worry – the group captain's bite was much worse than his bark. Somehow this didn't seem to help!

By the end of my tour I had flown nearly 140 hours in the Sea Kings and been involved in a variety of trials. These included projects involving lasers, high frequency (HF) radio, infrared jamming, aircraft model drops and a really interesting trial landing on the deck of a frigate in the dark. Another activity was flying the Bedford Ferry during the days when the airfield at Farnborough was occupied by the international air show and we could not use the main runway for our own fixed-wing transport aircraft. But the best of all the trials were those involving kit known as 'Red Eggs'.

The Red Egg was the colloquial name given to an HF dipole suspended below a helicopter. They were used in conjunction with a reasonably sophisticated computer-based measurement system for calibrating HF aerials. The complete measurement system was used to calibrate the HF aerial array at RAE Cobbett Hill, which was about 8 miles east of Farnborough. Because of the radio characteristics of the test equipment, the Eggs had to be flown quite close to the aerials at Cobbett Hill, whose radio call sign was Cove Radio. This meant that above 2,500ft the test aircraft would be operating in one of the busiest bits of controlled airspace in the UK – London Heathrow's terminal area. Cobbett Hill was, in turn, used at much longer ranges to measure the polar diagrams of aircraft HF aerials and derive how much power was actually transmitted. The Red Egg equipment could also be used to determine the polar diagrams of ground-based aerials.

The electrical dipole within the airborne equipment (the Egg) comprised two half-wave elements, with the transmitter and battery pack enclosed in an electrically insulated spherical enclosure – painted fluorescent orange – giving the Red Egg its name. The radiating elements were hawser-laid steel cables cut to the discrete resonant length of the frequency in use, making up both ends of a vertical dipole. The continuous wave radio frequency transmitter was crystal controlled, nominally of 1 watt output power. The transmitter and dipole aerial were suspended 132ft below the helicopter on a nylon rope, with a 68kg lead weight attached, via a strop, to the lower dipole element. The whole shebang was limited to 60 knots maximum speed in forward flight and 40 knots when descending.

I had authorised a number of these trials and, because they involved a Sea King climbing vertically within the London control area, I'd been briefed on all the operating procedures and the essential coordination with Heathrow ATC. So when I was asked to spend an evening in July 1988 flying a couple of these sorties, I was delighted to accept. Accordingly my co-pilot, Major Paul Whitfield of the Army Air Corps and now one of our helicopter test pilots, set up all the arrangements with Heathrow and the Civil Aviation Authority (CAA). We agreed with them to start after the teatime rush of arrivals and departures from the airport.

After we had started up and taxied to the pick-up point, the Red Egg was hooked on to the helicopter by a brave soul crawling underneath. We then had to lift off vertically to about 200ft to ensure that the Egg was airborne and then, observing the speed restriction, take our precious cargo to a nominated position 8 miles east of Farnborough and about 10 miles south of London Heathrow airport. Once we had located this position, helped by our friendly boffin in the back, we had to hover over it at heights of up to 10,000ft. Initially we started at 2,000ft, but once the folks at the radio station had got the answers they needed and our on-board scientist was happy we had to climb to the next altitude – 5,000ft – and then hover there.

We didn't have any sophisticated navigation kit to help, just our young civil servant down the back with an Ordnance Survey map looking through a hole in the floor and calling for us to move forwards or backwards to stay over the feature he had picked. Simple! However, I had never hovered a helicopter at any more than a few feet from the ground. The first experience at 2,000ft was initially a bit unnerving, but I just concentrated on the hovermeter to make sure that we stayed still and acted on any corrections from the back. To make life easier we had consulted the weather forecast for the evening for winds up to 10,000ft and made sure we were pointing into them. That would help us hover most efficiently, as we would effectively be flying slowly forward through the air while staying over the same spot on the ground.

This led to the first interesting conversation with the man operating the radar at Heathrow. I called, 'Heathrow Radar, this is Nugget 02.[5] We'd now like to climb vertically in this position from 2,000ft to 5,000ft.'

'Roger, Nugget 02. What heading would you like to climb on?' was the reply.

'We'll be climbing vertically so we won't move forward,' I said.

'Roger, 02, but I need to know the heading you'll be climbing on.'

At this point it was easier to fulfil his fixed-wing fixation. '250 degrees,' I responded.

'OK, 02, you're clear to climb on that heading.' Great – now he'll be wondering why our blip doesn't move!

When we finally arrived at 10,000ft I noticed that all the needles on the engine gauges were pointing very close to the red bits. We were operating at our maximum ceiling for the weight and temperature. We had taken off with a fuel load calculated to give us the right weight to climb to and hover at 10,000ft and it was spot on!

After word from the HF radio station we descended again, pausing at the intermediate heights for further readings to be taken. Then we had to land to change this Red Egg for another one that would measure different things. Once we had been released by Heathrow and the boffins at Cobbett Hill, I had to fly back to Farnborough while being very aware that the Egg was trailing along almost 200ft below us. Once overhead the part of the airfield we had been given to operate from, I started a very slow vertical descent (I was well in practice by now) until the man in the back, now looking over the sill of the open door, told me that the Egg had landed. Then I continued the descent but with a bit of sideways movement so that the cable would not be all coiled up under our belly when the ground team came out to retrieve our precious cargo.

Once we had topped up the fuel and got our new Egg attached we were off again to repeat the whole exercise before it got too dark to see the ground. Things went much as before and it was fun to watch the sun get near the horizon and then lift again as we climbed to the next test altitude.

It was now evident from the reduction of chat on the radio that things were quietening down over at Heathrow airport. However, at one point, and

---

5. 'Nugget' was the very long-standing radio call sign allocated to the RAE for use at all its flying stations.

while hovering at 5,000ft, we received a call from Heathrow: 'Nugget 02 can you maintain your present height and position until further notice please?'

As we were there to do just that it was easy to give an affirmative answer. I just hoped that 'until further notice' wasn't going to be too long – it would soon be dark. We quickly found out the reason for the request.

'Nugget 02, there's a Boeing 747 that's going to pass about a mile from you, descending through your altitude. He's south-west of you at 5 miles and descending out of 10,000.'

We looked up and spotted the big airliner straight away. 'Visual contact.' I reported.

'OK, 02, don't move.'

I had no intention of moving. It was mesmerising to watch the Jumbo Jet get bigger and bigger as it closed on us. I used the yaw pedals to turn to keep the aircraft fully in view though the windscreen. As it passed majestically across the setting sun, in a gentle right turn around us, I swear that I saw a sea of faces peering out of the windows, no doubt astonished to see a big helicopter going by at 5,000ft. It was a magical end to a fascinating evening.

# 8 FAST NIGHTBIRDS

One of the main areas of research for the ten years before my return to Farnborough was that of giving pilots of fixed-wing, fast-jet, military aircraft the ability to fly safely and effectively at high speed and at about 250ft above the ground at night. As a test pilot in the mid 1970s I had been involved in the early days of that research and had flown many hours in a specially equipped two-seat Hunter and a similarly capable Varsity.[1] (More of which later.)

The Hunter, a single-engine, twin-seat, jet fighter-trainer, was then fitted with a low-light television (LLTV) camera in the nose and a screen displaying its view in front of the right-seat pilot. The screen was overlaid with flight symbology so that the test pilot could fly the aircraft by viewing one source of visual information.

---

1.   See *Trials and Errors* by this author (The History Press, 2015).

The research programmes at that time were progressing steadily towards the goals of achieving safe, low-level operations at night. However, there was one major problem. The aircraft always carried two pilots on low-level sorties, the pilot in the left seat being both the captain and the safety pilot. It was his job to ensure that the test pilot using the sensor did not stray into any dangerous flight conditions. The paradox was that the best view of what was going on outside could only be gained from the sensor. As the sensor was merely experimental at that point, using it to monitor overall flight safety went against all the premises of test flying; an independent means of monitoring the flight was necessary. When this was pointed out it was received with deafening silence. There was, at least initially, no way round it. The safety pilot could only use his judgement and gut feeling – not the best approach.

Meanwhile our rotary-wing brothers had been flying around at very low levels in the dark using a fairly new-fangled invention: night-vision goggles (NVGs). Eventually, and after my previous time at Farnborough, the use of NVGs for fast-jet pilots was investigated. There were all sorts of potential problems with having these rather bulky and weighty objects mounted on one's helmet. The first was the lack of head room in small fighter cockpits. Another was the destabilising weight that tended to pull the helmet forward, especially when positive g-forces were used, such as in steep turns and pull-ups. A third was the potential effect on the pilot's physiology from an ejection with the NVGs in place – this was (quite literally) the killer, with a broken neck as the potential consequence.

To overcome some of these areas of concern helmets were fitted absolutely correctly and kept tight to the head. To enable pilots to get the NVGs off their helmets before using the ejection seat an easily operated, quick-release device was incorporated. In static tests we proved that they could be knocked off the helmet with a swipe of one hand in less than a second, which was deemed to be an acceptable delay. After all, we operated in a world of measured risk.

Aside from all that, the NVGs, by their very nature, greatly magnified all incoming light so that normal cockpit lighting overwhelmed them, rendering them effectively useless. This drawback had already been overcome in helicopters by the use of very soft, green lighting of the correct wavelength and, because the NVGs were especially sensitive to red and orange light, there had to be special filtering of all warning lights. Another problem was the magnification of any reflections on the windscreens from within the cockpit. These could come from many sources and the only way to eliminate, or at least minimise, these was by observation and then correction. Our shiny white gloves and white plastic kneepads were out!

So, by 1986, the reliable old Hunter, still carrying the name of the mythical ruler of the night – the Greek goddess Hecate – had an IR camera in the nose and a HUD that showed the right-seat pilot what the IR was seeing, with all the flight information symbols on it as well. The cockpit lighting had been modified for NVG operations and both pilots would be wearing NVGs.

During development of this capability the over-enhancement of the HUD scene by the NVGs became a distraction and limited capability when the pilot was looking ahead. The General Electric Company (GEC) had come up with a solution. Small sensors detected when the NVGs were pointing ahead and switched them off so that the pilot could then use the IR picture for navigation and terrain avoidance. When he looked elsewhere the NVGs would operate normally and help him to see all around.

As there was no shortage of test pilots to fly the Hunter, I avoided putting pressure on anyone to let me gain first-hand experience of the changes that had been made over the past decade. However, in early 1987 I was asked if I would like to become involved. My answer was an eager, 'Yes.'

So in early March, Flt Lt Mervyn Evans and I flew two sorties in our Nightbird Hunter WV 383, with me sitting behind the large HUD showing me the world outside as seen by the IR camera in the nose. Ironically, the first flight was in daylight. A retractable blind had been raised over the face of the HUD lens so that I couldn't see through it, but only use the IR picture to fly at low level. Of course we did not wear NVGs and there were lots of orientation cues in my peripheral vision. It was, however, a very useful introduction. We flew the low-level parts of the flight at 250ft above the ground and at a speed of 420 knots; this would be what I had to try to achieve in the dark.

When Mervyn and I rendezvoused later the first event was to fit the NVGs to my helmet, and have the helmet's inner harness tightened to just below pain threshold to ensure that it didn't droop down and affect my view through the goggles. Having done all that, Mervyn made me practise knocking the NVGs off – after he had adopted a suitable catching position! I then practised putting them back in place – not that easy once you have the helmet on. The goggles have a hinge so that they can be pushed up out of the way and latched there when you don't need them. Next we went outside, I lowered the goggles and adjusted the objective lenses individually to get the sharpest possible definition. Then I took a couple of minutes to look up at the night sky. The view through the NVGs was mind-blowing: the number of visible stars increased; the sky seemed literally full of stars. There were barely any dark spaces anywhere, and then a bright but slow meteor crossed the sky; it was an airliner climbing out of Heathrow! After that small indulgence we were ready to go find our steed and get airborne.

As the occupant of the left seat and aircraft captain, everything up to the take-off point was Mervyn's business. He handed over to me as we entered on Runway 25 and I used the picture in the HUD to line us up on the centreline. The take-off was easy to accomplish and we were soon winging our way west at about 2,000ft. Once we were west of Boscombe Down we descended to an initial height of 500ft so I could get used to it. One thing I had noticed immediately on lowering the NVGs into place was a feeling that my IQ had been halved – and as that wasn't huge to start with, it was a worrying effect! The cockpit was suddenly all very unfamiliar. The slightly offset view the NVGs gave me and the very low lighting level made me less confident about what was going on. However, like all new experiences, time and practice usually overcomes these uncomfortable feelings.

As we headed into the Welsh foothills I initially had a little difficulty in discerning clearly the rising ground, so I asked Mervyn to take over while I looked around without worrying about flying the aircraft. A few minutes later my brain had recalibrated itself to the images it was receiving and I took back control. As the flight went on I was feeling more and more comfortable and Mervyn seemed happy to let me fly down to our height limit of 250ft. All too soon we were leaving the low-level areas and had to head back to Farnborough. I wanted to try landing using the system. I had done this in 1976 using the LLTV system, and Mervyn agreed. Just to make sure I couldn't cheat, he called ATC, asking them to turn off all the runway lights.

I looked to the area where I judged the airfield to be; it was visible by its absence. Being in a built-up area the black oblong among the green spots of light to my left was undoubtedly where the runway could be found. We descended to 1,500ft, I completed the pre-landing checks and when I judged the runway to be in the correct relative position I turned on to the final approach. As I turned the runway came into view in the HUD, it was clearly visible and I could line up with it easily. The only trick now was to judge the 3-degree approach angle correctly. However, the view was so clear that experience took over and we arrived in the right place at the right speed.

There was no doubt in my mind that this was the basis of an acceptable operational system. However, the MOD's equipment procurement and training empires would have a lot of work ahead to translate it across to the RAF's offensive aircraft fleet.

In addition to this ongoing research and development programme in the Hunter, we had received a Harrier and a Buccaneer to help with type-specific, fast-jet research and development – all of which became known as the Nightbird Programme. Both these latter aircraft were modified to carry the latest iterations of IR sensors, which, thanks to miniaturisation of their electronics and their cryogenic cooling systems, were now much smaller than some of the previous models.

The Buccaneer had been modified not only to accept the nose-mounted IR sensor, HUD and NVG-compatible cockpit lighting, but also had a second control stick installed in the rear cockpit. This work had been done at the Cranfield Institute of Technology (later Cranfield University) and made the aircraft unique as the world's only dual-control Buccaneer; in fact, it was given the official nomenclature of the Mark 2C. I flew this unique aircraft only a couple of times, once in daylight and once at night. The system worked really well and the software included target-marking cues in the HUD. These had first been developed in the Canberra B(I)8 that I had flown in the mid 1970s, and then refined in the Hunter. The only drawback in the Buccaneer was that the viewpoint given by the NVGs, with its lenses about 10cm ahead of one's eyeballs, was badly affected by the Buccaneer's very wide canopy arch. However, the aircraft's excellent low-level handling made contour following using the IR picture in the HUD easier than in the Hunter.

The Nightbird Harrier XW 269 was similarly equipped and equally capable. With the Buccaneer, it took part in a large exercise over several nights called Grand Design. This took place on Salisbury Plain, in May 1987, using the military training area there so that quantitative and qualitative data could be derived while the aircraft were flying operationally realistic attack profiles against mobile armoured vehicles, including tanks.

One of the potential problems that particularly affected the use of NVGs in the Harrier was that of the pilot divesting himself of the goggles should a major malfunction occur while hovering – a mode of flight unique to the 'jump jet'. The delay involved was unacceptable hovering at 20ft or so. Because of this we had prohibited hovering at night when NVGs were worn. However, there was increasing pressure from above to extend the Nightbird Harrier's capability to carry out recoveries to off-airfield pads via a hover landing.

So the first thing to do was to investigate how we could get the goggles off the pilot's helmet reliably and quickly while his hands were full controlling the aircraft. Trials had been carried out using a static ejection seat rig in the USA, with dummies in the seat. A very small explosive charge had been installed behind the release mechanism of the goggles that was triggered by the operation of the ejection seat handle. This meant that the goggles would come off as soon as the pilot ejected and no delay would occur. That was very important if the jet was falling out of the sky to the ground only 20ft or so below. High-speed film footage showed that the goggles could impact the pilot's legs as the seat went rapidly up the rail. The medics at the RAF Institute of Aviation Medicine (IAM) based at Farnborough voiced their concerns that serious injury may occur, even to the extent of a broken thighbone – not a happy injury to take to a parachute landing. Their solution was to give the pilot extra padding to wear on his upper legs.

I could not help thinking that this was overkill, but I had no data to go on. Harrier pilots wore anti-g suit trousers and carried things in or over the pockets above their knees. That was already bulky enough in the tight confines of the Harrier cockpit. I discovered that more work was being done at Farnborough to test the NVG separation system so I asked whether we could set up a test with a live person rather than a dummy. I offered myself rather than press a valuable member of the test aircrew community to be the dummy. (If the cap fits!) So, a few days later a static ejection seat rig was set up in one of the hangars with a high-speed camera to record the outcome and I rolled up to once more be the guinea pig.

I strapped in, the goggles were put on to my helmet and the appropriate electrical connections made, via a wire attached to the normal intercom lead. Quite a crowd of aircrew had gathered to watch the 'wingco' catch the goggles in his delicate nether regions. Eventually the boffins decided that it was time to roll. So on a countdown I pulled the ejection seat initiation handle between my legs. Nothing happened! That is except the shrill whine of the high-speed camera. Things were examined; mutterings emanated from the boffins; connections disconnected and reconnected.

'Okay, let's do it again – but don't run the camera,' came the instruction from the man in charge.

'Three. Two. One – now!'

I pulled the handle and with a very small bang the goggles fell into my lap. They hit my left wrist and then dropped off the front of my legs on to the padded floor that had been laid beforehand. This success was sufficient to spur the assembly to cheer and the boffins to reload the goggles with its explosive cap and fit them back on my helmet.

'Right, let's go with the camera this time.'

This time everything worked and the event was recorded for posterity and analysis. The outcome was that, while there was still some uncertainty as to where the falling goggles might impact the rising pilot, we could go ahead with the system in the Harrier and drop the cricket pads on the thighs idea. We added the requirement for a positive electrical continuity check, between the micro-switch in the handle and the NVGs, after the pilot had strapped into the seat. This was easily achieved.

Early in 1987 we had received a task to examine the feasibility of recovering Harriers to dispersed, off-airfield pads at night and without lights. This operation was, and had been from the early days of the Harrier's service, a common daytime operation. Several aircraft and aircrew would be despatched to a pre-prepared area, usually in wooded countryside, to operate attack sorties from these dispersed sites. The landing pads were about 40sq. ft and made of pierced steel planking (PSP) firmly picketed to the ground. There were often also PSP 'taxiways' leading to camouflaged servicing pads.

One of the main difficulties for the operational Harrier pilots was making an accurate vertical descent over the centre of a pad they could not see. By day this was overcome by training pilots to use reference points, provided by bright red posts, arranged around the pad. Using these they could align themselves exactly over the centre. It required a period of high-intensity concentration but was part of the standard training package for Harrier drivers. The problem at night was that using lights instead of the posts would negate the covert nature of the operation; it was hoped that the pads and surrounding areas would remain dark throughout the exercise.

Enter a very clever man, whose name I can sadly no longer remember, from RAE Bedford who had invented the lighting system that helped aircraft fly visually an accurate approach slope to ground. A system that is now in worldwide use, and has been since the mid 1970s, it is known as Precision Approach Path Indicator (PAPI). This man's new discovery was fiendishly clever. He had discovered that when a 12-volt current from a battery was passed through a standard neon light tube no visible light was emitted. If, however, one observed the tube with NVGs it looked like a bright green line. So the cunning plan was to place the battery-powered neons in the same place that the daytime markers were located. The hope was that the pilots, using their NVGs, could then land safely on the pad in total darkness.

After much homework the trial was set up to take place in the Stanford Military Training Area in Norfolk during the last week of March 1987. The Harrier would operate out of RAF Wittering, then the UK home of the Harrier force, and ground support in the field being provided by the RAF from there. The test pilots would be Flt Lt Andy Sephton, who had joined the Experimental Flying Squadron from the Fast Jet Test Squadron (FJTS) at Boscombe Down, and Flt Lt Les Evans, an ex-Harrier pilot, from RAE Bedford. As the trial was deemed to be officially 'high risk', our new COEF, Gp Capt Reg Hallam, had to sign it off and he appointed me as authorising and supervising officer.

The preparations began in the days before the nominated trial date of Wednesday, 25 March. They started with Andy and Les getting familiar with the Nightbird Harrier by both day and night; I wanted them to have no doubts about how the kit operated and how they would manage any failures. I became involved with the scientists and the army, who managed the training area. On the Friday of the week preceding the trial I flew the Gazelle to RAF Wittering. There I checked on the logistic support that would be provided and I also picked up an old boffin friend, Mr Peter Tanner, who had been involved with fixed-wing electro-optical (EO) trials for many years. We flew to the site where I dropped Peter off and met up with the man from the ministry who had the final say on our operations, Colonel Baker. He came with me in the Gazelle and we flew a reconnaissance of the site and the approach paths for the Harrier that had been proposed. When the colonel had expressed his contentment with our plans I dropped him off and returned to base.

Wednesday, 25 March dawned bright and spring-like; the weather forecast for the night was good. The Harrier had been pre-positioned at Wittering and my job was to get myself there to authorise the two sorties that we had planned: one each for Andy and Les to take turns to fly in the front seat, with the other acting as safety pilot and captain in the back. In the meantime the trials management folk had asked for photographs of the site and approach paths so on my way I called in at Bedford and picked up photographer Peter Hudson and flew him to the training area to take a whole load of happy but informative snaps. I landed so that he could take shots of the pads and support facilities, and I took the opportunity to check in with the ground support folks. I would be spending the evening with them so felt it best that they knew who I was and what I was doing there. I then flew Peter back to Bedford and returned to the site ready for the evening's activities.

I had a pair of NVGs so that I could observe everything from a close but safe distance. The sun set and we waited. Then, when it was properly dark, we heard the Harrier pilots on the radio telling us that they were inbound for their first approach to the pad. We extinguished all our lights. An infrared beacon had been set up about a mile east of the pad and a portable Tactical Air Navigation (TACAN) beacon placed to help with the initial positioning. Soon we heard that distinctive Harrier noise as the aircraft was decelerating on its approach. The aircraft had no lights switched on so, visually, there was nothing to see – just the increasing jet noise gave us a clue as to where they were.

I put the NVGs to my eyes and searched in the direction of the ever-increasing roar. There it was! I looked round towards the pad and could clearly see the neon light markers. The noise was now thunderous and I pulled my ear defenders on. As the Harrier appeared over the trees at about 100ft it looked huge. I could now see the aircraft clearly through the goggles and saw a bright patch of green light towards the rear fuselage. What was that? Then I realised it was the heat of the jet exhaust acting on the rear nozzle. I slipped the goggles down for a second and I could see a cherry-red patch of light there. NVGs are sensitive to red light so they showed up the hot patch very clearly.

The Harrier had now come to a stop and was very slowly descending. It looked to be well positioned over the pad. It continued slowly down, the deafening roar of the jet efflux mixed with that unique Harrier sound – a fluctuating high-pitched metallic scream as the air came from the pitch and roll control nozzles. By the time the aircraft had descended to about 10ft I think everyone had stopped breathing – at least I had! Then it was down and the throttle was slammed shut and the engine made another unique Harrier sound, like the biggest intake of breath you ever heard; we all joined in!

Now came the really high-risk bit. The aircraft had to sit absolutely still with the engine at idle and the nozzles pointing rearwards so that our brave boffin, Peter, could go forward, crawl up to the nose wheel and make a chalk mark on the pad. This would happen after every landing during the evening and the location of each mark would be noted to give an overall average displacement from dead centre.

The exercise was repeated several more times before the guys said that there was insufficient fuel to do any more. After that last touchdown, and after Peter Tanner had made his mark, the next phase of the trial came into play: refuelling and servicing in the dark. All the ground crew involved had NVGs and, after the jet had taxied off the pad and shut down, they went to work. I used my NVGs to find the test pilots and chat about how it had gone. They both agreed that it was very hard work but manageable and they were happy to swap seats and do it all again. So I authorised trip two, slapped them on the back and told them not to crash!

The second sortie went much as the first and all the landings were successful in that they did not miss the pad. In fact, later analysis would show that the scatter of the touchdown point was not much different to those experienced by day. There were some concerns about the utility of the IR beacon but, overall, the outcome was that we could recommend that the Operational Evaluation Unit could take this method of night dispersed operation further to evaluate the equipment and training requirements.

I experienced one other interesting event during that evening. While I was keeping out of the way during the turnaround and refuelling I indulged myself in looking at the night sky through the NVGs. As I was marvelling at the awesome multitude of stars I noticed a dark, triangular shape moving across the green background. It was undoubtedly an aircraft, but it was not showing any lights. I watched it disappear from view to the south-east. I could hear no exhaust noise. To this day I am not certain what it was. However, when I first saw the Lockheed F-117 Nighthawk stealth fighter I was struck by the similarity in shape to what I had seen that night. Could the F-117 have been flying over the UK in 1987?

Andy and Les would be doing more Nightbird Harrier work later that year. In November a project office requirement arrived on my desk to test the firing of rockets at night while using NVGs. There was a worry that the flare from the rocket motors would swamp the goggles and prove to be dangerous. After all, diving at the ground in the dark was dangerous enough; and Harrier pilots came from the *day* fighter/attack lineage stretching back decades.

When I discussed how the aims of the exercise would be safely achieved it became clear that another detachment to RAF Wittering would be necessary – mainly for easy and efficient access to the weapons ranges in the Wash area of East Anglia. COEF was then brought into the picture, who appointed me the authorising officer for the sorties and I was to remain at the range while they were taking place. On 2 December I flew the Gazelle to Wittering, from where the Harrier would operate, so that I could authorise the flights, then flew to Holbeach Range to observe the firings. All went well and I stayed overnight at Wittering before returning to Farnborough the following morning. The outcome was that launching the rockets in sequences, from each of the pods carried under the Harrier's wings, starting with single missiles and progressing through pairs up to fours, had not proved problematic. Both pilots flew a sortie each to get two opinions.

When we returned to Farnborough the results were passed to the project office. This elicited the question, 'What about firing all the rockets in both pods simultaneously?' I passed this down the line and the response was that, based on the previous trial, it might be feasible. 'Let's try it,' was the considered response. I went to the group captain and proposed that we mount this sortie from Farnborough with me in the back seat, so avoiding all the complications of the previous week. He agreed and Andy Sephton and I mounted up on the evening of Monday, 7 December 1987, both equipped with NVGs. We made a medium-level transit to Holbeach Range and Andy flew a couple of dry runs to the target before he tipped in for the big event. I called the heights as we descended on the attack pattern and when his sight picture was right he let the whole lot go. From my point of view there was a very brief flare in the NVGs but they recovered quickly and by the time Andy had completed the recovery manoeuvre they were back to normal. With these latest generation goggles it was very much a non-event. We later recommended that NVG-compatible Harriers could safely carry out rocket attacks at night.

Another aspect of our Nightbird work was NVG familiarisation sorties in our Jaguar for nominated pilots from other units and organisations. I was fortunate enough to fly several of these sorties and, using NVGs alone, it proved perfectly feasible to fly successful low-level operational profiles using the proven techniques coupled with Jaguar's navigation and attack system. At that stage the equipping of the RAF's Jaguar force with an IR sensor was not envisaged; however, the modification of some operational Jaguars for NVG night ops followed later. It was very satisfying to see the maturity of this capability that had first started over a decade previously. Little did we know it, but the use of electro-optics in actual air warfare was not that far ahead of us.

# 9 A SLOW NIGHTBIRD

The Vickers Varsity was a bulky, twin-piston-engined training aircraft designed in the late 1940s. I had first flown it in 1976, when the Experimental Flying Squadron had been allocated three of these venerable flying machines to operate on research programmes: two for IR and one for highly classified work related to the guidance of the Polaris intercontinental ballistic missile (ICBM) that armed the UK's fleet of four Resolution-class nuclear-powered submarines. By the late 1980s, the sole remaining Varsity at Farnborough was WL 679.[1] This airframe had rolled off the Vickers production line at Bournemouth in 1953 and had been transferred to the Radio Flight at Farnborough in January 1954. After further service in the research and development business at Pershore, Bedford and West Malling, it was transferred back to Farnborough on 28 March 1977; I flew that flight.

So what is a Varsity? In 1948 the Air Ministry issued a requirement to the UK aircraft industry to propose a twin-engine pilot and navigation trainer as a replacement for the Vickers Wellington T Mark 10 and the Vickers Valetta. Perhaps, therefore, it was no surprise that the Vickers Aircraft Company came up with the winning submission. The Varsity was a development of the military Valetta and the civilian Viking that had already been built and were successfully in service. The main differences were that the Varsity had a tricycle undercarriage rather than the tail-wheel layout of the Valetta; it had a wheel under the nose. Moreover, the company had added a ventral pannier under the already rather rotund fuselage; this lower protuberance housed a small, glazed, prone position cabin for a student bomb-aimer and his instructor and, behind that, a bomb bay that could carry up to a couple dozen 25lb practice bombs. There were hydraulically operated doors over this part.

The Varsity was about 68ft long, with a wingspan of around 95ft and the top of its tail reached 24ft into the air. It was equipped with two big, round Bristol

---

1.  Varsity WL 679 was flown from Farnborough to the RAF Museum at Cosford on 27 July 1992 and is still on display there. At the time it was the world's only airworthy example of its type.

Hercules fourteen-cylinder radial engines, each driving four-bladed, variable-pitch propellers and giving a total motive power of almost 4,000hp. That was sufficient to take the Varsity's 15-ton weight to a maximum speed of around 200 knots in level flight and up to an altitude of over 25,000ft. We, however, would be generally operating below 10,000ft and cruising at 130–160 knots. The overall impression of the Vickers Varsity was one of bulk. In RAF service it had picked up the rather rude sobriquet of 'The Pig'.

The entry and exit for all who would sail in her was via a ladder, carried on board, let down from the door aft of the wing on the port side. The flight crew, in our case usually a pilot and a navigator or two pilots and a navigator, would then make their way forward to the bit with forward-facing windows, where there was a rearward-facing navigator's station behind the two pilots' seats.

The instrument panels were pretty conventional and typical of the era. The central console had a wondrous collection of levers that were there to control the engines: propeller rpm, throttles and fuel cocks. The flying controls were manually operated from a control yoke and rudder pedals, and the usual set of three trim wheels fell easily to hand.

Starting the engines was a challenging procedure because one needed more hands and fingers than the good Lord had provided. As well as operating the throttles there were switches on the roof panel to manipulate in a set sequence. After turning the engines over with the fuel and ignition off (to ensure that any oil pooled in the lower cylinders was first expelled), the fuel cocks were opened, the ignition switches were selected 'ON' and the booster coil – for that added electrical *oomph* – was pressed. This usually resulted in a wonderful sequence of pops and bangs, accompanied by clouds of white smoke from the engine's exhaust, before the Hercules engine finally settled into a rhythmic rumble. For those of us with little or no experience of big, round motors it was an extraordinary experience getting to grips with the beast.

In 1976 the aircraft had been modified to carry both forward-looking infrared (FLIR) and LLTV sensors with a suite of operating stations in the capacious rear cabin for the scientists to use. By 1987 the IR sensor was GEC's high-resolution thermal imaging high-bandwidth system, a world leader in its resolution capability. Like the Hunter, the Varsity's cockpit had a screen let into the right-hand side of the pilots' instrument panel. However, flight symbology was not shown on the screen, which instead had to be gleaned from special flight instruments surrounding the screen.

I had not really expected to get back in the cockpit of this lumbering old aeroplane again. Though that's not to say that I didn't still hold a great affection for it – after all I had flown over 200 hours in it during my previous stint at Farnborough. But in March 1987 Sqn Ldr John Turner, who had taken over C Flight, which operated the Varsity, asked me if I could help out as the workload on his flight was now pressing. Naturally, I agreed and on Wednesday, 18 March 1987 I renewed my acquaintance with the Varsity's 1940s-style cockpit and the protracted and ambidextrously challenging engine-starting procedures. Yet again Mervyn Evans was the brave soul who accompanied me as my mentor and guide – very different to the Jaguar and Hunter time we had previously shared.[2] It really was like going back in time, and not just to 1977. The roomy cockpit, furnished with a large windscreen made up of a mosaic of Plexiglas panels, was reminiscent of wartime aircraft like the Wellington or Blenheim. The aircraft's response to control inputs was appropriately sluggish and the forces mostly moderate, but flying it accurately was not particularly hard – the Varsity had been endowed with good stability and control characteristics. Once up and away it was a very satisfying feeling to be cruising round the sky with those big engines throbbing away, easily in sight on each side of the cockpit. As with all big piston-engine flying machines, powerplant management was high on one's agenda. The other really splendid quality that I liked about the Varsity was the ease with which one could pull off a really smooth landing. Of course, as the saying goes, 'Any landing you can walk away from is a good one!' A good landing requires a good final approach, but when one had learnt all the correct techniques with power, flap and trim a very satisfactory touchdown was usually the outcome. On one occasion I even had one of the boffins down the back ask if we were down yet as I turned off the runway. Result!

During that summer I flew the Varsity regularly on a variety of data-gathering trial sorties, mostly by day. However, much more flying in this tubby, twin-piston engine plane was to come my way in the autumn.

2.  Because I had not flown the Varsity within the last three months I was not 'current on type' so had to be checked by a pilot who was certified to instruct.

At one of our Friday afternoon meetings, John Turner said that he had been asked to support a two-week detachment by Varsity WL 679 to West Germany for participation in a large NATO ground forces exercise to the east of RAF Gütersloh, which would be the base for our operations. However, he had a problem with manning it due to other commitments on his test pilots.

'Could you do it, boss?' he enquired.

Of course my instant reaction was to say yes. However, I knew that I would have to clear my absence for two weeks with my boss.

'Leave it with me, John. I'll let you know as soon as I can.'

I managed to catch a word with the group captain as we were leaving the office and he was not totally happy with me being away for a fortnight.

'Ask John if he could cover one of the weeks and you do the other. There's a lot going on right now,' was his reply.

We agreed that I would do the first week and that Flt Lt Rob Foulkes would take over at the end of that week. It was all set.

After lots of briefings with the scientists and Flight Test Observers (FTO), agreements with the ground support management and our hosts at Gütersloh, we finally started the engines, in the usual noisy fashion, on Friday, 9 October. Flt Lt Dickie George was my navigator and we had two scientists and two ground crew down the back, along with all our baggage, spare wheels, tools and other potentially useful bits and pieces. Two hours later, after a pleasant flight, mostly flown by our autopilot George (not the nav.) we arrived at RAF Gütersloh.

The air base at Gütersloh was most probably constructed in the mid 1930s, during the interwar German military expansion; it was used by the Luftwaffe throughout the Second World War, until it was overrun by US forces in spring 1945. They handed the base over to the RAF in July that year and it became the HQ of No. 2 Group. In subsequent years many squadrons had been based there. In 1958, No. 2 Group became NATO's 2nd Allied Tactical Air Force (2ATAF) and moved its HQ to the west to RAF Rheindahlen. RAF Gütersloh was the most easterly of the RAF stations in West Germany and became the home of the shorter range fighter and fighter/recce squadrons while the longer range tactical nuclear squadrons, flying Canberras then Buccaneers, Phantoms and Jaguars, were based near the Dutch border, at the RAF stations of Laarbruch, Bruggen and Wildenrath. By 1987 Gütersloh had become the base for the RAF Germany Harrier force, comprising Nos 3 and 4 Squadrons. Chinook and Puma support helicopters, of Nos 18 and 230 Squadrons, were the other permanent residents. The airfield had a single east–west runway of about 7,500ft in length, the usual radar and navigation aids, and a large technical support site to the north of the runway.

After landing and wrapping everything up, we made ourselves known to the folks in station operations and moved into our rooms in the Officers' Mess, where we could relax for the weekend and be ready for a busy week starting on Monday morning. So the first thing on the agenda was to attend the usual Friday evening happy hour in the Officers' Mess. During a very convivial evening with Harrier 'mates', we were shown some of the special features of the Teutonic building. The first of these were to be found in the gents' toilets. There was a couple of what looked like oversized urinals, set apart from the others of more traditional design. Each had vertical chromed handles on each side and a large chrome stud at head height. The lower edge was far too high for conventional use, especially for a 'short house' like me. After puzzling as to what these porcelain vessels were, our host told us that they were traditional Luftwaffe loo fixtures that allowed young, Aryan fighter and bomber pilots to divest themselves of surplus beer and sausages in a hygienic manner. The chrome stud could be pressed with the forehead while using the handlebars for straining; this action would flush the bowl. The Harrier guys christened these bizarre furnishings the 'honkertoriums'!

Then we were taken upstairs into the tower that was an outstanding architectural feature of the mess building. At the very top was a room of about 32sq. ft with chairs set round a large table. There was a large beam above the table and windows around the sides. The legend was that Reichmarshal Hermann Göring used to visit the base during the war and take his young protégés up there, ply them with beer and tell tales of his exploits as a pilot during the First World War. Apparently he would punctuate these stories of derring-do with the phrase, 'And if that isn't true may that beam above my head break and fall on me!'

The legend continued that some young blood had arranged to have the beam cut and a mechanism installed to allow it to fall part of the way, without presumably jeopardising the structure of the tower – quite an engineering feat. And just to prove it, our jump-jet guide pulled the required lever and, sure enough, with a sudden noise the beam appeared to break in two and drop a couple of feet. I imagine very few Luftwaffe fighter pilots were brave enough to do it when the *Reichsmarschall* was actually there!

After a quiet Sunday we gathered in the Operations Block on Monday morning to start work in earnest. Although our main purpose was to chase armoured vehicles, it transpired that the traffic in the exercise would not build up until later in the week. However, the boffins had a cunning plan to fill in the time until then. They needed much more data on FLIR images of operational air bases and especially those with hardened aircraft shelters. Accordingly we spent that first day flying from Gütersloh westwards, first to Laarbruch and then to Wildenrath, where we landed and refuelled ourselves and the Varsity, which became the object of much attention. Then we reversed the whole exercise to return, via Laarbruch, in the afternoon. During the transits, flown at low level, we collected imagery of canals, autobahns and various industrial sites.

We flew another two similar sorties the following day, except that the second one was by night. Following the Dortmund–Ems canal at 500ft in the dark, using the NVGs and the FLIR was fascinating. What we had to watch for were the very tall high-tension electricity cables and their pylons that stretched across the canal and, further on, the River Rhine. They were visible on the IR screen but at quite a late stage – okay for us at 130 knots but not so good for the fast jets! However, our target-marking cues – little arrows that appeared on the screen – picked up the hot spots of electricity sub-stations at a good distance: ideal targets for IR or laser-guided bombs or missiles. Knocking out the electricity supply is a clinical way to reduce the enemy's capability to wage war.

On our return from Wildenrath in the dark, I decided that I would try to land the Varsity without airfield lights using the FLIR and NVGs. I'd done this in the fast-jet Nightbirds but never in this slow one. When we were in contact with the Gütersloh air-traffic controller I asked for all the airfield lights to be extinguished and told him that I would be making a visual approach and landing. This was received with a soupçon of incredulity. However, I pressed the point and reassured the controller that I would take full responsibility for the outcome.

Flying at 1,000ft Dickie George navigated us to a point about 5 miles east of the airfield and I turned on to a westerly heading. As I did so the runway came into view of the FLIR and I could line up on the extended runway centreline. When we got to 3 miles out I lowered the landing gear and completed the rest of the pre-landing checklist. At this point, I lost sight of the runway on the FLIR screen because the nose wheel positioned in front of it now obstructed the sensor's view. However, I could see perfectly well through the NVGs and, with Dickie calling speeds and heights for me, we slipped earthwards. The last bit is always a bit of a guess, but I just eased the control column back, closed the throttles and waited. There was barely a noise, just a satisfying rumble as the wheels kissed the runway. Complete fluke – but it got a round of applause! Trying hard not to be smug, I told ATC that we were down safely and that they could turn the lights back on. And so to bed.

The week progressed in similar fashion. We chased armoured vehicles, found surface-to-air missile sites, and even got some IR images of various helicopters scuttling around below us. We were there to fly, and fly we did. By the end of Thursday we had flown seven sorties totalling over sixteen hours' flight time, four of them at night. The plan was for me to fly one more sortie on the Friday morning and then Rob Foulkes would be delivered by our Andover to take over for the afternoon and the second week's work.

On Friday, 16 October 1987 I arose and looked out of the window. It looked very grey and windy, but no sign of rain. Before walking up to the Mess for breakfast I put on my cold weather jacket (aircrew, for the use of). It was, after all, mid October and it looked cold out there. As I stepped outside I was astounded to find that it was actually very warm and quite close. *How bizarre*, I thought.

At the Ops Centre I notified our flight details for the morning's sortie to the east. This was necessary because we were going to be operating fairly close to the East German border. I also informed the duty man that an Andover with a Nugget call sign would be arriving, probably by late morning, to take me home and deliver a fresh pilot.

We then went to the aircraft and got airborne on my final sortie of the detachment. It was very windy and turbulent. The boffins hung in there bravely, despite the rocking and rolling. After an hour and a half they had had enough and we set off back to base. As I turned over the airfield I looked down to see if I could spot the red, white and blue Andover, but it wasn't there. Not overly concerned, I completed the circuit and landed. As we got out of the Varsity I was greeted with the news that nothing had been heard from Farnborough. I decided to return to the Ops Centre and there I discovered that there was talk about bad weather in the south of England and difficulties in communication with military units there.

All we could do was wait. Eventually I got a message that the Andover was unserviceable and a Buccaneer was coming, flown by Rob Foulkes with Flt Lt Martin Taylor in the back seat. I was to fly it back. I just hoped that they had thought to bring all my Bucc flying kit! After a quick lunch we reassembled by the Varsity and, not long after, one of Mr Blackburn's Banana Bombers hove into view. After it shut down and the crew vacated the cockpit I was handed the appropriate bits of flying clothing – along with the news that there had been a hurricane overnight and that most of southern England was in chaos. The Andover, which had been left outside as usual, had been damaged by the wind – hence the change of plan. Many more stories of local damage and sleepless nights followed.

After notifying the operations folk of the details of our return flight, Martin and I boarded Buccaneer XW 986, worked our way through the checklist and departed. The plan was to return at low level. Over West Germany this meant not below 500ft and over the Netherlands not below 1,000ft. Martin's route took us out over the southern North Sea and then, via a sharp left turn, down the English Channel. Now we could legitimately go down to 250ft. He said that we would turn right inland between Folkestone and Rye. As we cruised down the Channel, close to the English shore, we spotted what looked like a cross-Channel ferry on the beach.[3] Inland from there was a huge thunderstorm, so I decided to carry on further down the Channel until I could see that the overland weather was suitable. We finally turned right, crossed the coast and passed just to the east of Lewes in Sussex.

As we headed north-west towards Farnborough we came across acres of forest in which the trees had been snapped off at about a third of their height. It was a bit like images I had seen after volcanic explosions or after the meteor that touched down in Siberia at the beginning of the twentieth century. By the time we reached Farnborough we had seen much more evidence of the passage of a great storm. Back at base I discovered that gusts over 100mph had been recorded by our own Met Office. Electricity supplies had been off or spasmodic throughout the night and morning, explaining the communications difficulties we had experienced, and I found out that the Andover would need quite a bit of rectification to its damaged flying control system.

When I finally got home, I found that the brick lintel above my garage door had been blown off. Thankfully the car was not in the drive. Otherwise the house was undamaged. But the most amazing thing was that when I asked my wife, Linda, what it had been like she said, 'I've no idea – I slept though it all!' What hurricane?

---

3.  The ferry was the MV *Hengist*, belonging to the Sealink Company.

# 10 BOMBING THE ARCTIC ICE

One of the larger trials aircraft on the Experimental Flying Squadron was a BAC 1-11, military registration XX 919. This particular twin-jet airliner first flew on 7 April 1966 and was delivered, twelve days later, to Philippines Airlines with whom it served until May 1974, when it was purchased by the UK MOD and allotted to the Procurement Executive fleet at Farnborough. I had flown it as a co-pilot during my previous tour there, but I had not qualified as first pilot or captain.

However, in January 1986 and within a month of arriving at Farnborough, I was asked if I would make myself available as a BAC 1-11 co-pilot again. I accepted the offer with measured enthusiasm. I flew a refamiliarisation sortie on 22 January, during which I flew a number of approaches and landings that would not have spilt the passengers' drinks. The BAC 1-11 handles well and, as it has the same Rolls-Royce Spey engines as the Buccaneer, many of the power settings required were familiar – two Speys give over 22,000lb of thrust. The only flaw with the 1-11's handling is at low speeds. Because of the T-tail layout there is the danger of a loss of control if the aircraft stalls. Indeed in October 1963 the 1-11 prototype, with test pilot Mike Lithgow in charge, crashed on Salisbury Plain with the loss of all on board. The cause was what is known as a 'deep stall', when the disrupted airflow from the wings affects the tail surfaces so much that control is lost and the situation becomes unrecoverable. After the accident BAC installed a stick shaker and stick pusher that activated at pre-set angles of attack to warn of or avoid the stall.

The 1-11 cockpit is a pleasant working environment, although the field of view, as to be expected with an airliner, is not as good as the jets I was more used to. The only complicated bit of the aircraft is its triple hydraulic system, so I spent a bit of extra time swotting up on that before I flew. Little did I know how handy that knowledge would be later. We always flew with a four-man crew: pilot, co-pilot, air engineer and navigator. That meant that our on-board technical expert, the air engineer, could cover any gaps in our systems know-how.

The Farnborough BAC 1-11 was used primarily for a variety of radio trials, including high-frequency and the HAVE QUICK (HQ) secure UHF communications systems. There was also research and development on a system known as the Joint Tactical Information Distribution System (JTIDS). This is an L-band radio system that is designed to link multiple military platforms and, as it says on the tin, distribute data in a secure manner to aid tactical decision-making and action. Our boffins down the back looked after all of this; we just drove them about the sky. More flying experiments than experimental flying!

Over my first two years in post I flew as co-pilot on several of these types of trials, including a very interesting trip to the Azores, where we made a touch-and-go landing at an airfield whose runway was laid on a coastal plateau with high cliffs at each end. Our destination and night stop was at Lajes, the biggest airfield of the island group, operated jointly by the Portuguese and the United States.

On another radio trial sortie, at low level in the Scottish Highlands, we were flying down a steep-sided glen and I was looking out assiduously while the captain, Flt Lt Ken Mills, was concentrating on not hitting the ground. I spotted a four-ship formation of Jaguars flying from right to left across our nose, only a couple of hundred feet above us. The last Jaguar in the loose formation suddenly tipped his left wing down, presumably as he spotted us. I've often wondered since what he made of a red, white and blue airliner flying up a Scottish glen below him!

By April 1988, Sqn Ldr Alan Sheppard, who had taken over both B Flight and the squadron, put me in the left-hand seat and supervised me through a qualifying sortie as first pilot. It all went well enough for me to enter the qualification in my logbook. Alan had an amusing but slightly off-putting trick of making noises like tyres squeaking on the runway as I tried to find the ground during landing. Laughing as one is trying to pull off a smooth arrival does not help! Following this sortie I was allowed to share some of the trials sorties with the other B Flight pilots and log some captain time.

Another research project using the BAC 1-11 was development of the utility of the American military Global Positioning System (GPS) and went by the code name NAVSTAR. But the oddest role that our jet airliner had was that of dropping sonobuoys. A section of the Weapons Department at Farnborough was involved with the continuous development of sonobuoy technology. Sensitivity and discrimination of the sounds they detected were important factors in their utility in anti-submarine warfare. We were still 'fighting' the Cold War and Soviet nuclear submarines were roaming the world's oceans armed with weapons of mass destruction. It was therefore paramount that Western forces could locate and track these stealthy, dark intruders accurately.

The BAC 1-11 was designed with third-world airlines in mind, where support facilities could be scarce, so it had integral steps, one set on the left-hand side at the front, just aft of the flight deck, and another that lowered under the tail. It was into the latter that the sonobuoy ejection tubes were fitted. The buoys could then be manually loaded and released from the rear of the aircraft. Sonobuoys are about 3ft in length and 5in around. When dropping them the aircraft must be depressurised.

It was in early October 1988 that I learnt of a requirement for a series of test flights to be made so that sonobuoys could be dropped into Arctic pack ice. This was to get more data on the noise that the ice makes as it moves with the swell of the sea. This information would help in designing countermeasures to this background noise interfering with the primary sounds. Alan Sheppard had arranged a four-day detachment to Keflavik in Iceland to allow the boffins to use the pack ice off the east coast of Greenland, in the sea areas off the mouth of Scoresby Sound – the world's largest fjord system. Having gone through the flight trial protocol and checked all the possible risks and wrinkles, I signed it off.

It was only then that Alan said, 'How are you fixed for the week of the 12th, boss? I've got a relatively new pilot, Mike Bradstock-Smith, earmarked for the job but I think that it would be good if you could go along and share the workload with him.'

Of course I was not going to turn him down. I checked with management, both at work and at home, and gave Alan a favourable answer the following day.

Just to make sure that we were both up to speed and current on type by night, Mike and I flew together on 6 October. Because Farnborough was not planning to be open that night we flew to RAF Brize Norton, which is a twenty-four-hour air base, and then operated out of there until we had both done sufficient time and landings from both seats to feel comfortable. Actually the weather made things increasingly uncomfortable. The winds got stronger and stronger and the rain came in from the west. During the final sortie, when I was in the captain's seat, the turbulence was so bad that the stick shaker kept operating as we bounced around the circuit. It was definitely a time to add 10 knots to the threshold speed for the wife and kids![1]

The following week, early on Monday, 10 October, we gathered for briefing, authorisation and boarding of all the crew and boffins. One of the limitations of operating the 1-11 out of Farnborough was that we could rarely take off with the maximum fuel load. The runway length and its overshoot areas did not allow us to achieve what is known as 'balanced field performance'; we had to reduce our take-off weight until we could depart safely if an engine failed. Hence the first part of our journey to the Arctic took us only a few miles up the road back to Brize Norton. After refuelling there we flew direct to Keflavik, Iceland's major airport on the island's west coast.

Having arrived before lunchtime, we arranged for refuelling, booked our outbound flight plan and set off for points north of the Arctic Circle. Mike had taken over as captain so I looked after the radio communications and monitoring the fuel. But with a navigator and flight engineer on board there was little else for me to do. We climbed to around 30,000ft and headed north-west towards our operating area. As we flew up the west coast of Iceland I could not help but wonder at the scenery to my right: huge snow and ice fields, the serrated coastline and the small coastal settlements that had no apparent road connection to anywhere else. *What is life like down there?* I wondered.

'We've crossed the Arctic Circle,' said the nav. I wondered if there was an ancient ceremony equivalent to that for crossing the equator. I kept that thought to myself.

Looking ahead I could see more and more white stuff covering the sea, with patches of dark water between them. On the horizon was a grey smudge – Greenland.

'Top of descent,' announced our nav.

Mike throttled back the engines and we cruised down to our operating height of around 500ft. The 1-11 was not equipped with a radio or radar altimeter so we had to guess our height – never a good idea over the open sea. However, ice was now covering most of the water and we soon got a good feel for the distance between the sea and us. We also had a forecast surface pressure so, using that setting on our altimeters, we could get an approximate confirmation of how low we were. The boffins wanted to drop the sonobuoys

---

1.   A well-known adage among aviators to indicate a desire not to crash and burn.

at a speed not exceeding 180 knots so Mike set us up at that speed with 8 degrees of flap, just to help the wing when we came to manoeuvre.

As we came across more narrow channels in the ice, called leads, we alerted the team down the back to load a sonobuoy and be ready to release it on our call. We could only guess at the trajectory; the sonobuoy has a small parachute that deploys after it is ejected so the forward throw was not going to be much. The requirement was for the buoys to be close to moving ice floes so only fairly narrow leads were acceptable.

Mike had lined up nicely on one black line in the ice and he called for the buoy to be released. When we got the word that it had gone, we had to climb to a few thousand feet and orbit in the general area so that the team could listen for the radio signals from the sonobuoy. This pattern would be repeated over a period of about one and a half hours. We had the occasional failure when the boffins thought that the buoy had been dropped on to the ice instead of into the water, or when there was no signal received at all. Thankfully, these mishaps were rare and over the three days we dropped a large number of buoys and the scientists were increasingly happy with the results.

On the second day it was the aircraft that let us down. About an hour into the sortie, which should have lasted about three and half hours, a hydraulic system warning went off. The reservoir of hydraulic fluid in one of the two main systems was empty! As the system was duplicated this was not a huge cause for concern. However, we were a long way from a useable airfield, and that was Keflavik. So, as captain, I gave the guys in the back the bad news and we set off back to base. During the transit the flight engineer, who was monitoring things carefully, gave us more bad news. 'The fluid level in the No. 2 system is now going down.' We obviously had a leak that affected both systems.

If both hydraulic systems fail there is an emergency third system, driven by an electric pump. But that is there to obviate failure of both engine-driven pumps; it still needs hydraulic fluid to work. The aircraft can be flown manually and we practised that very occasionally. It was extremely difficult and arduous; the control forces were very high and much use had to be made of the electrical tailplane trimmer. I never fancied my chances of making a safe landing in manual.

The engineer kept monitoring the fluid level and calculated that we should be on the ground before it fell to zero. I was captain, so Mike was doing the radio and had alerted Keflavik to our emergency status. He requested a priority visual circuit and that was approved. I made it more in the style of a

Buccaneer than an airliner, and was very glad when we touched down and then cleared the runway. But it wasn't over yet!

As I taxied back to our allocated parking spot I felt that the brakes were failing. The hydraulic fluid was all gone! I asked Mike to request that we park in the next space along the taxiway; there was a separate apron there (probably a relic of the USAF presence in years gone by). That was approved so I turned into the area with the nose wheel steering, asked the engineer to be ready to lower the stairs and go out when we stopped and chock the nose wheel.

*Stop? How are you going to do that?* I thought. *Use reverse thrust? Why not?*

So as we came to the centre of this isolated parking area I eased the throttles into the reverse thrust gate and gave it a little burst. We stopped. I put the throttles back to reverse idle and we remained stationary.

'Off you go!' I called. And then I watched to make sure we stayed essentially still until I got a thumbs-up from outside. There was a collective sigh of relief on the flight deck.

Then our magnificent engineer went into action. Transport was despatched to us and we went to the terminal. After a quick lunch and discovering that the engineers of the national airline, Iceland Air, could help us, we set to work fixing the problem. It wasn't long before the burst hydraulic pipe was located, removed and a replacement supplied by Iceland Air. Then it was fitted and the reservoirs refilled with lots of Skydrol hydraulic fuel. Thankfully we had the 'company' credit card to pay for it all!

By the time we finished it was time to park the jet where it should be, then head to the hotel in downtown Reykjavik and pick up where we left off in the morning. That would be our final sortie and, with a full fuel load, we would fly off the last series of drops directly back to RAF Lossiemouth, where we would refuel before our return to Farnborough.

During that sortie we flew closer to the coast and even ventured up the wide inlet that is Scoresby Sound, flying at just a few hundred feet. There we came across some awesome icebergs, several of which were over 300ft high and as big as several football fields. There was also a township on the northern shore of the fjord, close to the opening into the Arctic Ocean. This turned out to be a settlement with a totally unpronounceable name,[2] with lots of colourful houses in the snow, a church and several larger

---

2.  Its name is Ittoqqortoormiit and has a population of around 400.

buildings. I supposed that fishing and sealing were the main occupations when the weather allowed. I was glad to be looking down at it from a warm, comfortable seat in the sky!

Our job was over, we had 'bombed' the ice (well, the water between the floes) pretty successfully, the boffins were happy (subject as always to deeper analysis at home) and we'd seen some awesome scenery. The patched-up hydraulics held together all the way back to Farnborough and we knew that the skilled technicians there would make sure that the correct part would be fitted for the future.

# 11 TO ARABIA

During 1985 the Royal Saudi Air Force (RSAF) started taking delivery of forty-eight Pilatus PC9 training aircraft. By then the Swiss-built PC9 had lost the competition for a new UK basic military trainer in favour of the Shorts version of the Brazilian Tucano; I had flown the Tucano in Brazil in January 1983. However, the close relationship that had built up between the two aircraft manufacturers, Pilatus and British Aerospace (BAe), during the tendering for that contract and BAe's strong trading position with Saudi Arabia led to the PC9 being adopted for the RSAF's basic training needs.

The aircraft for this contract were built by the Pilatus Aircraft Company at their plant in Stans, Switzerland, and then flown to BAe's airfield and manufacturing facility at Brough, East Yorkshire – the erstwhile home of Blackburn Aircraft. The PC9s arrived there 'green', that is unpainted and without all of the equipment specified by the customer. It was BAe's job to finish the aircraft to the required standard and ready them for the four-day delivery flight to Riyadh.

The completed PC9s were to be delivered in batches of six or eight, so there was a need for sufficient pilots to fly them to the kingdom. BAe had a couple of their own instructor pilots, employed to teach the British ex-military pilots who had successfully applied to go to Saudi Arabia as Basic Flying Training instructors. However, even including those pilots who were ready to take up their new jobs in Saudi Arabia, there was a shortfall of experienced and available aviators to ferry the PC9s. During the previous couple of years several military test pilots had volunteered to help BAe with this task and in July 1988 I was asked whether I would be willing and able to fly a PC9 to Riyadh. When I mentioned this to my boss, Gp Capt Reg Hallam, he was very supportive. He had flown on one of the earlier deliveries and, despite having suffered a lightning strike en route, was keen that I should participate.

My first task was to arrange to go to Brough and learn to fly the PC9 and gain sufficient technical knowledge for the delivery flight. I contacted my old ETPS classmate, Roger Searle, who was now the Chief Test Pilot at Brough, and made the arrangements. Roger said that he had set a week in mid July for me to do my training and that the delivery was to take place at the end of the month.

On arrival at Brough, on the morning of Monday, 11 July, I soon discovered that another of my old ETPS classmates, Vic Lockwood, was also going on the same ferry flight. There would be eight aircraft altogether and these were the last of the contract. Vic had already done one of these delivery flights before, so I took his wish to repeat the experience as a good sign. After a series of technical lectures and the use of very basic cockpit simulation, just to find our way around the switches and levers, we were told that we would be flying in the afternoon. My instructor was yet another old friend from my own days as a RAF flying instructor – Ian Wormald, now employed by BAe for the PC9 contract.

After lunch Ian and I donned our flying kit and walked out to our aircraft. It was very pretty in its RSAF livery of white upper surfaces, royal blue lower surfaces and red wingtips. I was interested to see that all the numbers and letters painted on it were duplicated in Arabic script. The PC9 is a single turboprop-powered, two-seat trainer with the seats arranged in tandem, which first flew in 1984. It is a more powerful evolution of its predecessor, the PC7; it retains the overall layout of the PC7, but it has very little structural commonality with it. Amongst other improvements, the PC9 features a larger cockpit, with lightweight Martin Baker ejection seats, and has a ventral airbrake. Up in the nose is the engine: a Pratt & Whitney of Canada PT6A-62 turboprop, giving a very healthy 950shp. With the PC9 weighing about 5,000lb, its power-to-weight ratio is very similar to the early marks of Spitfire, so good performance was on the cards.

Ian and I flew for almost two hours, running through most of the flight envelope. The cockpit was modern and light, with the instruments arranged in an ergonomic and pleasing manner. In the centre were two electronic displays giving easily read and interpreted versions of both the horizontal and vertical situations of flight. There were several short-range navigation aids and a good suite of communications. Everything fell easily to hand and I had soon arrived at the point of winding up the engine. That was also very simple and the propeller soon became a shimmering disc up front. The view from the cockpit was first class, much like that in the Hawk. The seat was comfortable and I could twist round and see the tail without too much trouble; there were two rear-view mirrors as well. Once I'd checked the flap operation and other post-start items I waved the chocks away and a judicious nudge on the throttle got us moving. I checked the toe-operated wheel brakes, which were quite sharp, and nodded the nose down a bit, and then applied rudder to activate the nose wheel steering and taxi out to the runway.

The take-off was quite eventful. As the full power of the PT6 came on and the prop really bit into the air, there was a torque-induced yaw and I had to quickly dance on the rudder bar to get us going straight again and keep us there. However, the lift-off speed soon came up and we were off, still slightly out of balance and a bit sideways! I was going to have to adapt my jet technique to make that part of the flight a bit smoother.

But once up and away, and I'd operated the handy electric trimmers on the stick, the little trainer was climbing at 4,000ft per minute. Nice! Once at a safe height Ian encouraged me to manoeuvre freely. It really was a delight to fly. Aerobatics were easily accomplished, although, as usual in prop-driven aeroplanes, I had to keep an eye on the slip ball to keep the tail following the nose as the speed changed.

'Right, that's enough fun time!' came the voice from he who must be obeyed. 'Now we'll do some stalls and then a spin or two.'

So, being an obedient student, I set up for a stall. After looking all around and checking several other items, I closed the throttle, now automatically trimming the rudder, and slowed down in level flight. At about 80 knots there was a clear rumble and I could feel the buffet from the air separating from the wings, and at 77 knots the nose dropped, even though I had the stick fully back. There was not much tendency for a wing to drop, although I suspected that if there was still any sideslip it probably would have. With the landing gear and flap down the stall speed was just less than 70 knots. I also tried stalling during steep turns and while feeling for the maximum turn-rate point.

'OK, Mike, let's climb up a bit higher and we'll spin it,' said Ian.

So we did and the little trainer behaved predictably and impeccably. In the fully developed spin we did about one turn every three to four seconds. The aircraft recovered in less than two turns following the usual recovery actions of full rudder opposite to the direction of the yaw and moving the stick centrally forward. All, as it should be for a basic trainer, very conventional. Ian declined my suggestion that we try an inverted spin.[1]

We then flew to the RAF training base at Linton-on-Ouse, the place where I had started my flying career as a glider-flying Air Training Corps cadet twenty-eight years earlier. There we flew an instrument landing system (ILS) approach, a practice forced landing and several visual circuits. Everything soon fell into place and I was beginning to catch up with, if not get ahead of, the 'squirliness' during the take-offs. After our return to Brough we debriefed and Ian told me that we would fly a second sortie together the following morning and then I would fly solo in the afternoon.

The next morning, after an excellent evening meal and a very comfortable night in our first-class country manor hotel (thank you, BAe), I reported for duty. Vic Lockwood and several other test pilot mates were there, including Bernie Scott from Boscombe Down. Ian and I were going to repeat some of the instrument flying events from the previous day as well as do some formation flying. The latter would be good practice before we set off as an eight-ship formation to the Middle East at the end of the month. All went well and, after a quick aircrew lunch, I flew on my own in what would be my aircraft for the delivery: tail number 4208. So that was that: I was now signed up as a PC9 pilot and I travelled back to Farnborough to await the call to return.

That call came about a week later, asking me to be back at Brough on Tuesday, 26 July for a briefing, a final refamiliarisation flight and getting all our goods and chattels organised for the trip. Linda drove me up there and stayed at the hotel with me that night, along with the other guys who were acting as BAe mercenaries! She was then going to visit my parents in Bradford, about 60 miles away, before returning to Farnborough.

So, on Wednesday, 27 July 1988 eight pristine and hardly used Pilatus PC9s were lined up on the tarmac at Brough. Roger Searle was going to lead, as he had already done several times before, so I had every confidence that he knew the way. I was to be number eight in the formation – so 'tail end Charlie'!

---

1. For more about inverted spins see Part 1, Chapter 5 of *Trials and Errors* by this author (The History Press, 2015).

Among the other pilots were four ex-RAF guys going to become RSAF instructors, and Vic and Bernie were somewhere up ahead of me. The first leg was from Brough to Nice on the French Riviera – and I thought this was going to be an arduous expedition!

We were to fly in two four-ship formations, so Roger's section took off ten minutes ahead of ours, which was led by one of the Saudi-bound BAe pilots. After we had headed south-west for a while we were soon entering the airways system and climbing to about 21,000ft. There's an odd fact about turboprop aircraft: for maximum range they fly best at about 21,000ft and 210 knots true airspeed. So that was what we aimed at. As we flew over southern England the sky was clear and I tipped my right wing down at the place where I might see Farnborough. Sure enough, there it was – I could clearly see the runway pattern and make out where my house was. *See you in five days!*

Then the English Channel appeared and we were passed over to the French ATC system. Several '*bonjours*' and '*au revoirs*' later we started our descent into Nice. Off to the left were the Alpes-Maritime and ahead was the bright blue Med: the Côte d'Azur beckoned. At about 3,000ft we turned left to line up with the runway at Nice and started to drop back from each other so that we would land about thirty seconds apart. By now we were talking to the local controller in the tower and our leader had convinced him that we were happy to land with someone else occupying the runway ahead of us (not normal practice with airliners). After landing we had to taxi for what seemed like miles, not towards the airport complex, but to an area reserved for military aircraft on the south side of the airfield; an area that occupies land reclaimed from the sea and juts out into the water by a mile or so.

We parked with the other PC9s and joined up with the rest of our party. I got my bag out of the handy luggage compartment in the fuselage, behind the wing, and we waited for our transport, which Roger assured us he had requested. It was very pleasant waiting in the summer sun; it had taken just under three hours to get there from Yorkshire.

As we had already learnt at Brough, BAe don't use crummy hotels and this was the case in Nice. We were driven to the Hôtel Maritime on the promenade des Anglais. My room overlooked the beach and the Med stretching to the horizon beyond. I got changed and made my way down to the waterfront, picking up a couple of the chaps on the way. But there was no sand – like Brighton, just pebbles. More of our party appeared and we repaired to a restaurant for food and drink. Roger got a bit schoolmasterish to ensure that we were all going to be fit for the next leg in the morning – from Nice to Iraklion on the beautiful Greek island of Crete.

Roger took care of submitting the flight plan and by 11 a.m. on 28 July we were winging our way south-east and climbing to heights around – yes you've guessed it – 21,000ft. We passed Corsica and Sardinia on our right, reminding me of all those trips I had made in my Canberra in the same direction over twenty years beforehand, but now flying over twice as high and fast. Over Sicily we turned left and headed for Greece's largest island. This was the longest of the four legs of our journey and so was a bit fuel critical. We were expecting to take about three and three-quarter hours on this transit and the PC9's maximum endurance was four and a half. So, barring an uncharacteristic headwind, there should not be a problem. Nevertheless, Roger told us that if anyone's fuel consumption started to look dubious we were to inform him and an appropriate diversion decision would be made.

I just held loose formation on the other three and tried not to move the throttle too much. I checked the fuel against the plan every half-hour and things were going well. Soon enough the slate grey smudge on the horizon grew mountains, then a coastline and we started our descent after we had passed over the east coast. Just as at Nice, we landed a safe distance apart and I was again the last man down. It had taken me three hours and forty minutes to get here and I had enough fuel to fly for at least another half an hour. After parking up and retrieving our baggage we were taken, via the terminal to file tomorrow's flight plan, to another very nice beachfront hotel, with pool and bar terrace. The evening's entertainment was assured!

Roger told us that the next leg was the most navigationally challenging: it was a straight line from Crete to Luxor on the Nile. Our short-range navigation aids would not be much good to us until we were within 100 nautical miles or so of our destination. We had over 400 miles to cover. One aircraft was fitted with a longer-range device and Roger would use that to help him stay on our direct line track to Luxor. On this leg we would join up together as a loose gaggle of eight so that we at the back should be able to see the leading aeroplanes ahead of us. Once we had settled at our cruising altitude, about ten minutes after leaving Iraklion, there was just lots of blue water ahead. I started to wish that this little machine had an autopilot!

An hour later the sky ahead started to look distinctly yellow. *Must be sand,* I thought. *Where there's sand there's land.* At last, perhaps something to look at again. Ten minutes later I could make out the North African coastline in the haze below. Then we were back over terra firma, albeit endless desert. Roger called us on to a new heading, not much of a change – just a small swing to the left. A while later I could see off to my left and converging with our projected track a long, dark line. Then I realised what it was – the Nile. Way off in the distance to the east was the conurbation of Cairo and I peered hard at it. Sure enough, just this side of it I could make out the unmistakable shapes of the pyramids – so small from this distance and so surprisingly close to the city.

As the next half-hour passed the great river and its accompanying broad shadow of green came ever closer until I could see much more detail of the fields, palm groves, reed beds and the boats with their triangular white sails on the river. There was an occasional longer vessel – the Nile cruise ships. We were now descending towards Luxor airport, which was about 5 miles from the city on the ochre desert plateau to the east. Roger had told us to space ourselves out again so our section of four manoeuvred to be about two minutes behind the leading four. As we descended for a direct approach to the north-easterly runway, dropping the landing gear and flaps, I spotted something Roger had spoken about. It was the blackened wreckage of an airliner, with its tail still pointing forlornly to the sky, resting ignominiously about a mile short of the runway. The Egypt Air Airbus A300 had been there since the previous September, when it had crashed during a training flight from Cairo; all five crew on board were killed. A great signpost to welcome us to Egypt!

We taxied towards the airport terminal and parked in another neat line; this was getting a bit like the Red Arrows! After opening the canopy and climbing from my nicely air-conditioned cockpit I was bowled over by the sticky heat. The temperature gauge had shown 38°C as I landed and I guessed that the mid-afternoon humidity must have been well over 90 per cent. After liberating a large bottle of water, still fairly chilled, and my baggage from the locker, I walked to the rather cavernous and almost deserted terminal. There we were met by uniformed officials, who examined the visas in our passports and made us hang about while transport was arranged. I looked outside and noticed that scruffy armed guards had been stationed near our smart little aeroplanes. I guessed that the Arabic writing probably conferred them with a bit of brotherly credibility. I now had an urgent need, as did some of the others. We went hunting for toilets. They were easy to find – just follow the disgusting smell! Once inside it was overwhelmingly worse – but chaps in need must hold their breath and do what a man has to do. A revolting experience I can unfortunately recall with clarity, even today.

Thankfully the transport had arrived and we boarded the courtesy bus to our next hotel. We travelled west, down into the valley, through small towns and hamlets on the south side of the city until we came to a bridge across a small river. On the way I had looked into an open door. In the gloom were a woman and several children, sitting on a mat on the earthen floor. There were people in the scrappy fields on each side of the road and biblical scenes of carts overladen with palm leaves or sheaves of reeds, pulled by undernourished donkeys, urged on by skinny men with sticks. These scenes screamed 'poverty' at me.

The bridge from poverty to riches was on to an island that was the entire hotel – announcing itself as the Mövenpick Jolie Ville. I knew that Mövenpick was the name of an ice-cream company and in the ever-oppressive heat and humidity this gave me hope! I had long since finished my litre of water. Checking in brought relief and more hope – the place was air conditioned and had wonderful huge, colonial-style ceiling fans turning lazily over our heads. The rooms were in circular blocks scattered around the island and, having been issued with my key, I set off in search of mine. There had been a call for those who wished to go on an excursion to the Valley of the Kings to change quickly and report back in time for the transport into Luxor. I looked at the time and decided that a shower and a lie down in the air conditioning was a better option than rushing around in 40°C heat. A rendezvous was agreed for cocktails on the terrace as the sun set over the Nile; that would be at about 7 p.m.

After my refreshing rest and changing into the lightest clothes I could find I wandered down towards the river. It was still only 4 p.m. As I stood by the water two men in a low-slung boat came into view. The one standing in the bow had a net in his hand and, with a dextrousness born of a lifetime's practice, he spun it out into a circle that descended into the water ahead of him. After a short pause he pulled it towards the boat and lifted it quickly aboard. Silver flashes glinted in the sun among the delicate white of the net. Another biblical scene.

A motorboat came into view and moored nearby. People disembarked and walked toward the hotel. The man in charge called to me in English, 'You wanna go to Luxor, sir? See the temples?' I asked him how much and he told me it was 'Compliments of the hotel'. It seemed a fair fare, so I climbed aboard. It wasn't long before we set off and the zephyr of air that the boat's movement induced was most welcome. It was fascinating to watch the riverside scenes go by: lots of folk working on or near the life-giving water, kids tumbling down the bank to swim, boats of all sizes plying the river or moored up, and frequent chutes of rubbish and detritus spilling down into the brown water. Nearer Luxor there were several of the large cruise ships moored, awaiting the start of the tourist season later in the year.

At the quay in Luxor the captain told me I only had half an hour and that the return sailing would be the last of the day. So a very quick walk around the Karnak temple and back in time for tea or cocktails. Sipping sundowners while watching the orange orb descend into the desert west of the Nile was an experience not to be missed. Those that had gone to the Valley of the Kings said that, while interesting, it was far too hot in that confined bowl of rock and sand to enjoy the visit. I felt vindicated, but tried not to show it.

After a very nice dinner I was ready for an air-conditioned sleep. The next morning would see the start of our last leg, to Riyadh. I slept well, arose, showered and dressed ready for breakfast. As I stepped out of my room I was greeted by an amazing sight. All around the place, on the manicured and well-irrigated grass, were birds prodding the ground with their long straight beaks. They were wonderfully exotic birds, with pink upper bodies, large crests and black and white wings and tails. Having been interested in birds from an early age I recognised them immediately: they were hoopoes. As a youngster I had seen them in my *Observer's Book of Birds* with the note that they were very rare visitors to southern England. As a Yorkshire lad I thought I would never see one of these wondrous birds, and here I was surrounded by flocks of them! A great omen for our final push to Arabia.

A couple of hours later I was back in loose formation, at 21,000ft again, crossing the 120-mile width of the Red Sea; Saudi Arabia lay on the other side. We were headed initially for the city of Häil, then a right turn on to a south-easterly track would take us towards Riyadh. As we flew further inland the terrain below became increasingly bizarre. Areas of black, uneven and pockmarked rock lay like islands in seas of yellow, ochre, white and pink. Then there would be patches of desert on which were drawn circles of green irrigated fields and small towns with white buildings. As we turned towards our destination I noticed that the little LED instrument that showed me the outside air temperature (OAT) was indicating +21°C – at around 20,000ft that bordered on the ridiculous. Back home, even in July, it would be nearer -21°C. *If it's this hot up here, what's it like down there?* I wondered.

Well, it wasn't that long before I found out. After finally getting landing clearance for all eight aircraft I touched down as 'last man flying', three hours and ten minutes after lifting off at Luxor, and joined the crocodile of PC9s trailing the 'FOLLOW ME' truck to our parking area. We parked in a neat line and shut down. As I did I noticed that the OAT gauge was showing +48°C. It was going to be hot when I opened my canopy!

Sure enough it was – not unlike standing in front of an open furnace. I stepped over the side and noticed that everyone else was staying by their aircraft. My neighbour came over and passed on the delightful news that we had to remain here until the Saudi customs folk had searched each aircraft. I walked out, looked down the line and noticed that the aforementioned officials were just moving from the lead aircraft to the number two. I decided to empty the luggage locker and rescue a bottle of water. I then lay down under the left wing in what little shade there was; the sun was now more or less vertically overhead. That didn't really help because the concrete was even hotter than the burning air!

I took a drink of water – it was warm, verging on hot. Now I had to wait. Eventually, about half an hour after we had arrived, the customs men reached my position. They looked at all the things I had laid out under the wing, searched my bag and asked me to open the engine compartment, all without a word. When they were finished they signalled that I could join the rest of the team in the terminal. I was burning up. I had finished the warm water but the odd thing was that I was not sweating that much. The humidity must have been so low that any perspiration was drying as soon as it had formed.

Inside the air-conditioned terminal I found the others. Roger Searle was involved in a vigorous discussion, in English, with a uniformed official. The problem seemed to be that the latter was concerned about the 'drugs' that were in the first-aid kits carried in each aircraft. Roger was trying hard to convince him that the morphine was solely for pain relief after an accident; his argument wasn't carrying the day. Eventually it was pointed out that these aircraft were destined for Saudi Arabian use and that everything about them had been specified by the RSAF. Moreover, Roger said, we were not in the business of delivering drugs – just aeroplanes. Mollified, the official left us to carry out the very last act of the whole expedition: taxi the aircraft from this civilian side of the airport to the military area.

So back we went, put our baggage on board and started our engines. *Great,* I thought, *now I can put the air conditioning back on!* So I did – nothing happened except that it blew hot air at me. I checked all the selections but to no effect; after over twelve hours flying with an unblemished technical record RSAF PC9 4208 had fallen at the last fence. I turned the conditioning off and raised the canopy on to its short strut, which made a small gap and allowed slightly cooler air to blow on my face. Sadly I had to enter this failure in the aircraft's log when I handed it over to the BAe engineering team that ran the technical support contract.

After that we were taken to another luxury hotel downtown. After a well-deserved and much needed shower I joined a few of the guys on an expedition to the downtown shopping area. I bought some gold and marvelled at the ladies walking about covered from head to toe, but obviously wearing top of the range high-heeled shoes and carrying equally expensive handbags. Later we enjoyed dinner with some of the UK military people connected with the El Yamamah contract that covered the purchase of the PC9s, as part of a complete defence package for the kingdom. After a good night's sleep we were taken back to the airport and our British Airways flight back to Blighty.

It had been a wonderful experience, which was nowhere near as demanding as I had thought it would be. All the preliminary work had been done, I just literally had to fly the little plane to its destination. However, it did make me think back in wonder at those pioneers of aviation who flew vast distances across the old British Empire to South Africa, India and Australia in short-range, slow, tiny, unreliable flying machines which were horribly vulnerable to wind and weather. They had no navigation aids, other than a map and compass, and could take months to reach their destinations, often spending six or eight hours a day in the cramped, open cockpits. Bravo to the likes of Amy Johnson, Amelia Earhart, Wiley Post, Jean Batten and Alan Cobham. And more recently to modern aviatrix Tracey Curtis-Taylor who flew her Boeing Stearman from Capetown to Goodwood in the UK to commemorate her predecessor, Lady Mary Heath, who made the same journey in an open cockpit biplane in 1928. Compared with these folk, we had it easy.

# **12** OTHER OVERSEAS JAUNTS

In September 1987 Gp Capt Reg Hallam, our helicopter flight commander and I visited several test-flying facilities in the USA, for an exchange of ideas. We concentrated mainly on the low-speed end of the flight envelope and also learned about the latest cockpit technology. We started the tour on the east coast, at the US Navy Test Center at Patuxent River, Maryland. After two days there we travelled to the USAF R & D establishment at Wright Patterson Air Force Base near Dayton, Ohio, then on to the US Army's equivalent facility at Fort Rucker in Alabama and, finally, spent a couple of days at NASA's Ames Research facility near San Francisco.

At Fort Rucker I flew in the front seat of a Bell AH-1G Cobra helicopter. The warrant officer test pilot in the back was very trusting; I think he assumed I was a full-time professional 'rotarian'. He let me do almost everything, while talking me through the specifics. We flew at very low level around the neighbourhood of Fort Rucker, along a river valley with sandy banks, on which lay fat alligators basking in the Alabama sunshine. By the time I had taken us back to the landing spot I hoped he hadn't noticed anything that might disabuse him of the opinion that I was a 'real' chopper guy!

It was while we were at Fort Rucker, which is primarily a huge army aviation training base with four airfields and over 1,000 helicopters, that my British accent caused some amusement. We were not lodged on base but in a motel in the town of Daleville, just outside the main base gates. The motel's front desk was run by two blonde Southern belles who smiled broadly every time I spoke to them. On the second morning I came down and bade them good morning. This elicited more broad and beautiful smiles, showing off their splendid, and no doubt expensive, dental work.

Then one of them said, 'Why, Mistah Brooke, can you say some moah? We jus' love yoh accent! Where y'all from?'

So I obliged them with some polite conversation, before taking my leave as we were now all gathered and ready to move.

During our final day in the Bible belt we were invited to dinner by the British Army Air Corps colonel on an exchange tour at Fort Rucker. So when we returned to the motel I asked the ladies where I could purchase a bunch of flowers or similar hostess gift. I received this puzzling reply.

'Why, y'all should go on down to Piggly Wiggly's.'

I had not yet seen the film *Driving Miss Daisy* (probably because it wasn't released in the UK until 1990), so I had no idea what this strange name meant.[1] My puzzled look evoked an explanation and directions. I followed the latter and then there it was in all its porcine glory – and they had just what I needed.

At the other R & D places, we saw and experienced a variety of advanced technologies, including so-called synthetic and virtual reality cockpits. One of these I viewed through a huge headpiece and visor, while wearing motion-capture gloves so that I could operate the various virtual switches and levers on display. It was a bizarre experience at first and the headset was so heavy that it had to be supported by a cable. Intriguing as it was, it was not yet a practical proposition. No doubt the huge resources the USA could place at the disposal of their scientists made them world leaders in some of these advanced technologies. Back home the conservative Thatcher administration was hiving off all the core research done by Government establishments, like the RAE, to universities and industrial companies; privatisation was all the rage. I had doubts as to whether it would be beneficial to UK plc.

I had reason to make another visit across the Atlantic, but this time for a very different purpose. In October 1988 the first RAF Chinook Mark 2 helicopter, fitted with a full-authority digital electronic engine control system, known as FADEC, was undergoing a final ground test at Bell-Textron's manufacturing and test facility at Wilmington, Delaware. The test was ended when the helicopter's rotor blade speed went out of control to 322rpm – the design limit was 244rpm – because of a loss of engine speed governing. This caused the rear end of the tethered helicopter to get airborne, despite all the efforts of the pilot and technical crew to stop it. There was severe damage to the helicopter's rotor drive system.

I was selected from a cast of one by our senior master in London, erstwhile COEF, Gp Capt David Scouller, now the Director of Flying for the MODPE, to go and find out exactly why the incident had happened. A civil service aeronautical engineer would accompany me. I was told firmly

---

1.  In the film Jessica Tandy asks her chauffeur, played by Morgan Freeman, to take her to her local supermarket, Piggly Wiggly's, for her weekly shopping.

not to allocate blame, but simply report all the facts we discovered. In the event we uncovered a failure state that could cause uncontained engine runaway if two specific electrical or one electrical and one mechanical failure happened simultaneously. Our report, based on ten days of interviews and visits to engineering simulation facilities, pointed out the failings inherent in the design. We left it up to those much higher up the food chain to decide what to do. I later discovered that the MOD had instigated litigation against Textron, but I did not find out what, if anything, had changed in the design.

In June 1994, two months after I had retired from the RAF, Chinook ZD 576, one of the same batch from Bell-Textron at Wilmington, fitted with FADEC, crashed on the Mull of Kintyre. All those on board, including twenty-five of the UK's top intelligence personnel, were killed. When the pilots were blamed for the accident and a posthumous finding of gross negligence was brought (itself a very rare finding), I could not help but wonder whether that same FADEC failure case had occurred. It was some years before I discovered that knowledge of our inquiry findings had not been disclosed to the Chinook ZD 576 Accident Board of Inquiry.

To my mind, it was a travesty to hold those two pilots totally to blame – an element of doubt should, at the very least, have lifted the 'gross negligence' verdict. There were three further parliamentary inquiries and reports –mainly at the instigation of the pilots' families – all of which criticised the finding of gross negligence. In June 1994 my erstwhile colleagues testing the Chinook Mark 2 at Boscombe Down refused to fly the aircraft until a thorough investigation had been carried out into the integrity and safety of the FADEC system. As the Chinese say, 'It is a curse to live in interesting times.'

On 24 June 1988, in response to an invitation from the station commander at RAF Gatow in Berlin, Gp Capt Peter Eustace, we launched our Douglas DC-3 Dakota eastwards to attend the air show that would commemorate the fortieth anniversary of the Berlin Airlift; the Soviet blockade of Berlin had started on 24 June 1948. The DC-3 was well represented among the many military transports that took part in the airlift. Sqn Ldr Peter Hay, OC ATF, kindly invited me to go along as co-pilot. I then persuaded Peter and the group captain that it might be useful to take along someone who had been, not once but twice, the resident OC of the Station Flight at Gatow, Sqn Ldr Mike Neil. Mike flew the two Chipmunks stationed at

Gatow to exercise the right to overfly the whole of Berlin, including the Soviet-controlled east. I knew Mike from the past and he was OC AEF at RAF Abingdon. He would be very useful in helping us find our way around the restricted skies of Berlin. I had flown the DC-3 as co-pilot a few times and even been allowed to land it – not an easy proposition at first, especially with any appreciable crosswind. I had also learned the knack of operating the undercarriage lever on the floor between the pilots' seats.

So, on Friday, 24 June we set off for Berlin. We flew at heights between 6,000 and 8,000ft, and were soon entering the special air corridor over East Germany within which we had to remain. By then I was talking on the radio to the Berlin Air Safety Centre, the unit manned by military personnel from the UK, USA, France and the USSR that controlled all flying over Berlin. When we arrived at Gatow we parked in our spot for the air show and were invited to repair to our rooms and change into our best uniforms for the early evening official reception. After drinks and nibbles Mike Neil sidled up to me and said, 'Would you like to go downtown for the rest of the evening. I know a few ex-Luftwaffe pilots and I've arranged to meet up with them, I think you'll find them very interesting.'

'OK, I'll go get changed. Will we need to get a taxi?' I asked.

'No, stay in your uniform and we'll get a bus,' came the unexpected reply. 'If we do that we can travel free and we can even go into the East.'

Well, here was a man who had spent six years in Berlin, so who was I to argue? Off we went, out through the main gate and soon arrived at the bus stop. Sure enough we travelled free. Then we got off the bus and went to a train station. This was the U-Bahn; Mike had by now explained the difference between this rail network and the S-Bahn. The latter is the overground elevated rapid transit system and U-Bahn, perhaps not unexpectedly, is the predominantly underground system. Eventually we arrived at our destination and I followed Mike through the streets to an apartment block. There I met a group of about six elder statesmen who were members of the *Berliner Jäger Kreis* (literally 'Berlin hunting circle'), an association of Second World War German fighter aircrew. They all knew Mike very well and were delighted to see him again; they were equally warm towards me, even though I was wearing the uniform of their erstwhile foe. Their stories were fascinating and lots of moving hands and arms showed that they were true fighter pilots. During our time with them they shot down several wristwatches.

The air show was sadly plagued with low cloud. We were due to fly one or two parachute drops each day, with a small team from the British Army. We tried twice but could not climb to their minimum drop height so they had to do something that most professional parachutists don't like – stay on board for a landing! The most impressive item in what became a limited air display was a Boeing 737 from the local airline – lots of low passes and steep turns under the stratus clouds. Perhaps another ex-Luftwaffe fighter pilot?

In late October 1987 I was despatched to our outstation at West Freugh in south-west Scotland. Now I recognise that this locality is not strictly overseas, but for the following two weeks we pretended it was! I was to be the RAE's representative in a huge tri-service event called Exercise Purple Warrior. The scenario was that a joint task force, involving all three services, was to carry out amphibious and airborne landings to safely evacuate any UK civilians from a fictitious mid-Atlantic island that was under threat of invasion by a hostile government. West Freugh airfield was the airhead and the Dumfries and Galloway peninsular simulated the island. My job was twofold: I was to play the part, in a neutral capacity, of the airport manager and, for real, make sure that the relatively complex and much increased air operations were conducted safely, and ensure that none of the RAE's airfield facilities were put in jeopardy.

I persuaded my boss that as I was nominally a resident civilian for the exercise I should take my wife and lodge locally; surprisingly he agreed. So I called the friendly landlady, Julie, who was a regular home-from-home for many of us on our other detachments to 'The Froo'. She had a very nice house, up School Brae, overlooking the village of Portpatrick, and she readily booked us in. The exercise progressed mostly to plan. We received a detachment of half a dozen F-4 Phantoms from RAF Leuchars, acting as the air defence element. The 6,000ft runway and the distance to the best diversion airfields made life challenging for our fighter pilots and their supervisors.

Lots of memorable things happened during the two weeks of the exercise. While recovering a flight of four F-4s, an Andover carrying a bunch of VIPs arrived and, despite being told to turn off the runway at the first available point, which was well within the Andover's capability, it continued all the way down the runway at a leisurely pace to a point where it could not get back to its allocated parking space. The Phantoms were critically low on fuel and needed to land in turn and leave the runway clear for the following aircraft. But now the turbo-prop airliner, with its high-priced help on board, was blocking the way. We landed one F-4 and then got the Andover to scoot back across the runway and shut down. All we got from the captain were bleats about the lack of transport required to pick up his passengers. At this point I got on the radio and told him that real flying operations would take precedence and that we'd get back to him. We really didn't need sightseers, no matter how important they thought they were!

Another unforgettable event was the mass parachute drop before dawn in the fields near the airfield. I got up early to watch. Out of the south-west came a stream of fifteen C-130 Hercules, flying at about 1,000ft into the gradually brightening eastern sky. Then it started – bodies falling like poppies at the Albert Hall on Remembrance Sunday, blossoming as the parachutes opened. There were hundreds of them. Through binoculars I could see the troops gathering themselves from the grass and getting into a semblance of fighting order. It was a privilege to be there that day. Things like that don't happen often.

Towards the end of the exercise I heard that volunteer civilians were being sought to play the parts of potential evacuees. I told Linda and suggested she offer her services – along with our springer spaniel. So she attended the briefing and was taken off by service transport to the town of Castle Douglas. When her group had been assembled there, they were asked to dream up back-stories to provide to the soldiers involved in arranging their evacuations. Linda became an author travelling the world with her dog. When her details were taken the young man told her that the dog would have to be left behind, as it could not travel on the Hercules to the UK. She then went into some serious role-playing and made a big fuss. Shortly afterwards one of the generals turned up and, much to the staff's amusement, she confronted him with the fact that she would not go without her dog. This was a real test of the general's tact and diplomacy. But he found a solution – she could travel by sea, but it would be to Canada and not the UK. Linda told him that was fine by her.

All of this was to the great delight of the tired soldiers, some of whom concealed themselves behind screens and tent flaps, trying not to laugh too loudly. I think that, in reality, the general was not too put out; the top brass often appreciate a chance to lighten the atmosphere and reduce the stress levels for everyone involved. At the end of the day a friend was willing to take our spaniel back to West Freugh so that Linda could accept a ride back, at twilight, in a Gazelle helicopter, which she enjoyed greatly.

There was a delightful denouement to this tale. At the very grand end of exercise shindig, at Culzean Castle, we were introduced to the aforementioned general. He took one look at Linda and said in a loud voice, 'You're the woman with the dog!' For once it was 'the wife of' who was recognised and not her husband!

# 13 THE AIR SHOWS

The world famous, week-long international air show held biennially at Farnborough has its origins as far back as 1932. It was then that the Society of British Aircraft Companies (SBAC) held an exhibition of thirty-five aircraft from sixteen British manufacturers on the RAF airfield at Hendon, near London. After the Second World War, during which the industry had other fish to fry, the exhibition moved to the Handley Page Company's airfield at Radlett, in Hertfordshire. But after only two shows there, it moved again, this time to Farnborough, where it has been ever since.

When I took up my appointment in 1986 I knew that I would be involved in some aspect of the management of the air shows in that year and, if I was still in post, in 1988. It wasn't long before I found out how. The preparations for what is known as Farnborough International (FI) start in earnest about six months ahead of the show's opening in the first week of September. The first FI '86 meeting I attended was in April, by which time I had discovered my role was the on-airfield emergency coordinator. This meant that I was to be on duty in the control tower throughout the six hours of flying displays to ensure that any response to an accident or emergency that happened within the airfield boundary went according to our contingency plans. Any off-airfield crash or major incident would be the responsibility of the Hampshire Fire and Rescue services and the Hampshire Police. However, I would have control of a couple of fire-fighting, water-bombing helicopters that could also be deployed off the airfield should it be needed.

As the summer passed and we all got on with our normal duties, convoys of trucks would arrive on site with what seemed like the materials to build a small town. The 40ft-high hill to the south of the main runway, which had permanent brick and asphalt terraces, was gradually submerged in blue and white striped canvas, where the hundreds of exhibiting international aerospace companies would have their hospitality suites – the 'Chalets'. At the top of the hill huge marquees were erected to house the trade exhibitions. Meanwhile more meetings were held with all the key players involved.

As the time of the show approached, I noticed that the representatives of each agency got increasingly senior in rank (well, apart from me!). However, I also became convinced that there was a certain amount of overkill in the endless preparations. After all, the show had been running for nearly forty years, and since 1948 there had been twenty-six Farnborough air shows.[1] The procedures were well known and well rehearsed, so I likened it to a train being pushed off down well-used tracks. However, to be fair, there were lots of i's to dot and t's to cross – so we just had to get on and do it.

With a week to go the normal flying activity, apart from any very high-priority work and the daily ferry flights, was curtailed. Aircraft participating in the show, both static and flying, began to arrive and all the paper-work, especially their corporate insurance, had to be checked. Displaying pilots had to book their slots for rehearsals in front of the Flying Control Committee (FCC). The FCC was headed by my boss and consisted of invited doyens of the test-flying business. The FCC approved each pilot's routine, recommended changes if necessary, and watched every rehearsal and each display throughout the show's seven days. Their eyrie for doing this was a temporary greenhouse on the roof of the control tower, adjacent to that of the two commentators.

During the shows there was a daily briefing and non-attendance by any pilot would mean that his display would be scratched for the day. This put huge pressure on the teams to get to Farnborough by 10 a.m., despite the huge amount of traffic converging on the place. The pattern was that the first five days were for trade and press visitors, and the last three for the general public. It was on those last days that the flying display would contain additional items such as the Red Arrows, the Lancaster, Spitfires and Hurricane of the Battle of Britain Memorial Flight and other historic items.

I have many fond memories of those two frantic, long but very enjoyable September weeks. In August 1986 we learned that, following its first flight on 8 August, the BAe Experimental Aircraft Programme (EAP) technology demonstrator was aiming to fly in the show; that would be a coup for British

---

1. The Farnborough Air Show only became biennial in 1962.

Aerospace and UK plc. The folks organising the display programme gave it a slot, but with less than a month from its first flight there was a realistic chance that it might not appear. The EAP was a £10 million project to demonstrate and develop the systems that were projected for the future fighter, collaboratively designed, built and produced by the UK, Spain, Germany and Italy. This project, initially known as Eurofighter, was a highly advanced aircraft offering agility, multiple weapons systems and the ability to be operated by a single pilot.

The project pilot at BAe was Chris Yeo, yet another 1975 ETPS classmate of mine. He called me on the day he was due to fly in from the BAe airfield at Warton. He said that he was concerned about the forecast of north-westerly winds he had been given. We would be using the south-westerly main runway.

'What's your crosswind limit?' I asked him.

'Well we've demonstrated 15 knots so far, but we are concerned because simulation hasn't given much confidence to go far above that. The forecast I've got means that in some of the gusts it might exceed 15 knots.'

'Well, Chris, our forecast for today ties in with that. But in these conditions the touchdown area is downwind of the hangars and control tower, so while these give a bit more turbulence, they can abate the gusts a little. It's your call mate.'

'I'm going to give it a go. But you could do me a favour and be in the control tower when I arrive and give me a warning if the crosswind gets too much.'

I readily agreed and went to talk to the controllers and asked them to call me when Chris was starting his approach. I checked the wind and saw that it was indeed right on his 15-knot crosswind limit and, in the gusts, sometimes above it. When the time came I responded to the call and made my way up two floors to the local control room, with its all-round glazing. After a few minutes I could see the blue and white jet about 3 miles out. The local controller passed him the surface wind; it was such that the crosswind component was spot on 15 knots. Then, with about 2 miles to go, it gusted and the controller dutifully reported this to Chris. 'Roger,' he acknowledged coolly.

When Chris was at about 300ft the gust had passed and the wind strength dropped to give 15 knots across again.

'Tell him the wind now,' I said to the controller. 'Then don't say another word.'

I watched the final minute of Chris' flight, with one eye on the anemometer. As he came over the runway the wind gusted again – I noted its speed and direction. There was a barely discernable yaw as the aircraft touched down, smoothly and without much fuss. I got in my car and went over to the area where the EAP was to be parked. When Chris had disembarked from his unique flying machine I greeted him with the news that BAe could now legitimately clear the EAP to a crosswind limit of 18 knots.

'How was it for you,' I asked. 'It looked very smooth from the outside.'

'No real problem,' Chris replied.

Later he told me that the simulation had been unable to model the one thing that made his job easier on the day: ground effect. The complexity of the fluid dynamics of modelling the 'squashing' of the air beneath the low-slung delta wing, which helped smooth out the landing, had been beyond the simulation design. The old adage of 'never mind the modelling, let's try it for real' won again! Later in the week Chris was kind enough to give me a guided tour of the EAP's cockpit and, with power on, demonstrated many of the unique features of the aircraft's systems and how the pilot could use them.

Another big event of the 1986 show was the arrival of a Lockheed SR-71A Blackbird. This had flown in from the USA in just less than four hours, not quite breaking the New York to London record of three hours and forty-seven minutes set by one of its predecessors in 1974. The landing was very precise and, when we went to meet the crew, my deputy, Sqn Ldr Alan Sheppard, uttered these memorable words to the USAF pilot, 'Welcome, Major, let me shake that golden hand.' Perhaps a bit cheesy but very apposite!

Sadly, the SR-71 was only with us on static display, but it drew enormous crowds. The downside was that after the Blackbird roared off to RAF Mildenhall at the end of the show we discovered that, despite the use of multiple drip trays underneath it while it was parked there overnight, the special fuel that the Blackbird used had eaten into the surface of the secondary runway. We had just resurfaced that runway – not a cheap venture. The SR-71's design is such that when it is cold there are tiny gaps in the structure that only close up when it reaches its operational speed of Mach 3 and the atmosphere heats it up to between 230°C and 500°C. Nevertheless it was great to have it at the show. We got the tarmac machines out again later!

Certainly the biggest item in the 1986 show was the Antonov An-124 Ruslan transport aircraft. This was the first entry directly from the USSR at any SBAC show. At 226ft long and with a wingspan of 240ft, it was by far the biggest machine that our technical support folk had handled. It was disappointing to discover that the Ruslan was for static display only, but the Russians surprised us all by opening the An-124 at both ends and allowing the crowds to pass through its cavernous interior; 'oohs' and 'aahs' were much in evidence. I got a conducted tour of the cockpit as well. It was a roomy place to work and, in traditional Soviet fashion, was finished in duck-egg blue. The technical intelligence folks had expressed interest in discovering whether it was truly a fly-by-wire machine. I didn't get a clear answer from the pilot but, on the evidence I could glean, decided that it probably had a high-authority, electronically stabilised, hydraulic flying-control system.

On the morning of this vast flying machine's post-show departure it seemed that no one was in in their place of work at Farnborough; they were all out on the roadsides and verges watching. I exercised my privilege by climbing on to the roof of the control tower to see the Ruslan taxi out, like an island of aluminium on a sea of wheels. It then lined up at the very beginning of the runway and went through an elaborate process of running up the engines individually before finally declaring itself ready to commit aviation. When all four D-16T turbofans were run up to full power I hoped that the Fire Section in the Black Sheds at that end of the runway had shut their doors. Huge clouds of dust blew up downstream of the now shuddering aircraft, then it lumbered forward and, like a big guy that's light on his feet, picked up speed remarkably quickly. However, the big bear still used a lot of the runway before it broke the surly bond and soared off into the bright blue yonder. At that point we had no idea that it would be back two years later.

The 1986 show was notable for many other things: the largest number of exhibiting aircraft to date, the massive contribution from France, including the unique Mirage 4000 prototype, a very impressive display by the fly-by-wire Airbus 300 and a flypast by Concorde on several days. There were lots more items that made the show a great success – all we had to do was repeat it in two years' time!

Sure enough in spring 1988 we set off again down the tracks towards the destination of the first week in September. Roll out all the previous paperwork (just change the dates!), have the same meetings, talk to the same folk – or their replacements – how difficult can it be? By now the RAF man in charge had changed – Gp Capt Reg Hallam had been in post as COEF since taking over from David Scouller just after FI '86. He was well briefed for his role as head of the FCC. One of the two crucial items for the FCC to oversee was that no aircraft crossed the display line or came below the minimum height limit. The display line was shown by a series of large bright red markers on the grass, parallel with the main runway on the opposite side to the crowd. The control tower, with all the high-priced help, the air-traffic controllers and my office, was somewhat vulnerably right on the line. All the regulations pertaining to the conduct of flying displays had been dusted off and were in place. By mid August we were as ready as we could be.

On Sunday, 28 August 1988, at Ramstein US Air Force Base, in West Germany, at 3.44 p.m. (local time), a complex formation manoeuvre by the ten aircraft of the Italian Air Force Aerobatic Team, *Il Frecce Tricolori*, went horribly wrong. One of the Aermacchi MB-339 jet trainers used by the team crashed into a formation of four others. That aircraft continued its trajectory towards the crowd line, hitting the ground and then, as it exploded, carried on tumbling into the crowd. Its pilot was killed on impact. The aircraft it hit crashed into the emergency medical evacuation helicopter sitting at its standby location. The Italian pilot had ejected but was killed on impact with the ground. The severely burnt helicopter pilot died from his injuries a week later.

The scenes of devastation and carnage among the crowd were truly horrific. Of the thirty-one people who died at the scene, twenty-eight had been hit by debris from aircraft parts and other items on the ground. Sixteen of the fatalities occurred in the days and weeks after the disaster due to severe burns. About 500 people had to seek hospital treatment following the event.

The disaster revealed serious shortcomings in the handling of large-scale medical emergencies by German civil and American military authorities. For example, US military personnel did not immediately allow German ambulances on to the base, and the rescue work was generally hampered by a lack of efficiency and coordination. The rescue coordination centre in the nearby city of Kaiserslauten was unaware of the disaster's scale, even an hour after it occurred – despite the fact that several German medical evacuation helicopters and ambulances had already arrived on site and left with patients. American helicopters and ambulances provided the quickest and best means of evacuating burn victims, but did not have sufficient facilities for treating them, or had difficulty finding them. Further confusion was added by the American military using different standards for intravenous catheters from German paramedics. Over 600 people reported to the on-site clinic that afternoon to donate blood.

The news of this disaster soon reached us and its implications for our international, commercial air show, which was due start in a few days time, were devastatingly obvious. Crisis meetings were quickly arranged. Much midnight oil was going to be burned. Doomsayers from on high were talking about cancellation. Knee-jerk reactions were rampant. Our well-rehearsed emergency procedures were re-examined in minute detail; air-display regulations likewise. Eventually the competing pressures of safety, commercial interest and the military drive to get on with the job reached consensus. The senior military and civilian folk were reassured that modifications to some of the display flying rules and regulations could be implemented and would prevent anything like a similar disaster impacting FI '88.

Most of the exhibiting pilots could easily adapt their displays to the changes made. I remember the conversation with the Red Arrows leader, when he was told that the team could no longer arrive in their usual fashion, over the heads of the crowd. He wasn't a happy bunny at first. However, when voices from ivory towers made it plain that no exceptions could be made, even for men in immaculately tailored red flying suits, he went away to work out the required changes to the Reds' routine.

However, by far the most administrative and diplomatic effort had already been made in the acceptance of SBAC's invitation to the Soviet Union for the appearance in the show of a MiG-29 fighter, the repeat invitation to the Antonov Company to fly their An-124 in the show having already been accepted. In fact, Mikoyan said they would send two MiG-29s, one single-seat and one two-seat model. The appearance of three USSR aircraft was undoubtedly a coup and likely to draw even bigger crowds. Although the processes of restructuring (*perestroika*) and openness (*glasnost*) had begun – under the direction of the Soviet Communist Party's new general secretary, Mikhail Gorbachov – the participation of a fairly large number of Soviet personnel was going to raise some interesting and challenging issues. But all that was well above my pay grade. I just had to do my best to ensure that our response to any emergency went as planned.

The MiGs flew in from the east, escorted by a VC10, carrying service and civilian photographers, and two RAF Tornado F3s. Once they were handed over to the Farnborough controllers the Tornados broke off and the MiGs were directed for a straight-in approach to the main runway. They were in very close formation and, as the leader landed, the second MiG went round and, without so much as a by-your-leave, went into his display routine. I was in the control tower so had a good view, but I was not sure the FCC, sitting on the roof, was totally ready for this impromptu surprise. In any case our rules, sent to all participants, stated that practice displays could not take place until all the insurance documents had been submitted and examined for compliance. Of course that didn't dampen Anatoly Kvochur's enthusiasm – his routine was eye-wateringly impressive. I noticed that he did what I often did in my Hunter and streamed the braking parachute just before touchdown.

Some weeks before the show I had been approached by Wg Cdr Nigel Wood, a fellow test pilot and the man who had taken over from me at Farnborough ten years earlier. He was now working in the shadowy world of Defence Technical Intelligence in Northumberland House in central London. He invited me to go up to town for the day as he had a job for me. This turned out to be to try my best to get into the cockpit of the MiG-29 and revisit the An-124, but this time with much more specific guidance on what bits and pieces needed to be identified. I was given a few Cyrillic words to learn, but wasn't told what they meant – I just had to spot them and remember where they were located in the cockpit. I was also asked to give my overall impression of the working environment in the cockpits and any interesting features. All I had to do was win a place in the MiG-29 cockpit without causing a diplomatic incident!

As it happened it was my job to go and meet the Russian aircrew and bring them over to meet my boss and the FCC. Delicate negotiations were going to be required, with a translator present, to explain the situation of practice demonstrations versus insurance inspections. However, I hoped that this was going to be a chance for me to meet the three pilots. When I arrived at the Western dispersal area, where I would normally see Buccaneers, Canberras and an Andover parked, there were two of the 'opposition's' best fighters; for an old Cold War warrior it was a surreal sight.

Of course, the three guys in flying kit were busy and surrounded by ground crew, company suits and 'minders', some no doubt KGB employees. The aviators were Chief Test Pilot Valery Menitsky, and company test pilots Anatoly Kvochur and Roman Taskaev. Menitsky proved to be aloof and hard to get near, Anatoly was more approachable and ready to engage, and Roman was obviously the junior guy and, while having a winning smile, seemed to be kept on a tight leash. Later in my life I would get to know Anatoly a bit better when we met at other air shows.

By the end of the show I had managed to sit in the MiG's cockpit and have a really good look at the exterior while the aircraft were being refuelled. One very noticeable thing was the lack of precise finishing on many of the panels on the wings and fuselage; it looked hand made – by a tractor factory! One of the big questions the intelligence folk had was, 'Just how far could the jets fly?' Immediately after the Russian aircraft had arrived a PR9 reconnaissance Canberra from No. 39 Squadron flew over to take IR images of the MiGs from above. That would hopefully show how much fuel was left in the tanks. I knew about that subterfuge, as we had to tell ATC that we could, exceptionally, accept a 'practice diversion' from RAF Wyton that day; they weren't told why, but I bet they guessed! Fuel uploads were recorded and when one MiG's engine needed changing there were quite a few of our 'technical experts' watching. As with all spying, it is a bit of a game. However, late in the week I was quite well dressed down by a senior and rather dour Soviet man in a suit; he did most of it in very broken English and bits of Russian. I smiled a lot.

The MiG displays were quite outstanding and included some manoeuvres previously unseen or unimagined. The very new features of the intake doors that could close on the ground and the supplementary air intakes on the shoulders of the wings were much in evidence. Very short take-off and landing runs started and ended each show. Anatoly's ten-minute airborne time was spent in very tight turns, loops, rolls and the rapid pull-up at low speed that later became known as the Cobra. Another outstanding and slightly worrying manoeuvre was a very slow, level flypast with the nose of the MiG about 40 degrees above the horizon. At the end of this the engines were slammed to full power, with afterburner, and the aircraft accelerated directly into a steep climb. One couldn't help but worry about an engine failure, or even poor response from one of them, during this event. Three years later, at the 1989 Paris Air Show, Anatoly's MiG-29 would suffer just such a failure (due to a bird strike) and he was unable to recover using the good engine; he ejected just two and half seconds before the jet impacted the ground vertically and burst into flames. He landed just 100ft from the fireball but, amazingly, walked away unhurt. I bet he was smiling.

The An-124 Ruslan flew several times, but on one occasion one if its huge turbofan engines hiccupped very loudly as it was run up for take-off. We were not surprised to hear from the captain that the display, ponderous but impressive as it was, would not be happening that day.

The following day I met the McDonnell Douglas Apache test pilot, 'Cap' Parlier, and struck up a conversation with him. As a bit of an amateur rotarian, I asked him to explain the dynamics and any handling problems with the loops and rolls that he did during his display, which showed off the

Apache's impressive power and manoeuvrability. Until the advent of what are called rigid rotors, looping helicopters was a very ill-advised practice. In the course of our chat he told me that he had a spare, post-display, customer demonstration slot at about 6.30 p.m. and that I could fly in the front seat and find out for myself. After a couple of microseconds I accepted and then starting working out how I would cover my absence from that day's wash-up debriefing. In the event my boss was his usual relaxed self and told me to go and enjoy the flight.

I met up with Cap by the rugged, rather ugly flying machine as arranged. He gave me a tour of the front cockpit, which is for the gunner/co-pilot. It was furnished with all the flight controls and instruments to enable me to fly the beast, when invited to do so. I wore my own flying suit but I had to wear the helmet provided. This had a helmet-mounted display (HMD) which was slaved to the nose-mounted electro-optic TV and IR cameras. This unit was, in turn, harmonised with the moveable rotary gun under the fuselage. I had offered to do the radio calls, like a good co-pilot should, and once I had practised using the HMD to look around I called for start clearance.

'Apache, you're cleared to start but hold your position as we have a heavy fixed-wing on final approach,' came the reply.

Cap started the engines but did not engage the rotors. 'I'll wait till we see the aircraft clear the runway,' he explained.

As we were on the south side of the airfield, well clear of the runway and pointing north-east, I engaged the sighting system and selected magnification to search for the approaching aircraft. I guessed that it might be the Soviet transport due to arrive with spare engines for the MiG-29 and, possibly, the An-124. I looked into the HMD and spotted the long wings, with drooping wingtips, supporting four turbo-prop engines and the double-ended tailplane of an Antonov An-22; those aircraft recognition lessons of twenty-five years ago had paid off! Not only that, but I had it in my sights, even if the gun wasn't loaded. As the An-22 came over the Farnborough–Aldershot road I realised that it was head on to me, but we were several hundred metres from the runway centreline. *Surely the crosswind isn't that strong,* I thought. I stopped using the HMD and looked around it to put everything back into perspective. As I did so the huge transport rolled alarmingly to its right – it was very near the ground now – then, as if in realisation, the wings came level and it made a very unceremonious arrival. As it did so a lot of dirt was kicked up by its left-hand set of wheels. As the 'airfield manager', my immediate thought was that I hoped they hadn't written off too many of the runway lights. As it turned out not much harm was done – except perhaps to the captain's reputation.

Now that was all over we could go flying. I asked for clearance to lift and depart to the south into an area, adjacent to the airfield, called the Long Valley Training Area, which the British Army used for vehicle development and driver training. Long Valley is an area of pine trees, scrub and many sandy tracks. I informed Farnborough ATC that we would operate over Long Valley up to a maximum height of 1,500ft; the controller cleared us to do so.

'Right, Mike, let's start with that loop you were so interested in. Here we go.'

Down went the nose, but not by much, then the stick came back and the collective lever came up. We were round in what seemed like no time and the g-level stayed positive all the way round. We used all of 500ft of sky. It was very similar to a loop in a light aerobatic aircraft, but noisier.

'OK, Mike, you have control, just try a few turns and general manoeuvres and then have a go at a loop yourself,' came the words from the back. I did what the man said and found that the Apache was very responsive and it was, initially, easy to over control a little. But pilot compensation soon kicked in and I began to really enjoy the way that the helicopter responded and the apparently huge power margins it had. Then I told Cap to stay close to the controls and set up for the loop. Following his example with power and control movements, I found that it was actually quite easy to achieve a passable loop – a bit of yaw pedal was needed to make sure that it stayed straight.

Then Cap took control again and told me that he was going to descend into a clearing in the trees. What came next really took me by surprise. He stood the aircraft on its nose and we seemed to hang there briefly while he selected the hole in the trees he wanted to use. Then we went into a tight turn, levelled out over the clearing, down came the lever and we followed it until we were a few feet off the sandy soil. It cannot have taken more than ten seconds to hide ourselves. Very impressive. I didn't expect that he would invite me to do that; he didn't. But we then played at anti-tank manoeuvring, popping up above the tree line, with me scanning with the HMD, picking a target on the airfield just to the north and simulating a missile launch from the stub wings each side of the cockpit.

When Cap reckoned I'd had enough fun (which I hadn't), he asked me to get clearance back over the fence on to the airfield. Once we had received that he handed me control and asked me to take this wondrous machine back to the 'spot' and land it. No pressure then! In fact, with a bit of guidance on speeds, it was not difficult and those nice soft tyres made the landing more comfortable than it might have been. It was a great way to end a very busy day.

FI '88 came to an end with no disasters, major or otherwise. There had been no problems with the weather or attendance of exhibitors, and visitors had once again been outstanding, and many friendships with other test pilots had been made and others refreshed. Each day I used to supply a cartoon to show before the daily briefing – like an OHP screensaver, long before PowerPoint. I later gave some of these to the pilots I chose to depict.

# 11 FLYING BACK IN TIME: THE SE.5A

In 1916 Farnborough's Royal Aircraft Factory[1] design team of Henry Folland, John Kenworthy and Major Frank Goodden were working on a new fighter. They called it the Scout Experimental Number 5 (SE.5), and it was built around a newly available 150hp Hispano-Suiza V8, water-cooled engine. The SE.5 was designed to be a stable gun platform that should be both easier to fly and outperform the rotary-engine fighters already in service – aircraft such as the Sopwith Camel. The first of three SE.5 prototypes flew on 22 November 1916. The original two prototypes were lost in crashes due to a weakness in their wing design. One of these accidents, on 28 January 1917, killed Frank Goodden, the Chief Test Pilot. The third prototype underwent modification before production commenced. The SE.5 was known in service as an exceptionally strong aircraft, which could be dived at very high speed – the square-tipped wings also gave much improved lateral control at low airspeeds. Like the other significant Royal Aircraft Factory aeroplanes of the First World War, the SE.5 was inherently

---

1.  With the formation of the RAF on 1 April 1918 the 'Factory' was renamed the Royal Aircraft Establishment.

stable, making it an excellent gunnery platform, but it was also quite manoeuvrable. It was one of the fastest aircraft of the war – faster than any standard German type of the period. While the SE.5 was not as agile in a fight as the Camel, it was much easier and safer to fly, particularly for novice pilots. The SE.5 had one synchronised 0.303in Vickers machine gun to the Camel's two, but it also had a wing-mounted Lewis gun on a Foster mounting, which enabled the pilot to fire at an enemy aircraft from below, as well as providing two guns firing forward.

Only seventy-seven original SE.5 aircraft were built before production moved to the improved SE.5a, the initial models of which differed from late production examples of the SE.5 only in the type of engine installed – a geared 200hp Hispano-Suiza 8b, turning a large, four-bladed propeller. In total 5,265 SE.5s were built by six manufacturers – 200 of them at the Factory. The troublesome geared 8b engine was prone to serious gear-reduction system problems. Sometimes the propeller and even the entire gearbox separated from the engine and airframe in flight. The introduction of the 200hp Wolsey Viper, a high-compression, direct-drive version of the Hispano-Suiza 8a, manufactured under licence, with a two-bladed prop, solved the SE.5a's engine problems and was adopted as the standard powerplant.

The SE.5 entered service with the British Royal Flying Corps (RFC) in March 1917, although it did not deploy to the Western Front until the following month. Everyone was suspicious of the large 'greenhouse' windscreens fitted to the first production models. These were designed to protect the pilot in his unusually high seating position, which was in turn intended to improve vision over the upper wing. The first SE.5 squadron did not fly its first patrol until 22 April, by which time, on the insistence of Major Blomfield, No. 56 Squadron's commanding officer, all aircraft had been fitted with small rectangular screens of conventional design – the problem of the high seating position was solved by simply lowering the seat, pilots in any case preferring a more conventional (and comfortable) seating position. No complaints seem to have been made about the view from the cockpit; in fact, this was often cited as one of the strong points of the type. RFC pilots, some of whom were initially disappointed with the SE.5, quickly came to appreciate its strength and fine flying qualities. However, at the outset it was held to be underpowered and the more powerful SE.5a began to replace the SE.5 in June 1917.

Major Sholto Douglas[2] who commanded No. 84 Squadron RFC, which was equipped with the SE.5a, listed the type's qualities as follows:

- Comfortable, with a good all-round view
- Retaining its performance and manoeuvrability at high level
- Steady and quick to gather speed in the dive
- Capable of a very fine zoom climb
- Useful in both offence and defence
- Strong in design and construction
- Possessing a reliable engine

Some sixteen squadrons equipped with the SE.5a remained in (by then) RAF service for about a year after the war. A number of these machines found roles in civilian flying after the war and became popular for racing and skywriting. Major J.C. Savage formed a company for the latter, using a fleet of SE.5as that was in great demand for aerial advertising throughout Britain. The first such use was on 30 May 1922, when Cyril Turner, a former RAF officer, spelt out 'London Daily Mail' in black smoke from an SE.5a at the Epsom Derby horse-race meeting.

Fast forward to 1955 and cue the appearance of another RAE and RAF test pilot: Air Cdre Allen Wheeler CBE.[3] While visiting the Armstrong-Whitworth flight shed at Whitley, near Coventry, he spotted a rather dilapidated SE.5a hanging from the roof. It had last been used by Major Savage's company and had the civil registration of G-EBIA. Newly retired Air Cdre Wheeler, who was a trustee of the Shuttleworth Collection[4] and an active pilot of their vintage aircraft, spotted this potential trophy to add to the collection's growing fleet. Using his renowned powers of persuasion, he acquired the SE.5a and had it transported to RAE Farnborough, where

2. Sholto Douglas was awarded the Military Cross and the Distinguished Flying Cross during the First World War and rose to become Commander-in-Chief of Fighter Command during the Second World War.
3. Between 1941 and 1943 Allen Wheeler commanded the Performance Testing Squadron at Boscombe Down and, later, the Experimental Flying Department at RAE Farnborough.
4. The Shuttleworth Collection of vintage aircraft and vehicles is located at the grass airfield of Old Warden, near Biggleswade in the English Midlands.

it was restored over a period of almost four years by engineering staff and apprentices. The aircraft was finished in the usual First World War RFC drab brown colour scheme and re-allocated its original military registration of F 904. It flew for the first time after this restoration in August 1959, equipped with a Hispano engine. An agreement was struck between the RAE and the Shuttleworth Collection that the SE.5a should be a shared asset, primarily housed, exhibited and flown at Old Warden, but transferred to Farnborough during the summer to be displayed at venues in southern and western England. During the latter detachments the aircraft would be serviced and supported by Farnborough personnel and flown by the two most senior RAE test pilots: COEF and OC Flying.

In 1975 the COEF at Farnborough, Gp Capt 'Polly' Parrat, suffered an engine failure and had to land in a field. Despite his best efforts, the aircraft was damaged and the undercarriage had to be partly rebuilt. A Wolsey Viper engine was found and the decision was made to install it, so bringing the SE.5a back up to its full specification.

My first encounter with this diminutive biplane had been at Farnborough in 1976 when I watched the COEF of the day, Gp Capt Reggie Spiers, fly it from the grass not far from the HQ of the Experimental Flying Squadron, where I was employed as a test pilot. It was a magical sight to see and hear a real First World War fighter, not a replica, soar into the late afternoon sky over the airfield from where the type had originated sixty years earlier: a sight and sound that would stay with me for a long time. That was the first of several such flights I watched, as the OC Flying, Wg Cdr David Bywater, also flew the SE.5 as part of his duties. Now, in 1988, it was my turn.

In the late 1970s, when I was serving at RAE Bedford, my erstwhile ETPS classmate, George Ellis, who was also test flying at Bedford, invited me to go along to the Shuttleworth Collection, with a view to becoming one of their regular pilots. Accordingly, on the next of their summer display days I bade farewell to my family, hopped on my Triumph Thunderbird 650cc motorcycle and rode the 20 or so miles to the grass airfield at Old Warden. I met up with George and he introduced me to the other pilots and some of the engineers. I soon learnt that I was expected to do an apprenticeship before I would get anywhere near a cockpit. This would consist of turning up regularly, helping push aeroplanes out of the hangars (and back again at the end of the day) and generally show willing to be a dogsbody while learning how the collection operated. If that's what it would take to get myself in these old flying machines that was fine by me.

At the end of my first season, 1979, I had not done any flying at the collection, but had become accepted as being keen enough not to miss a show day and being fit enough to push and pull when required. During the following year I flew several times, mainly due to the kindness of some of the other pilots, but not yet 'officially' as a collection aviator. At the close of the 1980 display season I felt that the promise of starting as a collection pilot the following year was now firm. The chief pilot, retired Gloster Aircraft Chief Test Pilot Wg Cdr Dickie Martin, had told me so.

However, that was not to be. In January 1981 I had been unexpectedly posted back to ETPS at Boscombe Down. As there was no married quarter available for me I had to take a room in the Officers' Mess and commute weekly. This led to understandable pressure from my wife and family for me not to disappear on every second Sunday during the summer. So I told Dickie Martin that I would regrettably have to step down until my life stabilised and I could travel to Old Warden from Boscombe Down. But that never came about. My wife left the family at the end of 1982 and I attained the status of single parent. I realised with sadness that I had probably burnt my boats vis-à-vis flying for the Shuttleworth Collection.

So when, five years later, in June 1987, the call came for me to present myself at Old Warden to be checked out to fly the SE.5a I was, to say the least, a bit nervous as to how I would be received. The fact that my job now gave me the privilege of flying the aircraft was small solace! I flew our Gazelle helicopter to Old Warden and met up with John Lewis, who had taken over as chief pilot when Dickie Martin had retired. I had met John briefly before and actually flown with him in his capacity as a test pilot at Filton.[5] His job today was to fly with me in the collection's Tiger Moth, to check my competency in open-cockpit biplanes, and then show me how the SE.5 worked and send me off in that flying machine. The 1,200 hours I had flown in a 'tail-dragger', during five years instructing on the DH Chipmunk, gave me confidence in the vagaries of aeroplanes of that configuration. Things such as: a marked

---

5.    See Chapter 7 of *Trials and Errors* by this author (The History Press, 2015).

lack of view ahead on the ground, lifting the tail before getting off the ground, needing to use the rudder bar as more than a convenient footrest and achieving a three-point landing. In the event our twenty-minute flight in the Tiger Moth seemed to satisfy John that I was a fit person to be allowed to fly the SE.5a.

After a guided tour of the tiny cockpit and wise words on what to watch out for, John gave me an aide-memoire to put in my kneepad and took me for a coffee in the collection's café. As we walked back out to the purposeful-looking fighter, the ground crew were ready and waiting. We walked around to check all was well visually, John showed me how to check the tensions of the flying wires and then it was time to climb aboard. This was achieved by using the recessed step on the lower longeron of the port side of the fuselage and then athletically swinging one's right leg into the cockpit. During this manoeuvre it is vital to keep a weather eye on the butt of the Lewis gun jutting out behind the upper wing. It was neatly positioned to give a nasty bump to the head of a careless pilot. Once sat down, the cockpit fitted snugly around my upper arms, almost at shoulder level. Four canvas seat straps secured me in place and I checked that the two sets of ignition switches were off and the throttle moved fully and freely, and then was closed.

The SE.5a instrument panel is, with a couple of exceptions, definitely of its time. The original pattern large airspeed indicator (ASI), centrally located compass and aneroid barometer (pretending to be an altimeter) are the flight instruments that remind you of the aircraft's age. To go along with these is a vintage oil pressure gauge and fuel and air selectors let into a varnished wooden panel. Below the compass is a 'level indicator', consisting of a bubble in a curved tube. This was the only pilot aid for flying in cloud, which thankfully we were not permitted to do! There are also various plates with instructions on them. Some of these are there at the insistence of our modern aviation regulators – the most unhelpful of which is one stating, 'NO SMOKING'! To enhance the vintage dials are a few modern instruments, situated high and on the right of centre, under the coaming: a more accurate ASI, altimeter, fuel tank air pressure and coolant temperature gauges. So as not to upset the purists who might want to look into or even photograph the cockpit in the museum, these modern interlopers can be covered with a matching wooden panel. At the top left is the breech of the Vickers machine gun; it must have been very noisy when in use.

In my preparations to get things moving I also made sure that the shiny lever on the left that operated the 'Venetian blind' radiator shutters on the SE.5's nose moved freely and then was set to closed. The most complex part of the SE.5 cockpit was the fuel system, which had two selectors, one for the destination for the fuel and one for the air pressure that fed the fuel to the engine. There was also an arrangement of brass pipes on the lower part of the instrument panel and a hand pump down by my left leg; this was there for emergency fuel tank pressurisation should the engine-driven pump fail. As a last resort there was a small reserve fuel tank in the centre section of the wing above my head – this contained 4 gallons and would give a maximum of twenty minutes' flying time.

I checked the full and free movement of those flying controls operated by the stick, which is topped with a loop, bound with string, and has in its centre two thumb-operated firing levers, one for each gun. As the tailskid was fitted to the bottom of the rudder, checking that would have to wait until we were on the move. The SE.5a was fitted with an innovative longitudinal trimming system for its time – a variable incidence tailplane. This was operated by a notched wheel down by my left thigh; I had checked it earlier and set the recommended seven divisions nose-down from fully up.

I then used the pump by my left knee to put the air pressure in the fuel system up to 2.5psi. The strokes on the pump had to be made at just the right rate otherwise a very rude noise would emanate from the pressure relief valve. I didn't want anything blowing raspberries today! When the ground crewman had finished turning the prop to prime the engine with fuel, he took up his position ready to swing the propeller and called that he was all set. I moved the throttle forward about an inch and switched one of the magneto switches to '2' and the other, starter magneto switch to 'On'. 'Contact!' I called.

He gave the prop a good heave and stepped aside. The starter magneto protruded from the right side of the cockpit and the man with the easier job wound that just after the prop has started to move. With a pop and a crack the engine burst into life. I immediately caught it with the throttle, checked that the oil pressure had risen and set about 1,000rpm to help the now throbbing Viper to warm up. Then I switched the starter magneto to 'Off' and the other magneto switch to '1+2'.

The first thrill of an open cockpit is the sudden gale that hits your head when the engine starts. While waiting for the radiator coolant temperature to rise above 60°C, at which point I could increase the engine rpm, I checked that the magnetos were both working correctly. Once I saw that the temperature had risen sufficiently, I stuck my left arm out into the slipstream and gave a rotating, wind-up signal. Then a couple of burly guys laid themselves across the rear fuselage to stop the tail rising. When I was given a thumbs-up from out front I wound the engine up to 1,500rpm, and checked that the oil pressure was what it should be. Then I turned off each magneto in turn to check that the drop in rpm didn't exceed about 100 and that it recovered when I turned each back on. It was time to go. With the throttle closed, I waved the chocks away and set off across the grass towards the runway threshold.

On the ground I found the SE.5a quite easy to manoeuvre; I just had to remember that there were no brakes. The knife-like tailskid dug into the ground and turns were easy to make, especially if I used a simultaneous, judicious and brief burst of power. The blunt, high nose meant that I had to exercise the steering by weaving along so that I could clear the area ahead of me and not bump into anything. I also made a mental note of where the near horizon intersected the nose; this would be the three-point attitude I would try to achieve just before landing.

Once at the holding point I completed the brief pre-take-off checks. Perhaps the most important of these vital actions was to make sure that the fuel was coming from the main tank, and not the little reserve one up in the wing. However, the coolant temperature was also worth checking; if it was getting near 80°C, then opening the radiator shutters was a really good idea, especially on a summer's day or when going straight into a display. The reason for this is twofold. First, it's not good for the health of the engine if it gets too hot. Second, the coolant header tank is alongside the reserve fuel tank in the wing root above and ahead of the cockpit. If the engine gets too hot the expansion of the now very hot liquid in the header tank encourages it to flow out through the overflow pipe, which terminates at the in-board wing trailing edge, not far from the pilot's head. In flight the hot water flows away in the slipstream, but after landing it drips into the prop wash and gets blown on to the driver's visage – ouch! 'Always land with one's goggles on' was a good bit of advice.

The take-off, especially directly into wind, was relatively easy and the aircraft accelerated well, the rudder was effective for keeping straight and the tail came up readily with just a light forward pressure on the stick. After lift off, at about 50mph, I accelerated to 60mph and climbed on full power, delighting in the fact that I was flying history; this little fighter was already

27 years old when I was born! I climbed to 3,000ft over Old Warden and set up for a straight stall. As with all biplanes, especially those with flat noses, the SE.5 slowed down rapidly when the throttle was closed. I tried to keep the deceleration to about 1–2mph per second by descending slowly, so that I could get a good feel for the way the aircraft responded to gentle control inputs. As I had been briefed, the effect of applying aileron at less than 45mph was about zero – the aircraft didn't roll at all. Rudder had been effective at rolling it until then, but I didn't want to go applying rudder so near the stall – spinning was not allowed, nor was it sensible at this height! The stall happened in a conventional way at 42–43mph, with the nose dropping despite my efforts to keep it on the horizon.

Recovery with forward stick, full power and rudder to stop any yaw was immediate and very effective. I lost about 200–300ft at the most. *Note to self: never fly below 50mph, except near the ground when landing.* Also, always land into wind. Kicking off drift with rudder just before touchdown will beget roll and the ailerons won't stop that happening. Result: probably dinging a wingtip or worse.

After that I tried turns and wingovers, flew to the maximum allowed speed of 150mph, which needed quite a steep dive and made a lot of noise and buffeting round my head. I then tried a loop from 120mph and followed that with a stall turn; they worked fine.[6] After that I practised an engine failure and was astounded how quickly and how far I had to push the nose down to keep the recommended gliding speed of 60mph.

Now it was time to go back and try to land this little beast. I flew into the circuit and set up for a downwind leg at 1,000ft and 80mph. After checking all the usual things and setting full nose-up trim (that would help during the landing), I turned towards the final approach at 70mph, then lined up with the runway at about 300ft and let the speed decay slowly from 60 to 50mph as I crossed the hedge. As I flew over the beginning of the grass runway I closed the throttle and slowly raised the nose to the three-point attitude that I had memorised from taxiing out, then held it there as the nice little fighter

---

6. About five years later the CAA reviewed all the Shuttleworth aircraft permits and stopped most of them from carrying out aerobatics. This led to yet more plaques in cockpits, the most ridiculous of which was the one declaring, 'NO AEROBATIC MANOUEVRES', in the 1910 Avro Triplane!

settled sweetly on to the ground. *I hope John was watching that one*, I thought. However, I throttled up to try another full circuit, perhaps pushing my luck. The second circuit and landing was fine; it just showed how well designed the SE.5 had been from the outset. I taxied back to the parking spot with a big grin. When I dismounted, trying to avoid the hot exhaust pipe en route to the ground, John was also smiling. What a wonderful day!

Over the next two years I would fly the SE.5a many more times, with displays at various locations, including RAF Odiham, RAF Abingdon and RAE Bedford, as well as flying several transits between Farnborough and Old Warden. It was during the first of these that I decided to test just how stable the SE.5 was. I was flying straight and level at 2,000ft and 90mph. Having trimmed the aircraft to maintain level flight, I took my hands off the stick. I kept my feet on the rudder pedals so that I could use those to correct any lateral upsets and even turn the aircraft through small heading changes. After twenty minutes the little warplane had not deviated from the height and speed one iota; well done Mr Folland et al.! Out of the 140 aircraft types I have flown, the SE.5a is one of my firm favourites, along with the Spitfire and the Lightning, where it stands high on the list of all-time great fighters. I once gave a lecture on the merits, and drawbacks, of those three warplanes and what they were like to fly. An interesting thought that I shared with my audience was that there were just forty years separating the first flights of the SE.5 and the Lightning, with that of the Spitfire sitting neatly in the middle.

My last flight in the SE.5a as OC Flying at Farnborough would not turn out to be my last in F 904. In May 1990 I returned to the fold at Old Warden and flew another check flight in the Tiger Moth with John Lewis. This marked the start of six years of flying with the Shuttleworth Collection; I hope to write about that part of my forty-two years as a pilot in the not too distant future. Oddly enough, my last flight for the collection was in that same Tiger Moth (G-ANKT), displaying it, along with other vintage aircraft, at the 1990 Farnborough International Air Show. *Toute ça change, toute ça même chose!*

# 15 A RETROSPECTIVE

In April 1988 I received a telephone call from the man who looked after my future, and that of many others like me. He was known as my desk officer, and as far as I was concerned he could keep looking after my desk – wherever it was. We talked, or at least I listened a lot, as he read my tea leaves or gazed into his crystal ball to tell me what Her Majesty's Royal Air Force had planned for my future. As time went on I actually started to like what I was hearing. My name was pencilled in for a job in the USA. It was an appointment with the title of 'Air 1', on the military staff of the British Embassy in Washington DC – a city I had visited a few times, and the bits I had seen I had liked.

'What exactly would I be doing?' I asked, secretly hoping that a job title including the word 'Air' might indicate some flying!

'As I understand it, old chap, you'll be the contact point between the Embassy and each and every RAF officer on an exchange posting to the States,' came the reply.

'How many are there then?' was my next question.

'Not sure exactly, but I think around fifty,' he said. 'So you'll be doing a lot of travelling, all paid for by Her Majesty of course.'

Well, it all sounded good to me. Accommodation would be provided in the environs of Washington, I would work directly for the air attaché and I'd be back in a country that I had grown to like very much. The plan was that my replacement would arrive in plenty of time to understudy me, especially during the 1988 air show, and I would leave immediately after the show, to be in post by mid September – only five months hence. I settled back to daily life with a happy grin and an impatience to give my wife the great news. There would be lots of family things to work out, but we had done that many times before.

A few weeks later my boss called me into his office. 'I'm afraid there's some bad news about you going to that job in Washington, old chap,' he said, with genuine sympathy. 'Your replacement will not now be coming in time for you to depart in September; in fact he's not coming at all. The reasons are confidential, but even worse, the folks up at the body shop [personnel office] can't find a replacement for him!'

'So what now, sir?' I asked, trying not to sound too downhearted.

'We're working on it – just hang on in there and we'll try to get you a good job, even if it's not in the USA,' he said. So I just got on with my job, and did as much flying as I could manage without dropping the paper-work ball.

In the event I got two bits of news in rapid succession. First, the boss told me that it looked as if my replacement would now be Sqn Ldr Alan Sheppard, presently at Farnborough as the OC of the Experimental Flying Squadron, who would be given acting rank so that I could leave at the end of the year. Then I got another call from my desk officer.

'Hello, Mike, we want you to move across to Boscombe Down and take over as Wing Commander Flying. The present incumbent, a naval commander, is leaving at fairly short notice on premature voluntary retirement. You're the only name in the frame with the right qualifications.'

I was knocked back a bit and it took a little while for the implications to sink in. Although I had never been much of a career officer, chasing the next promotion, I knew a sideways move when I saw it. Also, I was fairly sure that I had one more promotion in me, which could make me eligible for the senior test-flying job at Boscombe. Being his sidekick wasn't going to help!

'Well, it's a bit of a forked stick. I was hoping for a more challenging staff job out of the test-flying business for a change. While the possibility of continuing to fly attracts me, I know from my past time at Boscombe that the Wing Commander Flying job is a bit of a sinecure for ageing folks of the appropriate rank. Here I've been doing that job and functioning in a command role simultaneously. It's not just a sideways move – there's a downward gradient to it as well. I really do not want to go.'

'I'm sorry you feel like that, Mike,' came the bland reply, 'but I don't have a choice. We've worked with your own personnel folks up in town and trawled all the test pilots of your rank that we can find. You're it and we'll just post you there if we have to.'

Ultimatum time! Now I knew what it was like to be sitting in the bottom of the barrel – all on my own. So that was that – as usual, defending democracy from an organisation that doesn't make much use of it.

As the time got nearer and the administration, organisation and logistics of the move took over, I started to look back on my time as OC Flying at Farnborough with great affection. This and my first squadron tour in the mid 1960s were probably the best six years out of the twenty-six that I had now spent in the RAF. Although, having said that, most of the rest were pretty good too!

Looking back over my time at Farnborough there were many other interesting events. For instance, I became involved in the search for a replacement for our venerable DC-3 Dakota, used mainly for parachute trials, but also for heavier equipment transport. Through this quest I got to perform qualitative evaluations of the Short 330, Dornier 228 and the Cessna 208 Caravan. All were turboprop powered, so economical to operate, and they shared good short-field performance and were much more modern, and therefore more economically supportable into the future than the 'Dak'. The three contenders all handled well and were worthy of commercial consideration. I personally preferred the Short 330 – it was British and had the most internal space for the weight. The Dornier's performance was better but not sufficiently to justify what was likely to be a higher acquisition cost. In the event none of them were purchased and the DC-3 (ZA 947) soldiered on until March 1993, when its colourful red, white and blue paint scheme was replaced with RAF wartime camouflage and the aircraft was handed over to the Battle of Britain Memorial Flight, where it serves to this day – an incredible eighty years since the type's first flight!

Another event that is indelibly engraved on my memory stems from the day when my boss, Reg Hallam, called me into his office to tell me that the RAF contingent at Farnborough was to be awarded the Freedom of the Borough of Rushmoor. 'Hurrah and three cheers!' I said. 'Good excuse for a party, eh boss?'

'Well, you might not cheer so loudly when I tell you that you, my son, are going to be the parade commander,' he rejoined, with an impish grin.

Desperately trying to think of ways out of this I said, 'But, sir, I …'

'It's no good trying to get out of it,' he interrupted. 'The boss of the Queen's Colour Squadron and his warrant officer (WO) are coming here to meet you on Monday next week. Get your shoes polished and your best uniform pressed – and you'd better buy a new SD hat[1] if that one you're wearing is the only one you've got!'

The Queen's Colour Squadron (QCS) are part of the RAF Regiment; they provide ceremonial guards and have a display team for special events across the nation. Their ten-minute silent rifle drill sequence is a wonder to behold. The regiment's real *raison d'être*, however, is to provide ground defence and security for RAF airfields. Its members are mainly those folk who would

---

1. The Service Dress hat (officers for the use of) is the peaked variety as opposed to the 'chip bag' forage cap.

have joined the army but prefer wearing RAF blue. The regiment are really good at drill, shining boots and generally looking smart. There is a legend, no doubt started by one of them in years gone by, that the RAF would disappear if the regiment was disbanded – much like the parallel adage that the British Empire would collapse if the Barbary apes left the Rock of Gibraltar. The legend backfired, however, because throughout the RAF, members of the regiment are known as 'rock apes'!

I knew that I should not mention any sort of primates when I met the two senior men from the QCS. The OC turned out to be a squadron leader I had met during a staff course, which felt like a good omen. The WO was straight out of the drill manual – tall, ramrod-straight back, stick tucked under his right arm, cap peak folded down almost over his eyes and a powerful voice. Virtually every sentence ended with 'Sir!' and his boots were a pair of ground-level mirrors that could be used for looking for explosive devices under his car!

They had done their homework and were obviously well versed in the normal sequence of events for Freedom Parades. They gave me an outline of all the likely moves and commands. Then they went to see the squadron leader in charge of the RAF Administration unit, to discover how many airmen and airwomen could be called upon to form the flights needed to make the whole thing worthwhile. The QCS would form the leading two flights; they would escort the standards and be the first formations behind me. We had about three months to work up a decent show and I could tell from the outset that OC QCS and his sidekick would take no prisoners in their search for perfection.

From then on a programme of regular practices took place. A lot of shouting happened, some of it part of the process and mostly by me, but the majority from the WO by way of 'encouragement' for us all to do better. Slowly it all came together. I went on a diet to make sure that I fitted my best uniform easily, number one son (who revelled in this sort of thing) took over the shining of my shoes (Oxford pattern, black, officers for the use of) and I took my aluminium dummy sword home at the weekends to practise in the garden!

On the big day it went off well. My mentor only had to prompt me once and all the lads and lasses looked great. We had handpicked a trio of tall, slim RAF test pilots to carry flags and collect the illuminated scroll from the mayor, and the march-past rounded things off to a tee – actually it was to a lunch, a really splendid day. I was more relieved at getting through those two hours than through any test flight I had ever made. To round it all off, we were on the local TV news that night.

Another really important feature of our time at Farnborough was the growth in our spiritual lives. In July 1986, after we had moved into our married quarter, we sought a church home; we found one a few minutes' walk from our house in Cove. There we were welcomed with open arms and were soon absorbed fully into our new Christian family. Over the next two years our journey of faith saw us learning more and leading house group meetings, the church youth group and starting, and running a Christian book stall. We also joined the Officers' Christian Union (OCU) whose HQ was just down the road in Aldershot. This would play an important part in our lives for many years to follow.

In 1988 I had become a member of the Guild of Air Pilots and Navigators (GAPAN),[2] a relatively modern element of the ancient guilds of London. The man who had introduced me to GAPAN, a senior scientific officer at RAE called Freddie Stringer, became the Master of the Guild the following year. He asked me to organise an air show for the guild's annual garden party, to be held on the airfield at White Waltham, west of London. I contacted folk that I knew from the air-display circuit and called in a few favours. The day was a great success – apart from one of the marquees collapsing on to the strawberries and cream teas! Later I was inducted into the Livery at Guildhall in the City of London and was put forward to receive the Freedom of the City of London. The rather intimately conducted ceremony was done in a way that brought home to me the long and distinguished history of the London guilds. Being a Freeman of the City would apparently allow me to drive my sheep over London Bridge and make citizen's arrests within the square mile!

I joined the technical panel of the guild and met many distinguished pilots from that 'other' world of civil aviation. In 1999 I was honoured to be given the guild's Master Pilot Certificate and it was a real pleasure to be handed it

---

2. Since 2014 the guild has been given honourable status by Her Majesty the Queen and is now known as the Honourable Company of Air Pilots.

by a doyen of the test-flying business – Duncan Simpson, the erstwhile Chief Test Pilot of Hawker Aviation, latterly British Aerospace Dunsfold. I had the honour to be introduced to the Grand Master of the Guild, His Royal Highness the Prince Philip, at several GAPAN functions.

There were many more high points of this tour, but they could fill another book. Suffice it to say that in the three years I was there I flew over 800 hours on thirty types of aircraft and we did not have a major accident. I could leave my desk to my successor, Wg Cdr Alan Sheppard, with a clear conscience.

# PART 3

# BOSCOMBE DOWN

# 16 BACK TO THE FUTURE

So, after yet another Yuletide house move, here I was again, back at Boscombe Down for the third time. This time my office was in the old control tower that overlooked the huge aircraft parking area and the airfield from its north-west corner. There I met the outgoing occupant, an irrepressible naval aviation officer and sea-dog character, Commander Ed Horne. He introduced me to things in his usual relaxed way, showed me the essentials and said the job was easy – it was the interruptions that were difficult. He didn't stick around long because it seemed that he was anxious to get settled into his new role in life as a school truant officer; a job that would, I thought, really suit him!

By now I had made the rounds of those essential departments and offices where I needed to show my face as the new 'wings'.[1] One of those was the man at the top, Air Cdre David Bywater, who was the Commandant – the senior military officer at the establishment and therefore my boss' boss. This was the third time we had served on the same establishment together – he always retaining a position two levels above me, and deservedly so. When I got past his ADC into his office I think that we were equally pleased to see each other again, although he did admit that he had expected me to move into a 'better job'. I told him the sorry tale and he sympathised. We shared tales of flying the SE.5a during our tours at Farnborough.

My last incarnation at the A&AEE had been as a fixed-wing tutor (instructor) with the ETPS. Over the six intervening years not a lot seemed to have changed on the airfield, except the rash of ugly, brown carbuncles that had grown all over the previously green and pleasant land that lay between the dispersal areas and the 10,000ft-long main runway. These blots on the landscape were the Hardened Aircraft Shelters (HAS) built under NATO auspices for the use of deployed flying units sent to Boscombe Down in times of tension or war. A new network of taxiways connected these unsightly but functional humpbacked buildings with the runways. There was also a large

---

1. A naval aviation term for the man in charge of flying and support facilities.

building being constructed in the centre of the row of hangars on the north side of the apron. This was the new aircrew building that would, in time, be occupied by the entirety of the fixed-wing test-flying units.

Another change was that the rotary-wing element of ETPS had moved across the airfield, from the misty distant horizon where the Rotary Wing Test Squadron (RWTS) lived to the ETPS hangar only a two-minute walk from my office. This move had been long overdue, as it brought proper cohesion to the two elements of the school. Over in the school itself, which I visited as soon as I could, there was a new boss, Wg Cdr Martin Mayer, the first helicopter test pilot to become OC ETPS. I made myself known to him and he was very pleased to see me. Over coffee in the familiar surroundings of the ETPS coffee bar, Martin explained that he had concerns over the fixed-wing side of his new 'empire'. It turned out that three of his four fixed-wing tutors were new that year and he could not yet take up any slack as he could only help out with the rotary-wing students.

'What aircraft of our fleet are you current on right now?' he asked.

'Let me see, fixed wing – the Jaguar, Hunter and BAC 1-11. Rotary wing – Sea King and Gazelle – but you've got those covered yourself. Plus I'm due to get re-qualified on the Hawk next week. Why do you ask?'

'Well, as you're an ex-tutor I thought I might be able to use you when I need help,' he replied.

'OK, it's a deal. The students don't start flying for another six weeks yet, so that will give me time to get back up to speed with the teaching bits. But I better have a word with the group captain first,' I cautioned.

When I had checked in with my new boss, Gp Capt Keith Mills, himself new in the post and to the rank, he had intimated that I should only fly the Hawk jet trainer and the Gazelle light helicopter, and that I should concentrate on the main elements of my new job. I took this to mean the oversight of all the airfield facilities: Fire Section, ATC, Met Office, Bird Scaring and Airfield Works Services. However, none of these came under my direct command and control – they were all civilian manned – so my role was very much a liaison and persuasion one. The group captain also said that I would be responsible for offering him advice on the clearance of flight trials when he needed it, as well as acting as his deputy. My direct command responsibilities were solely over my office staff of two squadron leaders, a serving squadron leader and a retired one. I was also chairman of the Station Flight Safety Committee. Any other work would be allocated to me on an ad hoc basis. Compared with my responsibilities at Farnborough it was definitely lightweight. However, it was a chance to spend time out of the office doing MBWA. (In fact, the walking bit wasn't true.) I had access to a yellow, radio-equipped Land Rover, so I could get out and about and still be contactable by radio. I made early visits to get to know the people in the ATC tower and at the Fire Section, both situated on the far side of the runway.

That reminded me of a perennial Boscombe Down problem: crossing the runway. It was a bit like Gibraltar, where the main road from Spain on to the Rock crosses the runway and lights operated from the ATC tower control all the road traffic. At Boscombe, it was the same arrangement and when there were more than a couple of aircraft in the circuit one could be stuck at the lights for ages. Eventually, when the queue of steaming vehicles had reached an unreasonable length, the controller would give ground traffic priority over air traffic and the lights would change to green. The variability in the timing could lead to a lot of unpunctuality. A solution was not easy or cheap. A tunnel had been suggested and some wag even proposed a bridge!

Early in the New Year of 1989, about a month after I had arrived, Keith Mills suggested that I fly the Harvard with him. I had flown the big, yellow American trainer with its 600hp Pratt & Whitney radial engine during my previous tour at Boscombe Down. He had already checked out in the back seat, so he said he would sign me up as current again, as long as I didn't frighten him.

It was a bright, sunny winter's morning when we walked out to the Harvard, sitting there reflecting the sunshine with its all-over daffodil-yellow paint job. We walked round the outside so that I could remind myself of the things that needed checking before we clambered up the wing for access to the spacious cockpits. I strapped into the parachute and seat harnesses, checking that the rudder pedals were adjusted for my limited leg length. Once aboard the smell of petrol and canvas reminded me of the Harvard's vintage.

The original 1935 design, by the North American Aviation Company, developed into the AT-6 Texan and was already in use in the US Army Air Force when the Second World War started. The RAF and Royal Canadian

Air Force bought some of the early models to use as advanced trainers – these became known as the Harvard 1. Later in the war, modified licence-built models from the Canadian Noorduyen company were used for the British Commonwealth Air Training Plan – these were designated the Harvard 2B. Over 15,000 AT-6/Harvard aircraft would be built and they would serve with the air arms of over sixty countries worldwide. Until early 1982 A&AEE Boscombe Down had operated three Harvards, predominantly in the photo-chase role (more of which later).

On 22 February 1982, Harvard KF 314 had crashed during a pilot conversion exercise and, very sadly, both occupants were killed. I later found the Board of Inquiry documents in my office. The exact cause of the accident was never ascertained. After the accident, in which the aircraft was written off, the remaining two Harvards, FT 375 and KF 183, continued to be employed by the establishment.

It was Harvard 2B KF 183 that I was strapping into, aiming to impress my boss that I was still a fit person to be allowed off the ground in charge of one of the oldest aircraft still on the UK military register. As I strapped in I noticed the maker's brass plate riveted to the canopy rail by my left elbow; etched into it was the date of manufacture. It was two days before my own! After checking around the cockpit that all appeared present and correct, including squinting down into the gloom below to read the two fuel gauges set into the floor, I was ready to start the big round motor up front.

To get it going there was an electrically driven flywheel, which once it had reached the right speed could be engaged to turn the engine. The correct speed could only be judged by the sound it made. So, after priming the engine with fuel and informing the ground crew that the propeller was about to rotate, I hit the appropriate switch. The low hum from up front soon rose to a treble C and I moved the switch in the opposite direction and turned on the ignition switches. The prop moved and, after a couple of rotations, there was a series of satisfying pops and bangs, accompanied by white smoke from the exhaust, and the engine burst into life. A few checks later and I was waving the chocks away and, with my canopy still slid back, I taxied out towards the runway in use.

As is normal with tail-wheel equipped aeroplanes that have big engines, I didn't move forward in a straight line, but rather tacked from side to side so that I could see the ground ahead – it's called 'weaving'. As I waltzed my way out, using the rudder pedals to turn and the brakes to control speed,

I could feel the Harvard's propensity to swing rapidly to one side or another if I didn't pay strict attention. It is very easy to let a rapid swing develop that can all too easily get out of control. This unfortunate event is called a ground loop and once it's going you just have to let it take you around. It's a very public demonstration that you need more practice! Fortunately I've only experienced the ground loop at the hands of others.

Our aim was to depart from and return to the grass strip that lay about halfway alongside Boscombe's long runway. I had last used this facility with the ETPS Andover and had also taxied a Jaguar (quite legally) across it. Before departing I parked out of the way of other aircraft that might be coming up behind us so I could check that the engine was functioning correctly. This check included holding the stick hard back and the brakes fully on, opening up the engine to high revs and making sure that the pressures and temperatures, magnetos and propeller rpm control were all up to snuff. Even with the canopies closed, it made a lot of very satisfying noise.

Once cleared to depart I lined up on the grass runway, released the brakes and smoothly pushed the throttle forward, all the while using the rudder pedals to keep straight. With a gentle forward pressure on the stick, the tail came up and we were soon in the flying attitude. With virtually no backward pressure on the control column, KF 183 lifted into the sky. The next job was to retract the landing gear and then reduce the engine speed using the rpm control lever, next to the throttle in my left hand. This stopped the harsh, high-pitched buzz created by the propeller tips travelling at supersonic speed. Because of this feature, during the 1940s this very aircraft had been used for research into supersonic aerodynamics.

The Harvard climbed at about 1,000ft per minute so five minutes later we were at a height where it was safe to manoeuvre, stall and do some simple aerobatics. These old ladies had to be handled gently so I kept the g-loads to not more than +3. It was delightful to be back in this big gentle throwback to the 1930s, making smooth lines in the Wiltshire skies. We did not usually spin the Harvards except on first conversion or check sorties like this one. So, to fulfil this requirement I climbed to 8,000ft and carried out all the usual checks, including a quick reminder about how to get out if the aircraft was not recovered by 3,000ft above the ground – and I mentally rehearsed it. Having made sure that there was no one around who we might bump into, I levelled the wings and closed the throttle. I had stalled earlier so at a good 5 knots above the stalling speed I simultaneously pulled the stick fully back and applied full-left rudder. The aircraft shuddered then made a quick tight barrel roll to the left before settling into the familiar rotation of a spin, going round a full turn in about five seconds. After three of those turns I moved the stick progressively and centrally forward and applied full-right rudder. After not much more than one further turn the Harvard obeyed and stopped spinning, and I pulled out of the fairly steep dive.

As we were now back down to about 3,000ft, Keith declared close of play and asked me to return to base to fly a practice forced landing and a few circuits and landings. We set up for the grass strip, doing our best not to disrupt things for our jet-borne brethren. It all came back quickly and after three safe landings I gave control to my 'instructor' so he could practise landing from the back seat – a much more difficult task, as the view ahead is even worse, as if that was possible! However, the group captain made a good fist of it and we turned off the strip to taxi back, both of us with satisfied smiles on our faces.

When we got back to the office I thought it an opportune time to mention Martin Meyer's idea of me helping out with some of the ETPS tasks. It was not well received by my boss – lead balloons came to mind.

'I want you available in your office or at least easily contactable by radio or telephone. You can fly twice per week in the Hawk, Harvard or Gazelle. Otherwise regard this as a staff tour with a bit of flying – not the other way round.'

The next time I saw Martin I let him know the rather disappointing outcome. He said that when the right opportunity came up he would raise the issue himself. To add fuel to this particular fire, it wasn't long before my very good friend and ex-colleague from ETPS, Wg Cdr John Thorpe, who was now commanding the Fast Jet Test Squadron (FJTS), known around the place as 'Fidgets', came to me with a similar proposal.

'Brookie, are you still current on the Buccaneer?' he asked. 'We need a bit of help with some trials.'

I checked my logbook; three months since the last flight was the rule. Any longer than that would require a simulator session and a check ride.

'Sorry, mate, my currency ran out about a week ago. Anyway you should be aware that I am not being encouraged to fly much,' I replied. 'If you have a strong case – I suggest you ask the group captain yourself.'

That appeared to be that. Proper staff work was a bit thin on the ground, partly because not much was coming down from above. Not having a great deal to do, I threw myself into management posture and did a lot of MBWA, liaising and persuading.

Not long after I had arrived one of the young test pilots I knew from Fidgets sidled up to me during the Friday evening happy hour. As the level in my glass was approaching critical, I assumed he was going to offer me a beer. Not a bit of it!

'Excuse me, sir,' he said. 'Didn't you do two flying tours as a squadron leader?'

'Yes,' I replied, wondering where this was leading.

'Now you're going to do two flying tours as a wing commander.' I couldn't deny it. 'So how does that work?'

A light bulb went on in my head. 'Well, Dave, don't tell anyone else, but I am the first Specialist Aircrew wing commander in the RAF.[2] It's supposed to be a bit of a secret until they work out if it's a good idea,' I responded, somewhat conspiratorially.

'Oh, I see … can I get you another beer, sir?'

I didn't deny him that pleasure. What was interesting was that at the following week's Friday happy hour it was the Commandant, David Bywater, who sidled up to me. And it was his glass that was now reaching minimum fuel level, so I expected to be buying.

But before I could offer he said, in a stage whisper, 'What's this I hear about you being Specialist Aircrew? I didn't know anything about it!'

I think my smile gave him a clue. 'I was wondering how long that bit of supposedly secret information would get around! No, sir, it's not true – but I do intend, regardless of any barriers being put in my way, to do as much flying as I can while I'm here!' I was safe in the knowledge that, aside from our difference in rank, David could be relied on to lend me a sympathetic ear.

---

2.  The Specialist Aircrew career option for RAF aircrew was introduced in the late 1970s. It gave those who wished to stay on in the service beyond the age of 38 (or sixteen years' service) the option of continued flying but with promotion limited to the rank of squadron leader; there were enhance salary scales attached.

# 17 THE YANKS ARE COMING!

June 1989 was the month during which elements of the USAF's 27th Tactical Fighter Wing would exercise their deployment from Cannon Air Force Base in New Mexico to the cooler and cloudier climes of Boscombe Down and the UK. They would bring with them eight General Dynamics F-111D bombers. I was allocated the job of liaison officer for all their flying operations and to be the man who delivered the arrival briefing.

The F-111's prime claim to fame was that it was the first production aircraft to go into full operational service with variable-sweep wings, known more prosaically as 'swing-wing'. The history of engineering variable-sweep wings goes back to 1931, with the British Westland Hill Pterodactyl design, whose slightly swept wings could vary their sweep through a small angle during flight. This allowed longitudinal trim in the absence of a separate horizontal tailplane. During the Second World War a German design, the Messerschmitt P.1101, was able to vary the sweep of its wings, but only on the ground. Post-war research on variable-sweep wings followed in the UK, the Soviet Union and France. After much experimental test flying some variable-sweep operational aircraft eventually emerged – among them the European Tornado, and no less than six Soviet bombers and fighters. The French Mirage G-8 variable-sweep fighter never went into production; the French preferred to stay with the elegant delta-wing solution.

In the USA the Bell X-5, which was based on the Me P.1101 design, could sweep the wings in flight. However, the rearwards movement of the centre of lift engendered some difficult control problems. Undeterred by the challenges, US research continued with the swing-wing Grumman XF10-F that flew in the early 1950s; however, it possessed extremely poor flying characteristics and rather vicious spin tendencies. But what was the rationale behind achieving in-flight variable sweep despite all the control problems?

The main motivator was to rationalise the ever-increasing need for speed, conferred by swept wings, with the increasing weight of aircraft and the resulting very high landing speeds. One solution was to introduce air tapped from the engines blown over the wings to fool it into behaving as if it was flying safely at lower speeds. The British Blackburn Buccaneer and the McDonnell F-4 Phantom were two aircraft that used this technique, known as boundary layer control. The other solution was to have the wings swept for high-speed flight and then bring them forward for the low-speed events of take-off and landing. A beneficial spin-off was that highly swept wings on fighters and bombers operating at low altitudes give a much better ride in turbulent conditions.

In 1961 the US Secretary of State for Defence, Robert McNamara, initiated the Tactical Fighter Experimental Program, known as TFX. This was an attempt to find one aircraft to satisfy the requirements of both the US Air Force (USAF) and Navy (USN) for a new fighter-bomber. As could have easily been predicted, the air force and navy wanted to keep these requirements separate. In the event they could agree only on swing-wing, two-seat, twin-engine design features. The air force wanted a tandem-seat aircraft for low-level penetration ground attack, while the navy wanted a shorter, high-altitude interceptor with side-by-side seats, to allow the pilot and radar operator to share the radar display. Also, the air force wanted the aircraft designed for +7g with speeds of Mach 2.5 at altitude and Mach 1.2 at low level. The navy had less strenuous requirements of +6g and speeds of Mach 2 at altitude and Mach 0.9 at low level. The navy also wanted the aircraft to have a nose large enough for a 48in-diameter radar dish. Design proposals were sought from industry: Boeing, General Dynamics, McDonnell, Republic, Lockheed and North American responded.

The Boeing design was selected in April 1962. After further reviews by the navy and much politicking, McNamara overruled the selection board and directed that the General Dynamics design be adopted in two versions: the F-111A for the USAF and the F-111B for the USN. A Congressional investigation was held but could not alter the decision. Development continued on both variants but, in 1968, the navy cancelled any further work on the B model. However, they did not give up on swing wings. They sponsored a new programme called VFX, which led to the production and eventual introduction into service of the variable-sweep Grumman F-14 Tomcat in the 1970s.

Back at Boscombe Down I was preparing for meetings with all interested (and some not so interested) parties. On the morning of the advanced party's arrival I received a call to say that the first aircraft was inbound. It was a Lockheed C-5 Galaxy, the USAF's largest transporter and one of the biggest aircraft in the world. After my encounters with the Antonov An-124 I was very interested to see this beast. It appeared over the western horizon, blotting out the sun as it came ever closer. The landing was almost graceful, the Galaxy's enormity making it appear to be flying much slower than it really was. After landing the crew were directed to taxi up to the large parking area outside the hangars, where our smaller aircraft had been despatched flying or put safely away. I went out to meet it, but kept my distance until it had been parked. I was glad I did so because the jet wash from the engines as it performed a spot turn on its 'sea of wheels' was something to be avoided!

Our engineers helped direct the offloading operation so that vehicles and crates of spare parts were sent to the right places. The people were led away to buses, which took them to the accommodation blocks provided. Later in the day the swing-wing F-111 Aardvarks started arriving until the full complement was finally put to bed in the hardened aircraft shelters.[1]

On the first full day of the detachment, all the USAF personnel were gathered into a large briefing room and the great and the good were there to welcome them, including the Commandant. Eventually the torch was passed to me and it was my job to brief them on the local area, base facilities, flying operating procedures and related matters. I started by welcoming them to the country where 200 miles was a long way and 200 years a short time. This had the desired effect of both amusing and relaxing them. Once the briefing was over our visitors dispersed to their places of work and I made my way to the specially hardened Operations Block, not far from my office, to make sure that the aircrews were settling in satisfactorily and answer any questions.

Before the detachment had arrived the Commandant had decreed that we should offer them some flying in our own jets. This would be good for transatlantic relationships, as well as giving the pilots an introduction to our local flying and radio procedures. It was my duty to fly the USAF detachment commander, Lt Col Braunhart, in a Hunter. This I did on 12 June and once the good lieutenant colonel had got over the tightness of the cockpit I think he enjoyed the experience. I noticed that he took some time to tone down his inputs on the control column to deal with the relative lightness of the Hunter's responses. However, once he had fully adjusted to the feather-light

---

1. 'Hardening' of airfields throughout NATO took place from the late 1970s onwards. Hardened aircraft shelters (HAS) were designed to withstand direct hits from conventional bombs and were constructed from ferroconcrete.

feel I turned the power controls off to let him experience the much heavier control forces in manual mode.

'Gee, that's better,' he said, with a twinkle in his eyes that suggested he was just kidding.

The trip ended with him having flown some aerobatics for the first time in some years, as well as low flying at 250ft above the ground, which I think he did a lot of, and trying to land a small jet, which he did successfully. As we walked back in he offered me a ride in his jet, to be arranged later in the month.

I also flew another two F-111 pilots that week, Capt Dunn in a Harvard, which he enjoyed enormously, and Capt Gunner in the Jet Provost, whose reaction to our funny little jet trainer was hard to judge – but he was very polite about it!

My turn at swing-wing aviation came on Friday, 23 June, and it was to be with Lt Col Braunhart in an F-111D Aardvark. I arrived at the required time to be issued with the American flying equipment and be given the safety brief. The F-111 is fitted with a crew escape capsule instead of individual ejection seats. If it became necessary to abandon the aircraft, the whole cockpit and a portion of the upper fuselage aft of the cockpit is ejected vertically by a 27,000lb thrust-rocket system. Once safe speed parameters have been achieved the whole cockpit structure, with the two-man crew strapped inside, descends to earth on parachutes. Air bags under the cockpit floor deploy to cushion the impact. It is then only a matter of egressing the cockpit, hopefully in the normal manner.

We walked out to our ship, standing in its slightly hunched posture awaiting our arrival. I walked around the black- and tan-painted machine as it was checked over visually. It was big to be called a fighter. It was 4ft longer in the fuselage than my old Canberra B(I)8, but, with the wings fully spread, 6ft less in wingspan. We climbed aboard, entering the cockpit via the gull-wing canopies, and I was very pleasantly surprised to find I was going to occupy the pilot's seat on the left, while the colonel was going to sit on my right in the weapons officer's place.

Our ground crew were hooked up to the intercom system and we worked our way through the pre-start checks with me not doing very much. I was then directed through the selection and operation of the necessary switches and levers for starting the engines. They were soon up and running and the cockpit had come alive with warning lights coming on and going out as things proceeded. After checking the flying control and flap operations we were ready to go.

'OK, Mike, as you know the lingo you can do the radio,' said the colonel.

I called and we were given permission to move out on to the main taxiway. The aircraft actually trundled along steadily! 'Trundled' was the only word to describe it. The big turbofan engines gave a satisfying low howl and the effect of the centrally mounted main gear made the aeroplane wallow a little as we turned corners.

When all systems were 'go' I called for departure clearance and lined up on the north-easterly runway. The two Pratt & Whitney TF 30 engines give about 36,000lb of thrust at full throttle and, with the afterburners engaged, just over 50,000lb of thrust. Our take-off weight was about 60,000lb so the acceleration was good and we lifted off at about 150 knots after thirty seconds on the runway. I held the climb-out angle to about 10 degree so that I could get the rather large wheels tucked away into the fuselage. As this happened the big flat plate of the landing gear door moved forward and down before closing over the now retracted gear. There was a definite sensation of decreased acceleration as this happened.

Once we had climbed to around 20,000ft for our transit to the west and the entry into the low-flying areas in Wales, I was able to get the feel of the Aardvark. The cockpit was reasonably conventional for the aircraft's 1970s vintage, with round, analogue instruments and a fairly simple HUD for the pilot. On the right side there was a radar screen and weapons selection switches, as well as a stick. The F-111 handled much like a well-harmonised airliner; it reminded me of the BAC-111 in its responses to control inputs, although it was a bit more agile and its increased strength and military demeanour allowed me to pull quite hard turns. It was stable around all three axes.

Lt Col Braunhart was using the mapping radar and navigation system to guide us to the start point for our low-level transit down through Wales towards the south-west of England. On his instruction I throttled back and we cruised down at 400 knots until we reached our operating height of around 250ft on the radar altimeter. As I levelled off I was instructed to bring the wings to a sweep position of around 60 degrees, which I did using a small lever next to the throttles, moving it forwards to sweep the wings back. That seemed geometrically odd, but made sense in relationship to our increased speed of 450 knots. There was no noticeable trim change with the change of sweep angle, which could go as far back as 72.5 degrees.

The Aardvark was now in its element. Like the Buccaneer it barrelled along smoothly, barely reacting to the turbulence off the mountains around us. The response seemed better now and I was able to follow the twists and turns of valleys with no difficulty. The stability in pitch meant I could easily follow the contours of the undulating land.

The colonel could see I was enjoying myself, back in my favourite form of flight, and so he said he would show me something else. He asked me to ease up to about 500ft and fly fairly level. Then he used the autopilot panel to engage the terrain-following mode and asked me to descend back to 250ft and then let go of the stick. I did so but didn't move my hand too far away from it. We were now flying under the direction of the terrain-following radar (TFR) and it was holding the height at 250ft. The severity of the ride could be selected to give some latitude on how hard the TFR's inputs would be; we had selected medium. It was fascinating to be there at low level and high speed letting the machine do its own thing. As I had never flown the Tornado, which had the same ability, this was a new experience. I could still steer the aircraft to follow our route and after some minutes I began to relax as I saw how good a job the system was doing.

As we crossed the Bristol Channel towards the hills of Exmoor I disengaged the autopilot and lit the afterburners for a rapid climb to around 25,000ft. That took not much more than a minute and we headed east back towards Boscombe Down. On the way back I was encouraged to test the wing-sweep mechanism throughout its full range. The F-111's flight-control system was impressive in how it handled the changes in trim that were inevitable from the shift of the centre of pressure that these movements caused; I hardly noticed it.

Back at base we carried out a radar-directed approach and I selected flap and gear on cue from the right-hand seat. Once more the change in drag and slight transient trim change were noticeable as the wheels cycled down. Touching down reasonably softly was quite easy, although I found getting the machine down in the right place a bit trickier. However, by my third and final attempt I was starting to get the hang of the relationship between power and stick inputs. With the wings fully spread, at a mere 16 degrees, the F-111 was very conventional and power could be brought right back during the last few feet. Once down those big wheels had equally big brakes and we stopped easily in a reasonable distance for a 30-ton flying machine.

We shut down back outside the HAS having flown for an hour and fifteen minutes: an experience that I had never expected when I was posted back to Boscombe, and one I still cherish.

# 18 HELPING OUT

By April 1989, just four months into my tour, the word had got around
that there was a qualified test pilot spending a lot of his day at a desk or
scurrying about the place trying to look busy. The bosses of ETPS, both
fixed-wing test squadrons and even the RWTS, had rung me on more than
one occasion asking if I could help out. They all received the same answer:
'I'd love to old chap, but you'll have to persuade the group captain that it's
essential that I do.'

The fundamental problem was that an increasing number of the trials
that A&AEE undertook were being run at other locations – usually the
manufacturer's airfields. So test aircrew were spending more time away. An
example was the Boeing E-3A Sentry project. This airborne early warning
and control system aircraft, commonly known as AWACS, was based on the
Boeing 707 airframe. The RAF had bought into the project in 1987, after
the cancellation of the AEW Nimrod. There were two RAF project test
pilots assigned to the E-3, but they had to spend all their flight-testing time
based at Boeing's airfield near Seattle, on the north-west coast of the USA.
Other projects were similarly being flown from other remote locations. This
frequently left holes in the manning of flight-test programmes for other, lower
priority trials. ETPS was also, as the boss Martin Mayer had predicted, getting
behind the drag curve, but for different reasons.

Eventually the collective pressure brought to bear on my boss meant that
things started to change and I could be more often found wearing my flying
kit. However, grudging noises still emanated from the adjacent office every
time I was seen heading out so attired. But he had agreed I could give a
hand when it was needed. I had also undertaken to work overtime to make
sure that I kept up with the paperwork. So by the beginning of June I was
regularly flying not only the Hawk, Harvard and Gazelle, but was back in full
currency on the Jet Provost, Hunter and Wessex helicopter.

Then in early June OC Heavy Aircraft Test Squadron (HATS) asked if I
had qualified on the de Havilland Comet during my time at Farnborough. I
was able to answer in the affirmative, but wondered why he was asking, as big
aeroplanes weren't my speciality.

'Great,' he said, enthusiastically. 'Can you spare three days out for a detachment around the 21st of the month?'

Cody's Tree at RAE Farnborough. (Author's collection)

Piper PA-31 Navajo Chieftain. (RAE Farnborough (OGL))

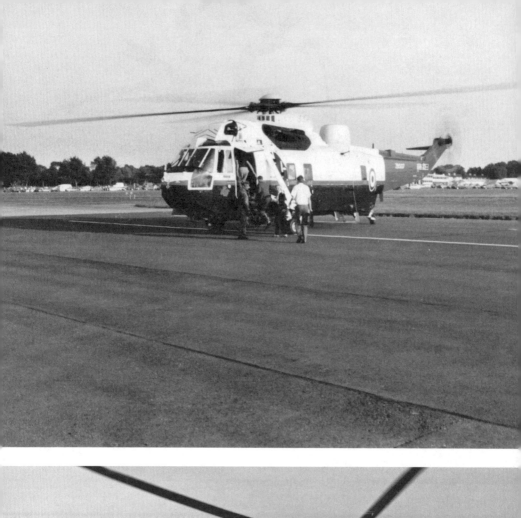

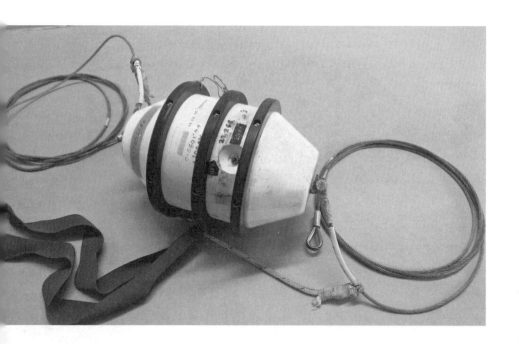

*Opposite top:* The author in Sea King 4 ZB 507 about to fly a ferry flight to RAE Bedford during Farnborough International Air Show 1988. (Author's collection)

*Opposite bottom:* Sea King HC4 ZB 507 in the fire-fighting role for a Farnborough International Air Show. (Peter March)

*Above:* A Red Egg. (Via Richard Cooper)

*Opposite top:* Nightbird Harrier front cockpit. (FAST via Phil Catling)

*Opposite bottom:* RAE Nightbird Buccaneer XV 344. (FAST via Phil Catling)

*Above:* RAE Nightbird Harrier XW 269. (FAST via Phil Catling)

*Above:* Nightbird Buccaneer XV 344 front cockpit. (FAST via Phil Catling)

*Opposite top:* RAE Nightbird Hunter XW 383 *Hecate*. (FAST via Phil Catling)

*Opposite bottom:* RAE Nightbird Varsity WL 679. (FAST via Phil Catling)

*Opposite top:* RAE BAC 1-11 XX 919. (Peter March)

*Opposite bottom:* RAE DC-3 Dakota. (Peter March)

*Above:* The author flying RSAF Pilatus PC-9 4208 over the desert en route to Saudi Arabia. (Author's collection)

*Above:* Lockheed C-130 Hercules W2 XV 208 of the Meteorological Research Flight, Farnborough. (Peter March)

*Opposite top:* Cartoon for FI '86. (Author's collection)

*Opposite bottom:* Cartoon for FI '86. (Author's collection)

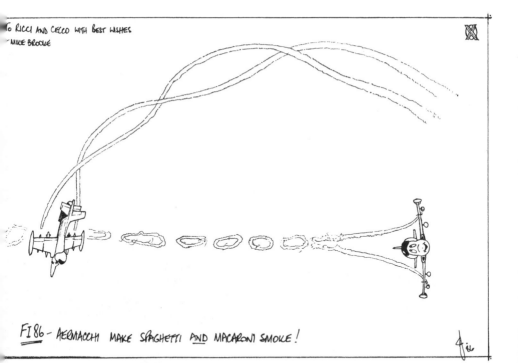

To Ricci and Cecco with best wishes — Mike Brooke

FI 86 – AERMACCHI MAKE SPAGHETTI AND MACARONI SMOKE!

" FANTRAINER – VERY NOVEL – BUT YOU'RE STILL TOO LOW!

Sep 86

The author flying the SE.5a. (Author's collection)

The author about to fly the SE.5a at the closure of RAE Bedford in 1994.
(Author's collection)

Just to prove that even test pilots can march and look smart! Leading the parade for the Freedom of the Borough of Rushmoor in 1988. (Author's collection)

Aerial view of Boscombe Down airfield in the 1990s – with 'carbuncles'! (Peter March)

F-111. (Peter March)

The author, flying Buccaneer XW 987, refuelling Dave Southwood's
Jaguar FGR 1A fitted with an over-wing AIM-9 Sidewinder missile, during
support for Operation Granby. (A&AEE (OGL))

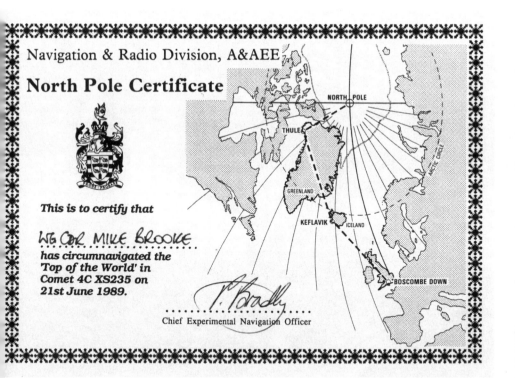

Navigation & Radio Division, A&AEE

# North Pole Certificate

*This is to certify that*

WG CDR MIKE BROOKE

*has circumnavigated the 'Top of the World' in Comet 4C XS235 on 21st June 1989.*

*T. Bradly*

Chief Experimental Navigation Officer

NORTH POLE

THULE

GREENLAND

KEFLAVIK

ICELAND

ARCTIC CIRCLE

BOSCOMBE DOWN

*Opposite top:* The Canberra T17A trials team. Left to right: project engineering officer, Nav./FTO Robin Smith, air electronics officer and pilot, and yours truly. (A&AEE (OGL))

*Opposite bottom:* Comet 4C *Canopus*. (Peter March)

*Above:* North Pole Certificate. (Author's collection)

*Opposite top:* A&AEE Harvard IIB KF 183 over Stonehenge. (Peter March)

*Opposite bottom:* Pushing the envelope! (A&AEE (OGL))

*Above:* A&AEE Hunter FGA.9 XE 601. (Peter March)

*Above:* Meeting the Grand Master of the Guild of Air Pilots and Air Navigators (GAPAN), HRH the Duke of Edinburgh. (Author's collection)

*Opposite:* Handing over 'wings' at Boscombe Down to Cdr Mike Swales RN. (A&AEE (OGL))

WG CDR. FLG.

*Opposite top:* The 'Barnabus' (and Dolly the Springer Spaniel). (Author's collection)

*Opposite bottom:* The Sukhoi SU-27 at Ramenskoye, Russia. (Author's collection)

*Above:* SU-27 cockpit. (Author's collection)

*Above:* ITPS Canadian Air Force students and the ex-ETPS Jet Provost XS 230. (Author's collection)

*Opposite top:* Slingsby T67M 260 Firefly G-BWXG on its second post-production test flight. (Author's collection)

*Opposite bottom:* The Slingsby T67M 260 G-EFSM company demonstrator at the Paris Air Show in 1997. (Author's collection)

Grace Aire Hunter T7 N617NL. (Author's collection)

Grace Aire Nanchang CJ-6 N22591. (Author's collection)

The author and his grandson, George, about to fly together in a Grob Tutor, No. 2AEF. (Author's collection)

My final jet flight: March 2004 in an ETPS Alphajet. (A&AEE (OGL))

Receiving the GAPAN Master Pilot Certificate from Duncan Simpson in May 1999.
(Author's collection)

'I should think so, why?' I asked.

'Well, we need a qualified Comet pilot to act as co-pilot to fly it to the North Pole. You'll be operating out of the US base at Thule in North Greenland.'

'Sounds great; I'll get back to you.'

A few moments later my phone rang again. It was Flt Lt Henry de Courcier, one of the fast-jet test pilots. My instant thought was that he was going to offer me something more up my street, but that was not the case. It turned out that Henry, an ex-Harrier and Red Arrows pilot, had converted to the Comet so he could fill in when the real Comet pilots were away. He gave me the proposed itinerary and suggested that we meet up so I could refamiliarise myself with the Comet's cockpit and checklist.

The trip to the North Pole was an annual event that had been started way back in the day, under the name Exercise Aries, and was a test of the performance of several of the latest navigation equipment. Flying this kit to extremely high latitudes was the most demanding test devised: GPS satellite reception was poor and magnetic compasses were virtually useless. On the morning of 20 June, we met up with our flight-deck crew – one navigator and two engineers – while an air commodore navigator from some ivory tower in London gathered the half-dozen rear crew for a briefing.

Henry led us out to our transport of delight, Comet 4C XS 235, named *Canopus*, resplendent in its grey and white livery with a red cheat line down the length of the fuselage. This aircraft had first flown in 1967 before its delivery to the RAF for transport duties. The only other DH Comet still flying in the UK was based at RAE Farnborough; I had first flown that in 1977.

We had decided that I would fly the first leg to Keflavík in Iceland, as first pilot, and that Henry would fly the second leg to Thule and act as captain throughout. Everything went to plan and after our refuelling in Iceland we climbed to our transit height of 36,000ft over the huge ice field that covers virtually all of the inappropriately named island of Greenland. Our destination, Thule USAF Air Base, had been active since 1943 in many roles. However, it was now part of USAF Space Command and its main function was the support of the huge radar installation a few miles east of the base. These immense and bizarre structures were part of the Ballistic Missile Early Warning Site (BMEWS) chain that included the similar installation at Fylingdales in North Yorkshire, England. Thule is supported mainly by air, but shipping can reach its purpose-built harbour during three or four months in summer. The average temperature in mid June would be 2–4°C. Thule was the only USAF installation with its own tugboat!

After a couple of hours we were in touch with the air-traffic controller at Thule and had started our descent. The most important thing we had to bear in mind now was that our magnetic compasses were showing headings and bearings that bore no resemblance to the geography. We were flying in an area about 500 miles east of the magnetic North Pole so everything had to be converted to headings related to true north.[1]

Because it was mid June, the sea near the coastal airfield at Thule was not covered in ice and there was little of the white stuff on the airfield itself. As Henry flew a very nice straight-in approach, I couldn't help but notice that the long runway was painted white and that all the usual white markings were red. Unique? Perhaps. We later learnt that this was done to reduce the absorption of heat that would occur with a black runway, causing it to sink into the permafrost.

After an enviably smooth landing we were directed towards a large hangar where we were asked to shut down, pointing at the doors. We were then quickly towed inside and once parked allowed to disembark. The hangar had large bore pipes set vertically to the exterior walls; I learnt that these sucked in cold air that was passed beneath the floor to stop, or at least reduce, the tendency for heated buildings to disappear underground as they melted the ground beneath them. This had apparently happened to some extent because the Comet was parked on a level strip of floor that sloped away to each side.

Once everyone had recovered their baggage we were transported by bus to the Officers' Club, where a delightful Danish lady booked us all in. Everywhere we walked outside was about 2in deep in soft, red mud and the floor of the entrance hall was a mess. My room was comfortable, if a bit bijou, and it had one tiny window. I could also see that the structure of the building had insulation as its primary *raison d'être*; it was constructed like an inside-out refrigerator! Once I had unpacked and changed I made my way back to the

---

1. The geographical North Pole is where we were headed but the magnetic core of the Earth is in the liquid inner core and moves about. Magnetic compasses point to the magnetic North Pole and not the geographical one. At the time of our flight there was a considerable difference between the positioning of the two.

entrance foyer, as we had been invited to participate in a tour of the base and the surrounding area.

The first destination was uphill to the BMEWS station, which stood in an elevated location on the edge of the permanent ice field, looking from below like some sinister futuristic citadel. En route we passed small, domed buildings on the roadside that had a light fixture on top. These turned out to be refuges that were to be used during ice storms. These weather events were caused by storm-force winds blowing down off the ice field, which reaches heights of 10,000ft above sea level, bringing ice crystals with them that can flay the skin and take the paint off vehicles in minutes. Should anyone be driving and an ice storm starts then the drill was to park downwind of the refuge, get inside and switch on the flashing light on top. Up at the radar site we were given a tour and briefing on how the BMEWS works. I had once seen around the installation at Fylingdales and it was much the same.

After that we were taken back to the base via a visit to a deserted settlement of wooden houses and its abandoned graveyard. It is hard to imagine anyone scraping a living in this remote and hostile place – a place that is in darkness for four months of the year, with savage winds and temperatures constantly tens of degrees below zero. I was grateful to get back to my warm, insulated room!

Thule is about 750 miles north of the Arctic Circle and lies 68 degrees west of the Greenwich meridian. What the local time was I had no idea. However, we had decided that we would work the whole detachment on GMT and had cleared this arrangement with the club in regard to meals, in-flight rationing and transport. Apparently the base was set up for twenty-four-hour operations so we weren't causing any unwarranted problems. During that 'night' I noticed that the sky looked exactly the same as it had done ever since we had arrived: blue and bright with passing cumulus clouds, some of which were giving out small amounts of wintry precipitation. The only thing that changed was the position of the sun. During our three days at Thule it simply passed around the sky, all the time about 15 degrees above the horizon.

The next morning, at 8.30 by our watches, we met up to brief for our trip north. All the folk down the back went to the aircraft to get the magic boxes working while Henry and I booked out our flight with the base operations staff. An hour or so later we were taxiing out to the westerly end of the 10,000ft runway. We were given clearance to go, with the unsurprising information that there was no other air traffic in the local sky. Henry lined up on the red centreline and gave me control of the yoke while he occupied his hands with the nose wheel steering handle and the four throttles, which he pushed forward smoothly to their full travel. The Comet accelerated just as smoothly and, once we had achieved 80 knots, he took over the yoke and I put my left hand behind his on the throttles. I called the appropriate speeds – V1, V2, rotate – and we were airborne. After I had retracted the landing gear and flaps, Henry accelerated to our climbing speed, selected autopilot on and we were en route to the North Pole. At least we knew what heading to steer!

The next couple of hours passed very quietly: not much to see, no radio calls to make, lots of white below. Eventually the word came from the back that we were approaching the top of the world. The master compass was still showing north, then it swung through 180 degrees – we were heading south but we had not turned. It was midday GMT on Midsummer's Day and we were as far north as you can get! I looked over the side – ice with a few dark lines was all I could see. It suddenly struck me, *how did everyone know we had actually crossed the North Pole?* Now we had to turn around to head north again and then a few minutes later head back to Thule.

Their work over, sightseers from the back came up to the flight deck, we dropped down to 5,000ft and cruised back to Thule. Just short of five hours after take-off we were landing on that strange, pale runway again. After another sunlit night we returned to Boscombe with a happy load of boffins and some special memories of life above the Arctic Circle.

Henry and I would fly the Comet together on more navigation kit trials. But in January 1990 it would be a special derivative of the Comet that we would climb aboard – the Nimrod. However, this Nimrod was not the normal maritime reconnaissance model but the Nimrod R1 – a version equipped for electronic intelligence duties (ELINT). Three R1s had been built and could be distinguished from the MR version in not having the long 'pole' sticking out horizontally behind the tail. Closer up there were a few extra aerials on the wings and fuselage. It was also fitted with an array of rotating dish aerials in the aircraft's bomb bay, with further dish aerials in the tail cone and at the front of the wing-mounted fuel tanks. On operations it had a flight-deck crew of four (two pilots, a flight engineer and one navigator) and up to twenty-five crew operating the special equipment down the back.

The reason we were going to fly this classified machine was that during routine air tests, following a series of upgrades and modifications, the RAF crews had noticed an increase in stalling speeds. The manufacturer, British

Aerospace, had been asked by the Nimrod R Project Office to evaluate the aircraft's new stalling speeds and then issue the changes to the speeds and performance data that were dependent on the new stalling speeds.

Apparently the manufacturer's tests did not find any changes, but the definition of the stall used by their test pilots was being questioned. So that's where we came in – to act as the honest broker in the argument. Boscombe Down had no vested interest in the results other than being truthfully objective. We would do two test flights: one at a forward centre of gravity (CG) and one at an aft CG. Henry would again be captain and lead test pilot, and I would act as co-pilot and second opinion. We briefed for the first test flight and took our test cards out to the aircraft. In keeping with its highly classified role, we were not allowed to see into the curtained-off main cabin. Our entry was via the crew access door behind the flight deck, and turn left only! I had noticed that the military registration of the big beige aeroplane was XW 666 – the devil's machine, I thought!

The tests went as planned. The stalls, especially with flaps and undercarriage down, were characterised by large amplitude vertical vibration (buffeting) but the usual pitch break, when the nose drops sharply, happened mostly after the loss of lateral control – the wing dropping with opposite lateral control applied. On one occasion, during the aft CG tests and full flap and landing gear down, the wing dropped so fast that Henry couldn't stop the Nimrod reaching nigh on 90 degrees of bank. I became very busy raising the flap and undercarriage while Henry applied all his skills at keeping the speeds and g-loads within limits. We lost a lot of height. Fortunately that was the last test point. Henry and the flight-test engineers wrote up their report and sent it up to head office. In keeping with the need-to-know principle applied heavily to the Nimrod R, I never heard the outcome. As a tragic footnote to this tale, the devil's aeroplane, XW 666, caught fire during a post-servicing air test from RAF Kinloss in northern Scotland. In a skilful piece of handling and captaincy, the pilot ditched the aircraft and all seven crew were able to board the life raft and were rescued unharmed. XW 666 sank to the bottom of the Moray Firth and into Davy (Mc)Jones' locker.

By the end of 1998 I was a fully integrated 'guest artist' with all the test squadrons and ETPS. I had got back into many of my favourite cockpits: Buccaneer, Jaguar, Hunter, Harvard, Sea King, Wessex and Andover. I was keeping the paperwork and routine management at bay and thoroughly enjoying the job. Occasional treats came my way too.

For instance, my chief fire officer, Mick Crawford, had received budgetary go-ahead to buy a new vehicle. Although we had two excellent big red fire engines, our rapid intervention vehicle (RIV) was no longer up to the job. So Mick showed me a catalogue with one of the vehicles he wanted to look at; it was made in God's own county of Yorkshire. I hatched a plot whereby I would commandeer a Gazelle helicopter for the day and Mick and I would fly up north to look at what was on offer. It was a grand day out. I landed at the small airfield at Crosland Moor above Huddersfield, where we were met by a company car and taken to the North Fire manufacturing facility to view their RIV. We later made a similar trip to Warwick to meet with the folks from Dennis Fire Vehicles. Test drives were offered and accepted. The brand-new RIV arrived a few months later, but I can't recall what make it was. I only remember that it went very quickly! We also managed to procure new dummy aircraft bodies, made out of heavy-gauge plate steel for the practice fire ground. If I was ever at a loose end I would ask Mick to tell me when he was going to call his boys out for fire exercises and would go and watch.

One day Sqn Ldr Keith Dennison, of the FJTS, called me to offer me a trip with him in a motor glider, the German manufactured Grob 109B. His test squadron was assessing the aircraft for use by the Air Training Corps' gliding schools, to replace the ageing Slingsby Venture motor glider. Keith wanted to get as much test-pilot opinion as he could for the final report. As ever, I was happy to oblige. I had never flown a motor glider before but I did have some experience of gliders and sailplanes; in fact, that was how my flying career started back in 1960!

We would be flying in the evening, after the airfield was officially closed, so we would have plenty of freedom and avoid upsetting the faster, daytime users of our bit of sky. The white composite construction Grob was attractive to the eye, in a long-winged fashion. It sat low to the ground and access to the cockpit was easy, via the upward opening clear panels on each side. The cockpit itself was modern but simply furnished and laid out very much as I had expected, with full dual controls.

The 95hp engine started electrically and we were soon on our way to the runway. Once the pre-take-off engine run and checks had been completed we were soon off the ground. Keith had given me control from the off and just cued me with speeds. The Grob climbed nicely into the May evening sky and handled very much as any sailplane of medium performance would. The

57ft wingspan made itself felt when testing roll rates and coordinated rudder inputs were essential to kill the yaw that was easily induced when rolling. The aeroplane handled very nicely in pitch and the stalls were predictable and easy to recover from.

After a while we found ourselves near some late-developing cumulus clouds so Keith told me to stop the engine and we would try some real glider flying. It was strange to be turning the motor off: it was the only one we had! I tried to centre on a thermal, using the variometer to show me when we were rising. But the lift at this time of day was pretty weak, so I used the time to see if there were any marked handling differences without the propeller wash. There were some, but nothing significant.

Restarting the engine was next on the menu. There was a lever that had to be operated to unfeather the prop before pressing the starter button. I found this quite stiff and wondered about small cadets succeeding. Anyway, it fired up and we returned to Boscombe to finish with a few circuits and landings. As the old song goes, it was a lovely way to spend an evening. A week later Keith checked with me that my civilian private pilot's licence was current; I assured him that it was.

'In that case,' he said, 'as the Grob is civil registered[2] then you could fly it again one evening and take Linda with you.'

I thanked him and when we were both home from work I told Linda. She said yes, so the following evening we went flying in the summery Wiltshire skies together. She was not too taken when I turned the engine off or during the multiple turns when I was chasing thermals. But she did enjoy the wonderful views especially when we flew over the ancient and mysterious megalithic site of Stonehenge on the way back.

Keith Dennison was also instrumental in an attempt to fulfil a couple of my outstanding aviation ambitions: to attempt in-flight refuelling and to fly the Tornado. I had approached him at happy hour to ask if this was possible, and a couple of weeks later he told me that he had booked the resident F2A Tornado, ZD 902, for a flight that would include an air–air refuelling (AAR) session over the North Sea. The day for this eagerly awaited trip was Thursday,

---

2.   German registration D-KNEO.

27 June 1991. The day dawned bright and clear, and I met up with Keith to go over the flight profile and get a guided tour of the cockpit – especially the bits required to start the motors.

Once I'd strapped in, Keith called out the checklist and we cooperatively got all the right things up and running. Another check of the time to make sure that we would arrive on the AAR towline at the time that our tanker was expecting us, and we were off. After taxiing to the end of the runway, holding while we went through the final checks, we received clearance to go. I lined up and gradually applied full power, with reheat, checked that all indications were good and that the green 'GO' light was on, then released the brakes. The acceleration was good, but not startling and, on cue, I raised the nose wheel. The jet lifted off cleanly and I selected the undercarriage up. As the red lights went out another one came on, accompanied by the loud warble of the master warning system.

*What did I do?* flashed through my mind.

'Damn!' sounded from the back seat.

A caption marked 'R VIB' was illuminated in red on the warning panel.

'I'm sorry, Mike,' said Keith calmly, 'that's an engine vibration warning and it's not one we can ignore. Shut down the starboard engine, please.'

Keith monitored me carefully while I stopped the right motor, adjusted the rudder trim and cancelled the reheat on the other engine. While I was doing that he called ATC and let them know that we would jettison some fuel and then return for a landing.

So we did just that. As I flew down the final approach I asked whether I should use reverse thrust on landing.

'Well, we probably don't need to on this runway length,' Keith replied. 'But I've never done a single-engine landing for real, so give it a try and we'll see what happens.'

*Real test pilot stuff!* I thought.

As it transpired, it was a total non-event. The auto-stabilised nose wheel steering system coped perfectly and we turned off the runway with lots of room to spare. So that was that: I got to fly a Tornado – for all of twenty minutes and I never did do any AAR!

I had a very different flying experience when ETPS hired a Hornet flexwing microlight aircraft to give their student test pilots a taste of a different mode of flight. Again it was a summer evening sortie and I met up with the pilot on the grass outside my office. The Hornet flexwing was what I expected:

a flexible kite-like wing from which was suspended an open-topped fibreglass capsule with wheels. We put it on rather than get into it. It was very cosy and the seat belt was just a diagonal car-type restraint over my left shoulder. I noticed straight away that the 'fuselage' was almost as flexible as the wing; I didn't feel that secure and we were still on the ground! The control of flight was via the trapeze bar across our knees. My captain started the engine and, although we had intercom in our helmets, the loud, rasping noise from just behind our heads cut its efficiency by half.

We taxied, not very far, just to a piece of grass that the captain judged long enough, applied full power and, with a twitch of the bar, we were airborne. I was surprised how quickly we seemed to climb and how slow our speed over the ground was. After a couple of minutes we were up at 2,000ft. I was invited to join in controlling this flying flea by putting my hands on the bar and following my instructor through while he showed me how it worked. It was all back to front! To turn right I had to push the bar to the left, and to climb I had to push the bar forward.

With the patience of Job, the man on my right cajoled and encouraged me to keep trying. That patience paid off as, strangely, I started to get my head round how it all worked and it started to feel natural. All was well as we returned to the airfield to make a few approaches and landings on the grass runway. I had very little difficulty as I made the adjustments to keep a steady approach speed and angle. However, as we got within striking distance of the ground my natural instincts overrode my recently acquired skill. I pulled the bar back instead of pushing it forward so we struck the ground with the little plastic craft's nose wheel, at which point I pulled the bar back and soared into the air with rapidly reducing speed. My instructor took over and avoided the impending disaster. I was instantly taken back twenty years to my days as an instructor on Chipmunks and those many occasions when my university air squadron students had treated me to the same manoeuvre! Not to be put off, I was allowed several more attempts and each was a little less scary than the last. Eventually Mr Microlight and his flimsy machine had had enough and we stayed down. Like parachute jumping, this was one aviation event that only needs to be experienced once. Thankfully, unlike the ETPS students, I didn't have to write a report, so I retired to the Officers' Mess Bar to slake my thirst and share the experience with anyone who would listen.

By the end of my tour I felt that I had been useful beyond juggling paper-work, learning the new-fangled rigours of executive responsibility budgets and the health-and-safety regulations that had just been introduced. I had flown lots of trials, predominantly in the Harvard, Buccaneer and Jaguar, helped out ETPS as a spare tutor in the Hawk, Hunter, Jet Provost and Jaguar, and been involved with lots of extracurricular work, such as a Battle of Britain 50th Anniversary Air Display, held at Boscombe Down in July 1990.

I was also, as part of my duties, the Hon. President of Boscombe Down's flying club. That meant that I managed to do a little light aviation on the side, flying the club's Jodel 1050, Glos Airtourer (a strange little machine) and, by very kind invitation, a replica ⅞-scale SE.5a – in fact there were two of them owned by the guys who built them.

They both came to my office not long after I had arrived from Farnborough to invite me to come over and not only inspect their aeroplanes but also fly them, when the weather allowed. I was not able to take up the latter offer until late May. The full-scale SE.5 is not a big machine and the cockpit is quite tight, even for a vertically challenged person like yours truly. So I was expecting difficulties in boarding the little machine. It turned out to be no more difficult than the real thing. I think the cockpit was almost full scale! The replica was powered by a cunningly disguised 85hp Continental engine and weighed in at around half the weight of the RAF SE.5a, so the power-to-weight ratio was going to be about the same.

So it proved. Once I'd had the prop swung and the little motor was running well, I took off from the grass in less than 600ft and climbed away at 70mph, getting a rate of climb of about 900ft per minute. It was very much like the real thing but slightly less noisy and a lot less draughty. Up and away I noticed two things immediately. There was no elevator trim wheel. However, the very low control forces and speed stability and small speed range did not make this a problem. The second was more subliminal: as I flew around, manoeuvring in pitch and roll, I had a sense of reduced awareness, but initially I couldn't pin it down. Then I realised I could not see my hand on the control stick. Due to the scaling, the stick was forward of the bottom of the instrument panel. I had never before realised that the peripheral view of what I was doing with my right hand was part of my situational awareness. A very interesting result. The little flying machine was delightful to fly. I did a loop (with permission) and a couple of wingovers, then a stall turn. I knew that the aircraft's builders, Doug and Ken, were down there watching and they'd each taken around 2,500 hours to build their aeroplanes, so I thought it was time to take it back before I broke it. Landing was no trickier than the real thing and I was very thankful that I was able to pull off a decent three-pointer. When I had shut down I was bombarded with questions and I was happy to be able to tell them, 'It handles and performs just like the real thing!'

I want to end this part of my story with a special flying story. Special because it was my last ever flight in another favourite of mine, the single-seat Hunter, and it involved my favourite mode of flight: high speed at low level. It's one that comes from the month the Berlin Wall came down: November 1989. That was when my long-time chum John Thorpe, boss of the FJTS, called me. I was shuffling paperwork across my desk when the phone rang.

'Hi, Brookie, JT here,' came a cheery voice that I recognised. It instantly cheered me up because calls from John would, more often than not, include an invitation to fly something fast and pointed. I acknowledged that I was indeed present and eager to know what he had to say.

'Have you flown our FGA.9 Hunter before?'

'No,' I said.

'Well, my friend, we've got a job for it tomorrow and there's no one on the squadron available to fly it. Could you?' he explained.

'Yes,' I said.

'I thought you would,' he replied.

*You knew I would, JT*, I thought.

'If you can come over this afternoon, I'll show you round the cockpit and the special switches for the kit, and give you the task details. OK?'

'OK.'

The aircraft John was talking about was Hunter FGA.9 XE 601. It had been retained at Boscombe Down for a specific job. Geographically adjacent to the airfield at Boscombe Down was a large area of open land, fenced off and rigorously guarded; it was known as Porton Down. This was the home of the UK's Chemical Defence Establishment (CDE) – a very secret place. In addition to its classified analysis and research work, one of the CDE's tasks was to oversee chemical defence training in the UK armed forces. That drove a need to have a method of the airborne delivery of a harmless liquid that would activate chemical warning systems and give personnel a fairly realistic experience of an aerial chemical warfare attack. The Hunter carried two large tanks for dispersing the 'chemicals' on its inner-wing pylons and two 100-gallon fuel tanks on the outer pylons.

I sat in the fairly familiar cockpit (it had been around seven years since I had flown a single-seat Hunter) and checked the whereabouts of the operating switches for the radio altimeter and the tanks, as well as refreshing myself on the rest of the cockpit layout. Then I went to John's office where he briefed me on the task for the following day.

'RAF Brawdy is having a big assessed exercise and the inspecting team want to test their response to a chemical attack. Here are the maps of where they want the "chemical" laid down and the timings. You can arrange the rest yourself. Any questions?' John asked.

'Standard questions,' I joshed.

'Standard answers,' he responded. 'Now get out of here – good luck tomorrow.'

The morning of 27 November started with winter sunshine clearing away the overnight mist lying in the hollows on and around the airfield. The weather forecast was good – broken cloud with a slight risk of showers towards the west. My planned flight profile was what on my first squadron we used to call 'hi-lo-hi'. I would climb out of Boscombe Down heading west towards Brawdy, which was in the extreme south-west of Wales, and fly there under radar control at about 36,000ft. Once across the civilian airways that were in my way I would descend towards Brawdy. There I would fly the patterns required to complete the task. The runs over the air base, during which I would deliver the 'chemical', were to be flown at 100ft above the ground at a speed of 450 knots. I would probably have enough liquid to complete three runs.

As I set up for the first of those attacks I kept an eye on the radio altimeter prominently positioned on the top of the instrument panel, and then waited until the start position before selecting the spray facility on. A very quick glance in the mirror at the top of the canopy arch was enough to confirm that a broad white curling trail was behind me. Once past the stop point I switched the spray off, throttled back, eased up, turned around and went down the run the other way. I finished that attack and set up for a third and final run. I wound the speed up to 500 knots for this one and could imagine the typical howl that my jet was making over the invisible heads of my 'victims' 100ft below. The noise had a name – the 'Blue Note' – and was unique to the Hunter.

I pulled up and called for handover back to the military radar unit for my transit back to Boscombe Down. As I approached the westerly airway north-west of Boscombe Down I was asked to hold my altitude.

'Gauntlet 03, you have Concorde in your ten o' clock. He's climbing through your present altitude. Tell me when you have him in sight, please,' said the controller.

'Roger,' I replied. I looked hard to the left quarter and there was the beautiful flying machine. 'Contact,' I called.

'Roger 03, you're cleared to continue your descent and cross the airway.'

Concorde was making condensation trails, so I probably was too. I turned on to the heading I needed to cross the airway and the big delta passed right over me. I looked up through the top of the clear canopy. It was an awesome sight and I could hear the muffled crackle of the four Olympus engines in reheat.

After that experience, the rest of the trip was a bit of an anti-climax. But I did finish with a run-in and break at 500 knots at 500ft; I promised to tell myself off when I got back to the office. I taxied back in thinking, yet again, how blessed I was to be doing something so brilliantly challenging, exciting and fulfilling for a living. And I got paid for it! What a wonderful life – thank you God.

# 19 MY VERY OWN TRIAL

In early 1990 my boss, Gp Capt Keith Mills, asked me into his office; this was almost a daily occurrence and was, more often than not, to do with upcoming trials requests from project offices up in London. If not that, then the mysteries of the new-fangled budgets we were all now working with. Today it was the former.

'You probably won't believe this, Mike, but here we are starting the last decade of the twentieth century and we're being asked to do quite a lengthy trial on a Canberra,' he said. 'You flew Canberras didn't you?'

'Yessir,' I responded, trying not to grin.

'Well, as this high-priority trial is estimated at about fifty flying hours, and they want a rate of one sortie per day, I want you to find someone else to do it. I'm not having you tied up with it for weeks on end,' he rejoined, sternly.

'OK, sir, leave it with me,' I responded obediently.

I retired to my office and picked up the phone. I rang the bosses of both fixed-wing test squadrons and asked them to let me know of anyone who had flown the Canberra, how recently and what their total hours on type were.

A day later I was able to give the results to the boss. 'There are three pilots here who have flown the Canberra. One has only done a few sorties and never flew anything but the trainer version; there's another that has just over thirty hours and there's one with about 2,500 hours. There are also a few people who've actually seen a Canberra!' I added flippantly.

'Well, that makes it an easy choice – just a minute – the one with the 2,500 hours is you, isn't it?'

'I cannot tell a lie, sir,' I said, this time deploying the grin.

He called me something impolite and told me to leave the office. Later he sent me the appropriate file with a covering note indicating that I should assume the role of project test pilot. I could read the disapproval between the lines.

I called the project officer dealing with this trial, got a lot more information and left him my number. The trial was on an updated version of the T17 model of the Canberra, originally designed by the English Electric (EE) Company and now almost a year past the fiftieth anniversary of its first flight.

EE had got into aircraft manufacture during the 1930s with a lightweight, single-seat aeroplane called the Wren. During the Second World War, EE built and flight-tested aircraft designed by other manufacturers. In 1944 the Air Ministry issued a requirement for a successor to the de Havilland Mosquito light bomber and reconnaissance aircraft. The specification was seeking a high-speed and high-altitude capability, such that the bomber could outclimb and outrun the fighters of the day. In May 1945, EE were awarded a contract to build a jet-powered prototype. Four years later, after being dogged by post-war supply problems, on Friday, 13 May 1949, the EE B1 took off for the first time. It was soon given the name Canberra and successful development followed; the production version, known as the B2, entered RAF service in 1951.

Many further developments followed and the Canberra was successfully sold to the USA – a very unusual event in any era – where it was built under licence by the Martin Aircraft Company as the B-57. In all, 1,352 Canberras were built in a total of twenty-seven versions. It equipped the air forces of fourteen nations, including the RAF in which it served on no less than thirty-five squadrons. By early 1990, I had flown ten versions of the Canberra, but most of my time had been spent as an operational pilot in the B(I)8 interdictor and as an instructor in the T4 trainer. One of the versions, in which I had flown about twenty hours, was the T17.

This version had been in RAF service since mid 1966 with a specially formed squadron – No. 360. The squadron was created on 1 April 1966, from the merger of the personnel of No. 831 Naval Air Squadron of the FAA and B Flight of the RAF's No. 97 Squadron. Initially the unit was known as Joint Electronic Warfare Trials and Training Force before being given the official designation of No. 360 (RN/RAF) Squadron on 23 September 1966. The T17 was a B2 modified to train surface-based radar and missile operators and airborne fighter and airborne early warning crews in handling radio and radar jamming. Twenty-four B2 Canberras were modified to the T17 electronic countermeasures (ECM) specification.

One of the main changes was the addition of a new nose section containing an array of electronic kit in four protruding radomes arranged symmetrically around the nose. This made the front of the previously slick and smooth bomber less than attractive. On seeing it a certain royal personage could well have mentioned carbuncles! Other less visible modifications meant that the bomb doors of the B2 had been removed and panels covered the arrays of black boxes inside the old bomb bay. To power all this electrically hungry gear two turbo generators, driven by air taken from the engine compressors, were installed in each wing. The T17 could also be fitted with chaff-dropping pods on the wings.[1]

The Canberra coming to Boscombe Down in 1990 was to be the first T17A, an updated version of the T17 with improved navigation aids, a new spectrum analyser and a more powerful communications jammer. The trials programme would start with a test flight to discover whether the modifications, which included two new vertical blade aerials under the wings, had affected any of the aircraft's handling or performance. The rest of the trial would be spent working with the radio and electronic calibration and measurement station, sited on the south side of the airfield, to measure the effectiveness of the radio- and radar-jamming equipment.

There were the usual slippages on the original timescales, but in March 1990 I was told to expect the T17A to be delivered to Boscombe Down in late April. So I set up a visit to RAF Wyton in Huntingdonshire, where

---

1. Chaff is foil-backed paper strips dropped in bundles that then spread out and cause false echoes on radar screens.

No. 360 Squadron was based, for a refresher trip in the Canberra T4 with one of their instructors. I passed the test and was sent back as a person approved to fly the precious T17A. The navigator on that T4 flight was a chap called Dave Adam. He and I had done our officer training together in 1962 and I had not seen much of him since. Tragically, Dave was killed in the crash of a Canberra T4 at Wyton the following year.

Meanwhile, back at the ranch, I kept busy flying for ETPS, in the Jaguar, Hunter and Hawk, then I received the news that my steed would arrive by the middle of the month. This timing turned out to be accurate and on 17 April I took my navigator for the trials, Sqn Ldr Robin Smith, flying in a Hunter just to get him back in the mood – he was on a ground tour in the Radio and Navigation Department and held a current Flight Test Observer's (FTO) ticket. The following day we briefed for the first flight – the handling tests.

I had not strapped into a T17 since September 1974, but, as the midshipman on his first ship in rough seas said, 'It all comes back to me now!' After all my years flying Canberras, the cockpit was still familiar and I found my way round without too much difficulty. The best thing about sitting in the T17 cockpit is that you can no longer be offended by its looks! The man in the back called out the checklist for me and we were soon up and running. We taxied out sedately, held at the edge of the runway, completed the pre-take-off checks and then lined up ready to depart. It was at this point that I mentally rehearsed the drill for an engine failure: the most dangerous event that could occur in the Canberra. That was what killed Dave Adam and many before him. I reminded myself of the safety speed. That is the speed at or above which the average pilot, who has been trained correctly, should be able to control the aircraft following an engine failure. The problem was that the big, fat wing of the Canberra means that it lifts off before that speed. So the only course of action is to close both throttles and land straight ahead. Above the safety speed quick and coordinated use of stick and rudder, and possibly the throttle, is needed to retain control.

Having got my head and hands ready, I pushed the throttles forward until I had both engines at 7,600rpm against the brakes, a quick check of pressures and temperatures, then brakes off and full power applied. The T17 is not a sprightly performer. The extra weight of all the electronics and the air bled from the engines for the turbo-generators reduces its performance when compared with the B2. So it was a while before I could raise the nose and lift a few feet into the sky. I then reverted to my old practice and held the aircraft level while I accelerated to beyond safety speed and retracted the wheels. Once that had happened I raised the nose a little further and let the aircraft accelerate to a climbing speed of 250 knots.

The tests included flight at the maximum permitted airspeed and Mach number, stalling, pull-ups to the maximum permitted g-level and general manoeuvrability and handling. Then I descended to 4,000ft, which was the minimum permitted altitude for shutting down an engine. Having shut down the port engine by cutting off the fuel to it, I then flew in level flight gradually reducing speed and increasing power to maximum on the starboard engine until, with full rudder and 10 degrees of bank to the right, I could no longer hold a steady heading. At that point, I called out the indicated speed and my faithful nav./FTO wrote it down; the value of 135 knots was what I had expected. I then repeated the whole thing with the port engine running and the starboard stopped. Once more, the speed was acceptable. These minimum control speeds can vary a little as they are affected by the ambient atmospheric conditions (which affect the thrust of the engines) and the airframe itself. They usually vary from each other by a few knots and this is down to the way the control system works.

Once we had got that moderately hazardous bit of testing over, I flew back towards Boscombe Down to fly an approach using the Instrument Landing System (ILS) while my directional advisor checked out all the navigation kit. We were not carrying the third member of the T17's crew, an air electronics officer. An officer of that specialisation would be with us for the rest of the trial programme, because it was the kit under his control that was now of most interest to the project office.

The trial proper started at the end of April and progressed steadily through May and most of June. Much of the flying was unexciting, verging on the boring, often consisting of flying on steady westerly headings at around 30,000ft until the Boscombe Down radio-testing folks said that the signal had disappeared. A bit more interesting was flying racecourse patterns at much lower altitude on a particular bearing from Boscombe Down. After a couple of hours of this, repeated on several days, I expected to get back to my office to have yet more noise complaints to deal with; however, it was no worse than usual. We did fly several sorties against No. 360 Squadron's normal 'customers' to see how the new, now tested and calibrated ECM kit performed for real. These few trips took me back to my time at RAF Cottesmore in the early 1970s, when I used to fly with No. 360 as a 'guest artist'!

During the trial we flew twenty-six sorties and just short of fifty hours, culminating in delivering Canberra T17A WD 955 to its rightful home with No. 360 Squadron at RAF Wyton on Tuesday, 19 June 1990. This would be the last time I would ever fly a Canberra.

# 20 PUSHING THE ENVELOPE

One of the joys of my job at Boscombe Down was that I got to fly the Harvard on a regular basis. The main purpose was to carry a photographer, who would take videos of parachute systems under trial – often the multiple-canopy systems used for dropping a variety of heavy loads. Personnel parachute trials were recorded not by a chase aeroplane, especially one with a propeller, but by a chase parachutist. Boscombe Down had its own cadre of brave and experienced parachutists who carried out these types of developmental trials.

One Lockheed C-130 Hercules was permanently based with the Heavy Aircraft Test Squadron (HATS) and was used for all aerial delivery trials flights; on these sorties it was flown by C-130 qualified aircrew posted to HATS. The protocol of those tests that required a Harvard chase was as follows.

The pilot and photographer would be notified beforehand and given the time of the briefing. This would take place at HATS with all the trials personnel in attendance. The type of load(s) to be tested and the point(s) of interest under test would be described. The suspension system was the most common of these. The engineers would often put strain gauges in the suspension system and we provided photographic evidence of how the load deployed. Apart from the video from the Harvard, there would be footage from ground-based, high-speed cameras on the range, which was located only a few miles from the airfield, at Larkhill on Salisbury Plain.

The normal procedure was that the Harvard would get airborne from the grass runway and the C-130 from the main runway, and the two would join up during the short transit time to Larkhill. As the Harvard had only one UHF radio the C-130 would wait for contact to be established between the two aircraft before the trials protocol was agreed with the range controller. The delivery heading would be confirmed and the first pattern, always flown to the north to remain within the protected range danger area, would be a dummy run. This would allow all the players to get their eye in and the ground-based cameras to practise their tracking. If all went well then a 'hot' run would follow. Almost without exception, if two or more loads were to be dropped each one would be dropped individually and each chased down by the Harvard.

For the delivery run the Harvard pilot's job was to position their aircraft in an offset trail position so that a diving turn could be made alongside the load as the parachutes opened. The photographer in the back seat, having opened his sliding canopy, would focus on the point of interest. Getting the initial position right was essential and took a little time to learn. The steep descending turn, with reduced power, was continued from the usual drop height of 1,000–1,200ft down to 500ft, or until the man with the camera – we called them 'toggies' – said that he had got what was required. It was interesting work and a real privilege to be doing it in a 50-year-old aeroplane of true character.

I was not only a chase pilot but also one of the Harvard instructor pilots, so extra flying came my way as new pilots arrived on HATS and were nominated to fly it. I also used the Harvard, when it was not needed for any other purpose, as a communications aircraft. It was very cost effective for flights to locations that were not too distant where I had legitimate A&AEE business. Another thing we used it for was to help the Battle of Britain Memorial Flight (BBMF) with their pilot training. Each BBMF pilot came to Boscombe for a day during which they would fly two trips: one in the front seat and one in the back. It could be a bit of a baptism of fire, but we usually sent them back to their base at RAF Coningsby with a good appreciation of how to fly a big-engined tail-dragger. I used to do some of the circuit work with them at the grass Army Air Corps airfield at Netheravon, close by on Salisbury Plain. If they could land safely on the undulating, narrow and poorly marked runway there from the back seat, they would have no difficulty in a Spitfire.

In early 1991, I became peripherally involved in budgetary arguments over the number of aircrew on HATS. I was involved, for reasons best known to the occupants of a financial ivory tower somewhere, as the costs of Boscombe Down aircrew were allocated to my executive responsibility budget. However, I had no real executive control over this budget, because I could not hire or fire anyone; so where the 'executive responsibility' came in I know not! Nevertheless a decision was made that three aircrew – an air engineer, a loadmaster and a pilot – could be taken off charge if the Hercules was returned to the RAF. We put up resistance and cited the necessity to keep the aircraft (and its personnel) in-house for the aerial delivery trials. In the end all our arguments were ignored in the cause of fiscal propriety. We were told that by June the responsibility for aerial delivery for our trials would be taken over by the Joint Air Transport Establishment (JATE) based at RAF Brize Norton, about 40 miles north-east of Boscombe Down.

On 13 June 1991 I received a phone call from the HATS operations desk asking, 'We don't have any Harvard pilots here at the moment. Would you be available to do a chase sortie tomorrow afternoon, sir?'

'Yes, I think so. I have to fly a conversion sortie in the Harvard with Sqn Ldr Bill Ovel in the morning, but I think I can clear my desk for the afternoon,' I replied.

Bill Ovel was a HATS test pilot and it was to be his first conversion trip, so we met up for a briefing at about 9.30 a.m. While signing out I was updated on the afternoon's event, which would be the first flown using the JATE C-130 and crew. The briefing time was confirmed and I made a mental note not to get too delayed by the upcoming sortie and debrief.

After a successful first dual flight for Bill in the Harvard and a rapid aircrew lunch (aka cup of coffee and a biscuit), I turned up at the HATS operations desk for the afternoon's briefing. Peter James, one of the photographers I had flown with on many occasions, in many different aircraft types, was waiting for me; he was wearing his usual youthful and enthusiastic look. Instead of a room full of people he had a piece of paper and a telephone number. I read the written brief. There would be two loads – both 1-ton platforms with military cross-country, six-wheeled vehicles strapped to them. These had been transported the 40 miles by road from Boscombe Down to Brize Norton. *Is this modus operandi really going to be cheaper?* I wondered. Once more the point of interest was the suspension system. I noted that after the second load had been despatched eight personnel were to fall off the back of the C-130. I assumed this would be on a subsequent, third run after we had left the range area.

I then rang the phone number. This eventually connected me with the C-130 captain at JATE. I clarified with him that the personnel would be dropped on a separate run, which he confirmed. We arranged a rendezvous time, height and contact radio frequency overhead Boscombe. I then put the details in the authorisation book, checked with Peter that he was happy, and we walked out to the aircraft in the sunshine.

As we got airborne I heard the C-130 check in on Boscombe's local frequency and told him I was ready. I soon spotted him smoking in from the north-east and joined up on his starboard side. He called me to change to the range radio frequency; I did so and checked in after I had heard the end of an exchange between the range controller and the C-130. All went as briefed for the dummy run, during which I had swapped to the port side, and we turned outbound for the live run.

*Right,* I thought, *there'll be two loads, so two runs and then we'll fly away after the second to clear the area for the parachutists.*

As we ran in and were cleared to drop I moved into my habitual position, ready to turn and dive as soon as the load came over the sill. I watched and listened.

'Load away!' came the call.

There it is, turn … now! Then there was a strangled yell from the back seat – I couldn't make out what Peter had said (there was always a lot of noise after the canopy was opened). Then I saw the second load coming over the sill!

*Do I tighten the turn or straighten up?* I tried to tighten it.

Before I could do anything else it all went dark. We had flown into the parachutes. *I wonder what the sensation of flying backwards toward the ground will be like?* I thought. Time seemed to have slowed right down.

Then we were back in the bright, bright blue of a summer's day again. I kept turning, curious to see the load descending behind us. One of the canopies was a tattered rag but the other two seemed okay. It impacted the ground 1,000ft below us.

'Gauntlet 03. I'm OK – returning to base,' I transmitted on the radio, trying to sound unperturbed. I had by now worked out that there was no damage visible from where I was sitting and that the engine was working normally. I changed the radio frequency to Boscombe Tower and told them that I was going to climb to 3,000ft overhead the airfield and make a precautionary forced landing on to the grass runway. I didn't want the engine suddenly deciding that it couldn't eat any more parachute silk just when I needed it most!

The glide descent and landing went fine, and I taxied back up to our usual parking spot, where, as I parked and shut down, our ground crew were giving the front end of KF 183 some funny looks. Once out of the machine I could see why. Behind the propeller there was a big disc of solidified, olive-green parachute material. Other scraps were stuck in every slight gap in the metal panels around the nose and on the wing. Peter even brought a piece of shredded parachute out of the rear cockpit with him. Photographs were taken, including one of Peter holding up his piece. In a presentation about the incident that I gave at a Society of Experimental Test Pilots (SETP) Flight Test Safety Symposium, I said that this was a shot of my toggie with the pair of underpants he had been wearing on the day! It got a good laugh.

Of course, this event was not a joking matter; it could have been a fatal accident, so there had to be an inquiry. The cause was obvious – pilot error – and I was the pilot. So why did I get it wrong? In the final analysis it was down to expectations and assumptions. The decision to move the aerial delivery trials from an in-house activity to what was essentially a subcontractor was made with budgetary considerations in mind. The Cold War was over and the government had decided that the country no longer needed as much military manpower and equipment. Savings could be made in the Defence Budget, which could therefore be possibly spent elsewhere more directly beneficially for the nation – the usual candidates being health and education.

This drive filtered down through the Ministry of Defence as senior folk were asked to come up with savings in their areas of expertise. Someone had made the very logical proposal that the apparent duplication of effort, with both A&AEE and JATE carrying out aerial delivery trials, should be eliminated by combining the trials. This bright idea got the seal of approval and was implemented during the first half of 1991. The Hercules at Boscombe Down was withdrawn back into normal RAF service, as were its three established aircrew.

What we all missed in this move was the different philosophies that drove each trial's organisation. JATE aircrews were accustomed to dropping multiple loads, normally all at once. The test aircrew at Boscombe Down were not. Each load was a test item and so was treated at such, and special provision was made to ensure that the two or three loads could be dropped individually. When I spoke on the telephone to the JATE pilot I assumed he knew that, and he assumed that I knew their normal *modus operandi*.

There was no doubt that the final responsibility for the small amount of damage done to one of Her Majesty's flying machines, and for the premature ageing conferred on the man in the back, was down to me. I was the aircraft captain and the buck stops there. However, the inquiry found that there were organisational contributory factors that led to the rather frightening circumstances we found ourselves in on that sunny summer's day. Procedural changes were made to the briefing chain and radio communications before committing to a drop.

After that there were no other problems with the way that aerial delivery trials were completed, although the geographical separation of the major players did continue to reduce the cost-effectiveness of the imposed solution.

As for me, I could never comprehend the phrase 'Pushing the envelope' in the same way again!

# 21 OPERATION GRANBY

On 2 August 1990, at 2 a.m. local time, Iraq launched an invasion of its neighbour Kuwait using at least seven divisions of its armed forces. The assault was supported by attack and troop-carrying helicopters and attack aircraft. Kuwait was overrun in two days. The seven-month occupation of the country that followed led to the conflict that became known, inter alia, as the Gulf War.

There were several likely reasons for the invasion. First, Iraq had partly financed its eight-year war against Iran with a $14 billion loan from Kuwait and was unable to repay it; a request for the loan to be set aside had been refused. Second, Iraq believed that Kuwait was stealing oil from its territory by slant drilling under the border. Third, Kuwait had refused to cut its oil production, so helping to hold the world price down – a move disadvantageous to Iraq's GDP. Moreover, the dictatorial President of Iraq, Saddam Hussein, had always resented that Kuwait had been brought into existence by the Anglo-Ottoman Convention of 1913, whereby a portion of the Ottoman territories, later Iraq, was separated off as an independent sheikdom. Saddam also held that the Emir of Kuwait was highly unpopular with the general Kuwaiti population and so sought to justify his decision to invade as 'liberation'. In the event the puppet governing system that the Iraqis put in place on 4 August became much more unpopular.

On the day following the attack the UN Security Council passed Resolution 660 condemning the invasion and demanding the withdrawal of all Iraqi military personnel and equipment. The Arab League independently passed a similar resolution. Further UN resolutions imposed economic sanctions and a blockade on Iraq. The United States then started building a coalition of countries that would join them in military action to liberate Kuwait. The US envisaged three campaigns: the build-up of forces in Saudi Arabia and other Gulf locations; the liberation of Kuwait; and the withdrawal and subsequent security of the region. The liberation phase they named Operation Desert Storm. The name for British military activities during the conflict was Operation Granby.

Meanwhile back in England's green and pleasant land, the Wiltshire skies became noticeably busier as August passed and September arrived. All sorts of Urgent Operational Requirements (UORs) were rolling in from project offices and RAF sponsors. I had been stationed at Boscombe Down during Operation Corporate following another invasion: that of the Falkland Islands by Argentina.[1] Things felt very similar this time, but the technology was almost ten years further on. All the test squadrons were involved to a greater or lesser extent and the need for fast-jet photo-chase sorties in support of some of the trials increased.

The major developments over the four months from August to December 1990 would be many and varied. Perhaps one of the highest priorities was to bring a weapon-aiming system known as the Thermal Imaging and Laser Designation (TIALD) pod that was still under development up to an operational standard. TIALD was capable of acquiring and locking on to targets using TV or infrared imaging technology and then using a harmonised laser to designate the target for attack by laser-guided weapons. The pod and the on-board displays and recording equipment could also be used for stand-off reconnaissance.

TIALD's gestation had been a long one. The first trials had started in 1973 at RAE Farnborough using a laser/TV system known as Line of Sight Stabilisation Equipment (LOSSE) flown in a Canberra B(I)8; much of this work was in refining and testing the algorithms to give stable tracking. By 1977 the Canberra had an infrared turret installed under the nose, which was used extensively to test forward-looking infrared (FLIR) for aircraft navigation, target acquisition and weapon aiming. I had flown many of these trials sorties in the Canberra at Farnborough during my first tour as

---

1. See *Trials and Errors* by this author (The History Press, 2015).

a test pilot.[2] Later iterations in the 1980s led to the GEC Ferranti aerospace technology company being awarded a contract to produce a demonstrator pod for the RAE to fly on their Nightbird Buccaneer XV 344.

In 1986, following the success of the RAE trials the UK MOD issued Air Staff Requirement 1015 for a laser targeting pod for the RAF's Tornado aircraft. Thirteen companies entered the competition for the contract; in 1987 these were reduced to three that then received the Project Definition Phase award. The contest closed in May 1988 and the winner was GEC Ferranti; this was not a great surprise to anyone – after all they had done all the work! By the end of 1990 laser-guided bombs had been dropped and guided to their targets by the TIALD-equipped RAE Buccaneer aircraft.

During the build-up phase of Operation Granby the MOD initiated the TIALD Accelerated Programme (TAP) to give the RAF day and night laser-designation capability in advance of any conflict. The first technical meeting had been held on 30 November 1990 to define the equipment and its interface. Less than three weeks later GEC Ferranti delivered a modified pod to Boscombe Down for assessment. Within a day the folks in the Radio/ Navigation Trials Department had proved the feasibility of the TAP. On 19 December the MOD awarded the TAP contract to GEC Ferranti and the definitive trials began. The RAF immediately allocated five Tornados to the TAP to allow for the eventual installation of two pods, system integration and crew training. Meanwhile the software validation work carried on with very high-priority and strict security measures in place.

The weather that winter was worse than usual and caused delays. The A&AEE trials officer, Flt Lt 'Taff' Morgan, was often to be seen tearing at his fine mop of ginger hair. The urgency was exacerbated by the number of cancelled or weather-affected sorties – to such an extent that I was asked to explore the possibility of the civilian ATC and fire services being prepared for operations right through the Christmas holiday. Negotiations were not as difficult as I had expected and the final position was that we would close the airfield only on Christmas Day itself. The Tornados and their crews flew on most of the other days around Christmas, although some days were lost to the appalling weather.

---

2.   Ibid.

Thursday, 17 January 1991, marked the start of the Operation Desert Storm air campaign and the beginning of the Gulf War. We were all glued to our TVs when the pictures of the 'shock-and-awe' bombing of downtown Baghdad were beamed into our living rooms. As an aside, I was particularly taken by a shot from what I recognised to be the lower targeting FLIR screen in a Lockheed F-117 stealth fighter. It showed the automatic lock-follow system keeping the aiming point cursor on a dark point in the centre of a flat roof. Seconds later the tall building below that roof exploded. A 2,000lb Paveway 2 bomb had been dropped down the central ventilation shaft using the sort of equipment I had worked on since 1976. The finale of the first *Star Wars* movie came to mind! It was also the ultimate in vicarious job satisfaction.

From a few days before the start of the air campaign a TIALD-equipped Tornado, with all the necessary software changes incorporated, was ready to start trials in earnest. This work would now be handed over by the A&AEE staff to the resident Central Trails and Tactics Organisation (CTTO). By the end of the following week the TIALD task force of five Tornados and four crews from No. 31 Squadron were fully installed at Boscombe Down. Despite yet more bad weather, within fifty days of the start of the TAP, the system was operational and the five aircraft, with two pods and their crews, deployed to the Gulf. There they operated from the Royal Saudi Air Force Base at Tabuk, and the force of five TIALD and fourteen bomber Tornados achieved the previously unheard of total of 229 direct hits in eighteen days. As the RAF detachment commander at Tabuk said, 'It was a triumph of cooperation between the RAF and GEC Ferranti engineers.' There were many folk, back in the relatively safe environs of Wiltshire, who played their part in that triumph and did so with pride.

Meanwhile a lot of other work directed at the Gulf War was going on, such as the equipment of Tornado with the high-speed anti-radiation missile (HARM), and the purchase and clearance of the Canadian CVR-7 70mm unguided rocket pod for use on the Jaguar and Harrier. Another modification to the Jaguar was the installation of AIM-9 Sidewinder air-to-air missiles on over-wing pylons. The detachment of a dozen Jaguars to the Gulf War had led to the Air Staff issuing a UOR to give them a self-defence capability, without losing one of the four under-wing hard points for carrying offensive weapons, such as the CVR-7. BAe had successfully engineered and cleared this on their Jaguar International model, aimed at overseas customers in the mid 1970s. When we irreverent young test pilots had first seen this arrangement at the 1976 Farnborough International Air Show we reckoned that the missiles should have been mounted the other way round – facing backwards. Our rude rationale was that any Jaguar pilot could easily fight his way into someone's twelve o'clock position and so shoot down the attacker from there. The kit to allow fitment of the pylons was procured from BAe, and within days flight-capable, unarmed Sidewinders were received so that firings could be made. Jaguar GR1 XZ 385 was the trials aircraft and carriage flights were soon followed by the first firings on the large over-water range in Cardigan Bay, off the west coast of Wales, under the control of Aberporth Radar.

I actually got some flying out of this programme; sadly not in the Jaguar, but in one of the ex-RAE Buccaneers XW 987, an old friend from my past. This aircraft had been transferred to Boscombe Down and had received the now standard red, white and blue colour scheme. However, as time had gone by several panels had been changed but not painted to match. So XW 987 had a bit of a patchwork look. Once I flew it to RAF Lossiemouth for a simulator slot and as I got out one of the ground crew said, 'How can you fly around in something that looks like that, sir?'

'I don't mind flying it at all,' I responded, 'because once I'm strapped in I don't have to look at it!'

The first flight was acting as a tanker aircraft[3] to allow the Jaguar more time on the range. That was followed by flights as the chase aircraft for two of the live firings. Flt Lt Dave Southwood was the Jaguar pilot and one of the test points was a deliberate entry into the white smoke trail of the missile immediately after launch. I noticed a flash from the starboard exhaust as Dave turned into the smoke. He said that there was what is known as a pop surge: a very brief instability of flow in the engine. Not something to worry too much about. My toggie Peter James, who by now had forgiven me for our encounter with a parachute, got some good video of the incident. I also flew several other photo-chase sorties in the Buccaneer, Jaguar and Hawk.

And that, grandkids, is what I did in the war!

---

3. The Royal Navy had specified a refuelling capability for the Buccaneer, which had been retained. The refuelling pod was operated by the navigator while the pilot monitored the fuel off-load.

# 22 SETP AND A BLACKBIRD

I joined the Society of Experimental Test Pilots (SETP) in 1982. This organisation had started after some US aircraft company experimental and engineering test pilots, operating in southern California, decided to share their experiences across industrial boundaries. By doing this they hoped to vastly improve flight-test safety, which in those days was not great. It was not a popular move with some of the captains of industry, who thought that their competitors might learn things they didn't want them to know! Some of the sixty-five SETP charter members are still well known in aviation today, Neil Armstrong, George Cooper, Scott Crossfield, Tony LeVier and Joe Walker being just a few.

In time the SETP expanded its reach out of California across the USA and gladly welcomed military test pilots alongside their civilian counterparts. It wasn't long before the organisation started to become known around the world and it then became truly international. As it grew the 'experimental' in the title gained a less rigorous definition and membership flourished.

The SETP's vision is to be the recognised world leader in promoting safety, communication and education in the design and flight test of aerospace vehicles and their related systems; and to maintain a viable professional and prestigious international society for all test pilots and aerospace corporations. Its mission statement is to broaden professional relationships through sharing ideas and experiences, which promote and enhance safety, communication and education; to prevent accidents and loss of life by improving safety, design and flight test of aerospace vehicles and their related systems; and to provide a forum to disseminate information to those in the aerospace industry for the benefit of all aviation users.

The society has formed two charitable arms. First is the SETP Scholarship Foundation, whose primary purpose is to receive, acquire, manage, administer and expend property and funds for scholarships and other forms of educational assistance to children of deceased or disabled SETP members.

The second charitable arm is the SETP Foundation, which aims to provide flight-test educational programmes by sponsoring symposia and disseminating educational material. This is done to increase the safety and efficiency of flight-testing and enhance the professional knowledge of test pilots, astronauts, cosmonauts and other aerospace professionals in the field of research and development. The foundation also provides mentors for educating young people, while encouraging them to enter flight-test or aerospace-related profession. The foundation also aims to enhance flight-test safety by initiating and sustaining a flight-test-related safety organisation. Its activities aim to reduce the risk of mishap, promote risk-reduction management and continually improve the profession's communication and coordination. SETP also develops, implements and maintains a computerised database, readily available to all members and member organisations, containing flight-test-related data collected from the industry. The SETP aims to be the world's leading source of history relating to test pilots and to preserve the historical significance of the accomplishments of test pilots, the SETP and the aerospace industry by displaying memorabilia, written and oral records, reports, photographs, video and other artefacts. Finally, its aim is to archive and display such history in a manner that supports and enhances the efforts of flight-test education and flight-test safety for current and future generations of flight-test personnel and the general public.

By the time I was an experimental test pilot in the late 1970s, SETP membership was well over 2,000. Its aims remained the same – to share information and lessons learnt from test programmes and the inevitable mishaps that occur from time to time. The SETP does this by organising flight-test symposia in many locations every year. It also publishes its own quarterly magazine, *Cockpit*, and circulates members with selected papers from the annual main conference held in California. Through the wonders of modern communication technology, a huge amount of flight-test information and experience is accessible by the membership.

When I joined SETP in 1982, I was teaching at ETPS – anagrammatically speaking of course! The SETP President who signed my certificate was Lt Col William 'Pete' Knight – a one-time X-15 hypersonic research vehicle pilot. I met him once during a visit I was making to Edwards Air Force Base in January 1981. It was at a dinner in the Officers' Club, with several other distinguished test pilots present, including Chuck Yeager, that Pete told the story of a total electrical failure during one of his flights in the X-15. Absolutely gripping and fascinating! (The full story is related in Chapter 32 of my book *Trials and Errors*.)

Through the SETP I met numerous test pilots from many countries, sometimes at the international air shows of Farnborough and Paris, sometimes during visits to the USA, but more often at various European and American symposia. In 1990 a small group of us from Boscombe Down attended the annual European SETP Symposium in France and decided that we would organise the following year's event, due to be held in the UK. We got together, formed a team and I was volunteered to be the chairman. As I was still at Boscombe Down we decided to make it south-west-based and chose the beautiful city of Bath as the location. The A&AEE Commandant, Air Cdre David Bywater, came up trumps by allowing us to make a visit to Boscombe Down, where we were also able to hold a short flying display. In September that year, 1991, I attended, for the first time, the annual symposium in Los Angeles and gave a thirty-minute presentation on some of the test programmes we had undertaken during the Gulf War. That year my very good friend and Lockheed Skunk Works test pilot Tom Morgenfeld was the SETP President.

In 1995 I was elected as a Fellow of the society and was presented with my certificate in Los Angeles by someone who had also become a friend: General Dynamics test pilot John Fergione. I stood alongside six others who seemed far more worthy of this honour, including Space Shuttle test pilot Bob Crippen and Joe Kittinger, who had jumped out of balloon at 102,000ft and set records that stood for fifty-two years. Part of the benefit of being in an organisation like SETP is the opportunity it gives to be able to talk to folk who share the same passion for flying and concern for flight safety, and to learn from others. Sometimes those opportunities allow conversation to take place with people one never thought one would meet.

One such opportunity came at the symposium in Los Angeles when my wife Linda and I chatted to Gemini and Apollo astronaut Jim Lovell and his wife Marilyn. He was, of course, most famous as the commander of the unlucky Apollo 13; but that was a subject I stayed clear of while we talked much more about his earlier naval test flying and the Apollo 8 out-and-back trip to the moon. He was delightfully open and friendly, and it was an honour to have been given the chance to chat to a man who has a crater on the moon named after him! The next time I went to LA for the Annual SETP Symposium, Jim Lovell's alter ego from the film *Apollo 13*, Tom Hanks, came along to a similar social event. He was mobbed so I didn't get to talk to him – but he wasn't a real astronaut or test pilot, so I wasn't that put out!

Another gang of us British 'TPs' organised the 1998 European SETP Symposium and I got the chairman's job again. This time we held it in Manchester and it was a success, thanks to the great team I had. The final event is always a formal black tie banquet with a special guest. We booked the impressive main hall of Manchester Town Hall and, having invited him well in advance, our special guest was HRH Prince Andrew, Duke of York. I had been one of his joint-service tutors during two phases of his Staff College training in 1993, so I thought we had an odds-on chance of getting an acceptance. His presence was a great honour for us all and went down particularly well with the ladies – especially the American ones!

Despite the reductions in worldwide defence spending and aircraft manufacturing, and the advent of pilotless air vehicles, the SETP remains a vibrant and truly international organisation. To this day I remain as active a member of SETP as my location and pension allow!

A very accomplished test pilot that I had the privilege to get to know quite well was Rogers Smith. I had actually flown with him in the Calspan Corporation's fly-by-wire T-33 demonstrator aircraft in 1981. By the early 1990s Rogers had left Calspan and was a NASA test pilot at their Dryden facility at Edwards. Among the aircraft he was flying there was the SR-71 Blackbird. It was one of three[1] used by NASA for a variety of high supersonic research trials and he and his fellow NASA Dryden test pilot Ed Schneider were, at that time, the two who flew them. During an earlier encounter with Rogers I had asked whether my wife and I could make a visit to see around Dryden; Rogers said that we could and that I should arrange it when we were next in California.

In September 1999, when we were living in Texas, Linda and I were again able to attend the Annual Symposium in Los Angeles. We flew ourselves there in a borrowed Cessna 210T. After the symposium we stayed on for a few days with our good friends the Morgenfelds. I had by then arranged for our day out with Rogers up in the desert. We arrived at NASA Dryden to a warm welcome and Rogers kindly gave up part of his busy day to show us around. After a presentation on Dryden's past and current work, we went to the hangars to examine up close some of the rather exotic flying machines. These included an F-18 Hornet and an F-15 Eagle, both highly modified for advanced aerodynamic research programmes. But the star of the show was the

---

1.  These were SR-71A (serial nos 17980 and 17951) and a SR-71B Trainer (serial no. 17956).

SR-71. My wife and I both got to sit in the cockpit of one and hear about its latest test programme.

Then Rogers said, 'I've got one last thing to show you, so follow me.'

He led the way out of the hangar and down a couple of passageways between other buildings before going through a door into one that had the look of a temporary, perhaps mobile, structure. It was the SR-71 simulator.

Rogers took me into the cockpit section and invited me to sit at the controls. There was no visual system, but the cockpit was a faithful representation of the real one that I had sat in only a few minutes before. My first impression of the SR-71 'driver's office' was that it was, like the U-2 I'd sat aboard in 1974, not state of the art. It was functional and had a brutal honesty in its use of familiar round gauges set into a black instrument panel. Having given me a conducted tour of the essential items – throttles, stick, trimmers and a few switches – Rogers shut the door behind me and went to sit at the instructor's console. We could now communicate through the headsets we were wearing. Linda sat behind me while I remained in excited anticipation at the controls of one of the world's most legendary flying machines (well, a simulator of).

Under Rogers' direction I worked through the engine start sequence and then he set everything ready for take-off. I slowly pushed the throttles as far forward as they would go, the engine instruments responded and I released the brakes. Reheat selection followed and the acceleration, judged only by the airspeed indicator as there was no visual in this simulator, was rapid. Rogers called me to ease back the stick to lift off at 210 knots. I did and the altimeter started to indicate. I lifted the gear handle and watched the undercarriage lights go out and accelerated to 450 knots. The climb became rapid and I was told to level off at 26,000ft and fly at a minimum speed of 325 knots. This combination represented the parameters during refuelling so that I could get a feel for the SR-71's handling at subsonic speed. In operational practice the crew's first event would be an airborne refuelling rendezvous to top off the tanks after the fuel-hungry take-off and initial climb. The normal fuel load for take-off was 45,000lb, but the jet can hold 80,000lb of the very special JP-7 fuel.

It is quite a fragile aircraft with a limit of only 1.75g at Mach 3 and a maximum airspeed limit of 500 knots. This speed is an equivalent airspeed (EAS), a measure of the dynamic pressure being felt by the airframe. This limit is displayed to the pilot by a red needle on the airspeed indicator. There is also a prominent red warning caption 'EAS' that illuminates when the aircraft approaches the limit. So gentle handling and strict attention to the structural limits is the order of the day. I found that the SR-71's flight-control system helped in this as it handled more like a bomber or small airliner than a fighter.

Then it was onwards and upwards. Rogers had 'refuelled' the jet so I relit the afterburners and continued the climb to 72,000ft. But on the way up there was a neat little manoeuvre. I had to accelerate to 450 knots equivalent airspeed (KEAS) and climb with full thrust to 33,000ft, then push over, descending to 30,000ft and accelerate through Mach 1; this helps the aircraft get rapidly through the high drag point at Mach 1. Then just trim and hold 450 KEAS all the way up to 72,000ft.

Levelling off was not too demanding and I let the jet accelerate to Mach 3. I still had to watch the airspeed and try to hold the altitude. In practice the autopilot would be selected and would hold the angle of attack (AOA) at its optimum value of 5 degrees. After I had selected the autopilot it worked well. On real missions its navigation mode could hold the SR-71 within 0.1 nautical miles of the pre-planned 'black line' on the map, along which you would be proceeding at 30 nautical miles per minute – a speed faster than the muzzle velocity of many well-known guns. Surface temperatures on the external structure were up in the 400°F range, with temperatures in the inlets reaching 600°F or so. The fuel was used as a heat sink and was pumped through the aircraft skin, which was corrugated to get more surface area for heat dissipation.

The autopilot turned the jet at a 32-degree angle of bank, when it would pitch up to a 9-degree AOA, but the turn rate was very non-fighter-like. The radius of such a turn was 75 nautical miles. Once the Mach number is set the altitude will drift because of variations in temperature and air density (not that it's very dense up there). I disconnected the autopilot and tried a turn using 30 degrees of bank. The roll rate response was good and it was not too difficult to hold the altitude during the turn, but I had to keep a good eye on that speed limit.

At this point it is worth describing the Blackbird's unique engine intake control technology. It is essential that the engine air intake slows the flow from supersonic speed to subsonic speed before it gets to the engine. It is critical for the stability of the airflow that the normal shockwave, after a series of oblique shockwaves, finally goes from Mach 1 to subsonic flow, at or close to the minimum area of the air intake duct. The shaped spike that sticks prominently out of the front of each of the SR-71's engines is positioned within the intake duct according to the aircraft Mach number. The spike moves from its fully forward, subsonic position back into the duct as the Mach number increases. It moves over 2ft back when the SR is accelerating to Mach 3.2: the Blackbird's 'design speed'. It is most efficient at this speed – about twice as efficient in terms of fuel consumption as it is at 0.9 Mach at 30,000ft. However, it does take a lot of fuel to achieve its cruise conditions of initially Mach 3.0 and 72,000ft, then cruise-climbing to as high as 85,000ft and accelerating to Mach 3.2. Rogers said that, if you are at Mach 3.0 and want to save gas, speed up to Mach 3.2 and achieve about a 10 per cent saving in fuel flow. Not many aircraft can do that!

Also critical to the proper operation of the intake duct and engines are the forward and aft annular doors. These are set to keep the critical normal shock in the proper place relative to the spike position. The aft door is set by the pilot according to the checklist at various Mach thresholds and the forward door is set automatically. Above about Mach 2.3, if one inlet 'unstarts' it means that the normal shockwave is 'spat out' forward, as far as the intake duct entry, and the airflow becomes totally chaotic behind it. At this juncture the other intake duct will sympathetically go into restart mode; otherwise the structural loads would break the rather fragile aircraft. An unstart is not a pleasant experience. Another SR-71 test pilot I knew, Tom Smith, once told me that when he had a double unstart his helmet was thrown from side to side against the inside of the cockpit canopy; it sounded hairy and scary. Rogers confirmed the unpleasantness of the event – he suffered a double unstart on his first flight in the SR-71B pilot trainer and his own head-banging experience. After an unstart or a restart the inlet will go through four auto cycles to get the inlet back working correctly.

When I was settled at about 75,000ft and Mach 3, Rogers warned me that he would now simulate an engine unstart. Because the simulator didn't have its limited motion switched on I would not be getting the full treatment. However, Rogers said that I couldn't fail to notice it. A couple of minutes later, as I was cruising at 75,000ft and Mach 3.1, there was a bang and a rapid change of heading. The autopilot tried to correct it and my job was to reach down to the left and hit the unstart switch for the appropriate engine. This would cure the problem and was the updated solution via the relatively new digital engine inlet computer.

After all this excitement I slowed the jet down and descended so that I could fly the SR-71 in the landing configuration. At about 250 knots I lowered the landing gear and just flew along until the speed dropped to 175 knots, which was the approach speed with 10,000lb of fuel remaining. There were no flaps or other devices: the Blackbird's big cranked delta wings provided all the drag we needed. As there was no visual system to give me a runway to land on, Rogers just froze the flight mode and we shut the simulator down. What an experience and what a privilege!

# 23 MOVING ON

Nearing the end of my tour, in November 1991, I was asked by OC RWTS, Commander Mike Swales RN, who was going to be my successor as 'wings', to fly a few Sea King trials flights for the Radio and Navigation Division. I was, of course, delighted to do so. Hence my final flight as a test pilot at Boscombe Down was on 25 November 1991 in Sea King Mark 4 ZF 115.

At the end of the month I was posted to the Directing Staff of the RAF's Advanced Staff Course, back at RAF Bracknell, where I had been a student seven years earlier. The irony was that I was going to 'teach' staff work to the up-and-coming officers of many air forces but, in almost thirty years in the service, I had only done eight months in a proper staff job! Moreover, this would be the fourth time I had returned to instruct at a unit where I had previously been a student; there must have been a message there – but I'm not sure what it was! And yet again, it would be a house move just before Christmas. I now wondered whether I would fly again as a test pilot, or would I be condemned to a series of staff tours for the next eight years, until I reached the normal retirement age of 55?

A part of the staff work that I was leaving behind, which was new to all military management was budgeting. This 'good idea', passed down to us from the Treasury's ivory towers, via the MOD, was the first step on the road that would lead inexorably to agency status and the eventual privatisation of the A&AEE – with a plethora of name and acronym changes still unknown (or even unknowable). The executive responsibility budgets (ERBs) that we were allocated were administered by the establishment's financial staff. However, we ERB holders had to be the executive managers. In reality, the flexibility to manage the ERB by changing anything was close to zero. One large element was the pay of all the aircrew. However, I had no influence over the numbers of aircrew we employed; that lay well above my pay grade. Another element I had responsibility for was to pay the charges made by the Civil Aviation Authority (CAA) for the personnel who manned our ATC facilities.

However, when I received the first invoice to authorise payment I noticed there was one controller position listed that I knew was not being manned. I sent the invoice back to the admin folks for correction. It never reappeared. About one month later the same thing happened. I was told that the invoices had been returned to the CAA for correction. About six months later I was summoned to a meeting with the Commandant and the Senior ATC Officer. Also present was a smartly suited gent with a big briefcase. He was from CAA head office and was complaining that Boscombe Down had now received six months' ATC services for free. I explained why I had not authorised payment; if I was the responsible executive then I wasn't going to pay for something we were not getting. Our visitor said that the adjustment would be made at the end of the annual contract period, but we should pay all the backdated bills immediately. I protested but was overruled.

The CAA were as good as their word and my ERB received a substantial refund. It just so happened that another part of my pot of gold was there to fund the support expenses of aircrew on overseas trials and that looked like it was going to run out before we had finished the plethora of such trials that year. By reading the rules I discovered I was able to transfer money between certain parts of the budget – problem solved!

However, I learned from other budget holders of an iniquitous Treasury rule that was being applied. Boscombe Down ran various facilities that were available, on repayment, to civilian companies, or even individuals. It transpired that any income earned from these facilities, such as the Blower Tunnel, the Radio Range and flights in our trainer aircraft, had to go directly to the Treasury ('do not pass GO and do not collect £200'). So the establishment paid the capital and running costs, but these could not be offset by their gainful use.

This, and some other financial issues, led to the Commandant and the Chief Superintendent going up to the Treasury to ascertain whether this unfair system could be changed. I happened to meet them both in the Mess on their return. They were not cheerful bunnies! Obviously they had not received a warm welcome.

But David Bywater did say one memorable thing: 'I did think that chap who was the chief secretary was impressive; he'll go far. What was his name again?'

'John Major,' replied the Chief Superintendent.

During this tour at Boscombe Down I came across a new sort of being: the consultant. This was the outcome of certain persons who occupied very tall ivory towers in London deciding that we – the UK military test-flying business – should be 'rationalised'. (I had always thought that passage through the rigours of test-pilot training had made us more rational than most!) The proposed scheme from on high was that all the MOD test and evaluation should take place in one location: Bedford/Thurleigh, Farnborough or Boscombe Down. I think another driver was purely financial in that if two of the main locations for military test and evaluation activities could be vacated then some very valuable real estate could be turned into more money for HM Treasury; perhaps that was cynical of me? A well-known City of London company was hired to carry out the evaluation and it wasn't long before I discovered that the MOD would have to save at least £3 million because that was the fee. Three of us still 'in the business' who had served at all three sites – Roger Beazley, Vic Lockwood and I – soon hatched a plot to apply to do the job for the highly discounted price of £1 million! In the end it was Boscombe Down that was chosen – we could have told them that for free.

Looking back over the past six years, I realised how lucky I had been to get to fly more than 1,200 hours in over forty types of aircraft. Not many wing commanders get to do that! During these two tours I had done lots of other things too. I had helped run three international air shows, been involved in a major joint forces exercise, been on the periphery of the nefarious technical intelligence world, been instrumental in organising the hosting of a large USAF detachment and receiving a party of multinational officers of the inspection team of the Treaty on Conventional Armed Forces in Europe (CFE).

The latter had been signed in Paris on 19 November 1990. The CFE treaty required Warsaw Pact and NATO nations to reduce their holdings of a variety of conventional force equipment to agreed limits. The implementation was verifiable by inspections and the protocols for these surprise visits were complex and delicate. We had very few qualifying aircraft on our permanent strength at A&AEE, but we had to be prepared. There was a clause in the treaty by which classified equipment could be described but not presented for visual inspection. The huge irony was that the two aircraft we nominated for this procedure were a MiG-29 Fulcrum and a Sukhoi SU-22 Fitter, which were loaned to us for test and evaluation following the reunification of Germany. These two machines were kept well out of sight, in a hangar and behind huge screens, when our Eastern European friends arrived.

During the six years that brought my military test flying to a close, the world order that I had known all my adult life had changed drastically. The first hint of that reordering was the appearance of Soviet aircraft at the Farnborough International Air Shows of 1986 and 1988. From inside the R&D business it was possible to see that some of the technological advances in the West – particularly cruise missiles and all-weather/day-and-night offensive aircraft capability – were outstripping the Soviet Union's ability to keep up. I'm convinced that Mikhail Gorbachev knew that and the collapse of communism happened essentially because the USA and its allies outspent the Russians. The irony was that the peace protesters camped outside the cruise missile bases at Greenham Common and Molesworth were totally unaware that those mute weapons behind the fences represented the final deterrent. The Russians had no answer to the threat that they posed. In the end those hardy souls in their tents and Cold War warriors like me were seeking, and had obtained, the same outcome. The fall of the Berlin Wall in November 1989 was the iconic end to the Cold War. We had won – medals all round! But by August the following year, with Saddam Hussein's invasion of Kuwait, a new world order was already taking shape.

During the two years after I left Boscombe Down I would see more of the upheaval following the downfall of Soviet communism. At the RAF Staff College we would receive our first students from Poland and the Czech Republic. In 1993 I was a member of a small team that visited the air force staff colleges in Poland and Hungary – something unimaginable only five years earlier. Many erudite and highly qualified visiting lecturers would point out new threats to world peace: migration, access to water, nuclear proliferation, the break-up of previously united countries, drugs, religious intolerance and fanaticism. It was becoming increasingly difficult to identify the place of the military in these threats. Questions as to whether NATO was still relevant and how future alliances would be formed were being asked.

But things were changing inside the RAF too. Politicians saw the fall of the Wall as a reason (or should that be excuse?) to cut defence spending even further. I was not very impressed with what I heard from our top leadership and management. I felt that the party I had enjoyed for so long was coming to an end. Was it time to leave? Then a man came to tell me that I was not going to be promoted after all. Shortly afterwards I saw the attractive terms of a redundancy scheme for officers of my rank and age. This coincided with Linda's bank offering her redundancy. So the decision was made. We said a collective 'Thank you and goodbye', and on 31 March 1994, having handed over two companions of thirty-two years – my ID card and my aircrew watch – I drove out of the gates of RAF Bracknell into the new world of civilian life. Somewhere on Civvie Street was my new address – a place I had not lived since the age of 17.

# PART 4

# CIVVIE STREET

# 24 CLUB-CLASS GYPSIES

During the last few months at the RAF Staff College, Bracknell, Linda and I had decided that we had no special place where we wanted to settle; our children were scattered around the UK and we had no real wish to return to the localities of our roots. The idea of travelling had come from a desire to see more of our nation – 'following the brown signs', we called it.[1] Our redundancy funds allowed us to look at buying a motorhome and we finally bought one of the large American types. With a few weeks to go before my last day of RAF service, we found a Winnebago motorhome that was exactly what we wanted. It was 10m long, had a separate bedroom at the back, all the usual bathroom facilities and its electrics converted to take UK plugs and deal with the national grid via a transformer. There was also an on-board petrol-driven generator. We bought a small Citroën AX car and had it modified for towing, which would give us the opportunities for sightseeing and shopping open to a smaller vehicle. We were ready to hit the road as club-class gypsies!

During this planning phase we felt led to offer ourselves to the Officers' Christian Union (OCU) as what they called honorary travelling secretaries. We were going to be moving around the UK, basing ourselves on caravan sites for two or three weeks at a time and then radiating out from those places in our car. Thus we could contact serving OCU members in that area and offer to visit them and find out how they were. It would be a networking exercise helping members to keep in touch with HQ at Aldershot, other OCU members and the associate prayer groups that supported individual serving officers. We also hoped that it would be a ministry of encouragement to folk of all three services. The OCU Council accepted our offer. One of the Apostle Paul's travelling companions was called Barnabas (his nickname in the early Church was 'the Encourager'). We called our Winnebago 'The Barnabus', or 'the bus' for short!

However, we soon realised that in the UK this could not be a truly year-round pursuit; very few caravan sites were open continuously and taking a

---

1.  In the UK brown signs point folk to tourist sites of interest.

6-ton vehicle on to a soggy field in midwinter would not be wise. Moreover we couldn't get all our stuff in the bus. So we needed a base for the winter. But where?

In 1991, my father had inherited a small 1930s bungalow from his aunt. She was my favourite great aunt and was called Alice. As a child I had visited her, often with my paternal grandfather, who would take me by train from the grimy, industrial environs of Bradford's Foster Square station, through the moorlands and valleys of the Pennines, to Auntie Alice's little house in the seaside town of Morecambe, Lancashire. A wondrous place for a 6- or 7-year-old boy!

My parents had put the bungalow on the market soon after Alice's death. But almost three years had passed with little or no interest from prospective purchasers. Linda and I decided that if the place was suitable we could help out by buying it. So, on a very wet day, we went to look at it. There was a lot of damp in the house too! It was small, but we thought that we could convert it to give us adequate living space for the time we would be there. I wondered about the location but, when I looked at a map, Morecambe was surprisingly close to the geographic centre of the British Isles, and it was only 5 miles from England's longest motorway – the M6.

We went ahead, had it surveyed, found a builder that we liked and, over a couple of months, the little bungalow was knocked about a lot, modernised and became a lovely, if bijou, residence. We could walk to the seafront, the local shops and the parish church in less than ten minutes. Within three months of leaving the RAF we held a house-warming party and got ready to go on our first trip.

Over the next four years we would spend the time between the clock changes, April to October, on the road, although we did return for the height of summer. This was because in July and August the caravan sites became overcrowded and much more expensive. It also gave our children and grandchildren the opportunity to visit us, and the seaside, in summer weather. One of the church members ran a small guesthouse and the family would stay there.

We travelled many hundreds of miles in our Winnebago, and covered most of the UK, including Northern Ireland. We often sited ourselves within reach of RAF stations and army and navy units. We met up with lots of really interesting people with whom we shared at least two things in common: our Christian faith and service life.

One of our cats died during our second period on the road but the other, a Siamese of great character (aren't they all?), took to travelling as if she had been doing it all her life. When we parked up she would come out and walk all around the pitch, usually talking loudly, before making short expeditions into the surrounding greenery. She never got lost, although she did stay out all night once, and would often return with a 'squeaky toy' that she would play with under the motorhome. When we left any pitch I would pull forward and stop so that Linda could collect and dispose of any small corpses. On one site, the manager warned us of moles on our allocated pitch.

'Don't worry,' I told him. 'If it shows its head above ground our cat will catch it.'

'If it does you can have a free night,' he replied. She did and we did!

Running the Barnabus was not cheap. It did about 12mpg and until I owned it I didn't realise that petrol pumps had a delivery limit of 100 gallons. The first time I filled it the pump just cut out and I was mystified. Fortunately Linda was in the filling station shop and could get them to reset the pump having assured them that we would pay in full. People took a great interest in the bus and nearly always asked three questions:

'Big isn't it?'

'How many miles to the gallon?'

'Do you live in it?'

I felt like making three placards with the answers: YES, 12, and YES, and just hold them up in turn!

During those four years that we travelled in our bus we visited many places that had brown signs. Among them were the Giant's Causeway, Rutland Water (England's largest lake) and a multitude of castles – often dominating the countryside. In retrospect we regard this time as one of the best phases of our married lives. But what about the flying? Was I missing it? Well, the answer was conditional – I was missing the sort of flying that had filled most of my time in the RAF. But I was not going to be 'grounded'.

During my time at Bracknell I had reapplied to join Mike Neil at the AEF at RAF Abingdon and I had managed to fly a lot of air cadets in the Chipmunk. But once we had moved to Morecambe this was not possible. However, my former colleague and friend from Boscombe Down, the erstwhile OC ETPS Martin Meyer, was running the AEF at RAF Woodvale near Southport – not that far from Morecambe. So when we were back in Lancashire I checked out in the Bulldog, which had replaced the Chipmunk, and flew there. I was also flying a variety of historic aircraft with various organisations. (More tales from that aspect of my flying life will have to wait!)

As well as that bit of 'dabbling' on the shores of light aviation, I received two offers of gainful employment. They were both part time so would fit with our peripatetic lifestyle. Linda and I decided that we would form a business partnership as consultants so we could receive payments – and pay tax – legitimately. So retirement was not yet on the cards – but flying was!

# 25 CRANFIELD UNIVERSITY

Roger 'Dodge' Bailey is an ex-RAF C-130 'driver', fellow test pilot and friend. We knew each other from working at RAE Bedford and through our activities with the Shuttleworth Collection of historic aircraft. After leaving the RAF, Dodge had taken up the post of Chief Test Pilot at the Cranfield Institute of Technology, which became a university in 1993. The major area of study for the students was aeronautical science; the origins of the institution went back to 1943, when it was known as the College of Aeronautics. The main campus was on the site of a former RAF airfield near the village of Cranfield, midway between the towns of Bedford and Milton Keynes, in the English East Midlands.

It was Dodge who had approached me to see whether I would be interested in helping him with some flying on an occasional basis. I was happy to accept his offer, especially as it would be remunerated. The task was to give Cranfield University students experience of flight in a light aircraft and, as part of the syllabus, show them some of the basic test-flying techniques used in assessing handling and stability. The aircraft that the university owned for this task were two Beagle Pups. However, there was one small hurdle to overcome: I had to have a commercial pilot's licence (CPL). In the 1990s the UK CAA had introduced a new level of commercial licence called the Basic CPL; this was to allow pilots of light aircraft to fly for, as the regulation put it, 'hire or reward'. I had taken all the exams and the flight tests for the Basic CPL. Because that level of licence was appropriate for the job at Cranfield, all I then had to do was to get type and instrument rated and, in due course, night qualified.

The Beagle Pup first flew in 1967 and was the forerunner to the Bulldog built by Scottish Aviation, which took over Beagle Aircraft's design. The company then produced the bigger and beefier 200hp Bulldog for the RAF in the 1970s; it replaced the DH Chipmunk on university air squadrons. I had flown the Bulldog with the AEF at RAF Woodvale. Both of the Cranfield Pups, G-AXIA and G-AXDW, were Series 1 models, manufactured in 1969 and fitted with 100hp engines. They were very attractive to look at in their blue and white livery, but not sparkling performers, especially when full of fuel and with two people on board.

Dodge had told me that the two flights each student was allowed in the Pup would happen in periodic two-week phases – hence the part-time nature of the job. During my times at Cranfield he said I could expect to fly three or four flights per day, each lasting about forty-five to fifty minutes. Many of the students were postgraduates from overseas nations undertaking Master's degrees.

Before I started with the students I had to update my civil instructor's and instrument flying ratings. So my first few flights at Cranfield were as a student myself. Dodge first flew with me to introduce me to the 'little doggy' and then I flew an instructional refresher flight with an instructor from the local flying school. This was an interesting trip because the gentleman involved was very large in all dimensions. I worried that we would be over the 725kg maximum take-off weight limit. However, he wasn't worried so we just got on with the job. The rate of climb after take-off was, to say the least, marginal!

I resurrected my CFS instructional patter on demand and taught my large, and rather taciturn, 'student' whatever he demanded. After he was satisfied with that he asked me to demonstrate a spin. After all the usual checks and lots of looking around I put the Pup into a spin. It went very nose-low quite quickly, so I guessed that, due to the presence of my companion, the centre of gravity was probably well forward. The recovery after a couple of turns was very rapid and it took more than a little extra pull-force on the stick to get back to level flight. The rest of the flight went well enough to satisfy my supervisor. The following day I flew with the chief flying instructor of the same flying school, who put me through quite a rigorous check flight, but signed my logbook afterwards with 'QFI test passed'. I completed my instrument test in a Piper Warrior later.

All the above had happened in late July 1995 and Dodge said that the first batch of students would be ready to fly during the last two weeks of October. Before leaving the area I met up with a farmer recommended to me by Mike Clarke, Dodge's very amiable and helpful ops officer. I was told that he might be willing and able to let me park our motorhome in his yard, which was within easy walking distance of the hangar from where we operated. He was amenable to the idea so I booked my 'pitch' for the last two weeks of October. That had the pleasing outcome, especially for a Yorkshireman, of saving on hotel bills.

I returned on 16 October willing and eager to get airborne. The first of the two flights with the students was simply a flight to give them the experience of being airborne in a light aircraft. A minimal amount of instruction was given, but I always encouraged them to take control. This gave them a feel for how small the stick movements are to control the aircraft in flight. The second sortie was aimed at showing them some basic stability and control test techniques, like slowing down without trimming and making sure that the stick force needed to hold the nose on the horizon was a pull and not a push: ergo static longitudinal stability.

Then let go of the stick and watch the subsequent behaviour of the aeroplane. If it is dynamically longitudinally stable it will perform a series of nose-up and nose-down pitching manoeuvres that gradually get smaller until the aircraft is once more steady and level from where it started. Having done that for themselves I would move on to show more basic test techniques for testing lateral and directional stability. These would include steady heading sideslips, using the rudder, to test the static stability and then releasing the rudder to examine the dynamic stability. Then there was the coupling of the lateral (rolling) and directional (yawing) characteristics in the Dutch roll. This is named after the motion generated by speed skaters – rocking and rolling their way across the ice of frozen canals in Holland. If airsickness was going to be an issue it usually manifested itself at this part of the exercise. Not that many of the students ever did feel queasy – or, at least, they didn't own up to it!

I found over the couple of years I did this flying that the students were, on the whole, enthusiastic and receptive. A few were less so and sometimes communication was difficult, especially when English was not their first language. I was and still am grateful to Dodge for having me on his team and allowing me the chance to taste another slice of the aviation pie.

# 26 SLINGSBY AVIATION

While attending a Historic Aircraft Association symposium at Duxford I was approached over coffee by an old acquaintance from my Boscombe Down days. His name was Bob Cole and he was the Civil Aviation's Chief Test Pilot (CTP) for general aviation and light aircraft. He gave me his trademark broad smile and asked how I was. After some small talk he went on.

'I understand you're living in the north of England now.'

I confirmed that, wondering why he was asking.

'You know Don Headley don't you?'

I confirmed that fact too. When I had first met Don in 1975 he was the CTP at Hawker Siddeley's (later BAe) factory and airfield in East Yorkshire, where he flew the Buccaneer and Phantom. We had shared several test-flying occasions since then. I had also flown with Don in a delightful little 1930s biplane, called the Blackburn B2, and written a magazine article for *Aircraft Illustrated*[1] about the experience. I was beginning to wonder where this rather one-sided conversation was heading.

'Well, Don's now CTP with Slingsby Aviation at Kirbymoorside in East Yorkshire. But he doesn't have a deputy, so I said I'd look you out and see if you would be interested in doing the job. It will be part time and you'll have to agree terms with the company.'

'Part time suits me fine, Bob, but it is a bit of a trek across the Pennines to get there from where I live,' I responded. 'Also, I travel about the country in my motorhome, but as long as I get notice of when I'm needed it might work.'

'Right. Give me your contact details and I'll pass them to Don.' So I did.

Not long after that, the phone rang and when I answered it the sound of Don Headley's voice confirmed that Bob had indeed passed on my details. After much reminiscing and a bit of joshing, Don got round to trying to pin me down about the job offer. I told him I might be interested, but needed to know more.

---

1.  Published by Ian Allan Ltd, February 1979.

'Well, that suits us all then. Can you come over for a meeting and a look around?' he asked.

I confirmed that I would be glad to and diaries were produced at both ends. We settled on a date and agreed that we would look forward to seeing each other again.

A couple of weeks later I set off for East Yorkshire. In those days, before in-car satnavs, I looked at my road map and decided that the most direct route through the Yorkshire Dales would be best. It would take me about two and half to three hours. I arrived at the factory and airfield site just in time to meet up with Don and a cup of very welcome coffee. After a chat and more reminiscences he introduced me to the managing director, Jeff Bevans, and then took me on a tour of the factory, to see how they made their latest product – the Slingsby Firefly T67 M260.

Slingsby Aviation gets its name from its founder, Frank Slingsby. It is also the name of a village about 10 miles south of the company's factory at Kirbymoorside. Frank Slingsby was a Royal Flying Corps pilot during the First World War and in 1920 bought a partnership in a furniture and woodworking factory, located in the east coast resort of Scarborough. Ten years later he was a founder member of the Scarborough Gliding Club. There his joinery and flying skills came together and he started repairing some of the club's gliders. In 1931 he built a glider using the design of the German RRG Falke (Falcon). This marked the start of his business as a glider and sailplane manufacturer.

Business grew rapidly and in 1933 a local landowner persuaded Slingsby to move to a site just outside Kirbymoorside. There a factory was built and an adjacent field had a 750m reinforced grass runway laid across it. During the war, Slingsby built parts for other companies' aircraft, as well as a military glider, which did not see action. After the war the company produced large numbers of training gliders for the Air Training Corps. I started my flying career in one.[2]

Slingsby also continued to make increasingly refined sailplanes for civilian use in clubs and competitions. Their greatest success was at the 1952 World Gliding Championships with the Sky, which finished in first, third and fourth

---

2. See *A Bucket of Sunshine* by this author (The History Press, 2012).

places. The later Skylark series was their post-war bestseller. Slingsby then began to move away from wood toward glass-reinforced plastic (GRP) and metal construction. However, in July 1969 the company, trading as Slingsby Aircraft Ltd since 1967, went into liquidation following a fire.

In November 1969, Slingsby became part of the Vickers Group, initially as Vickers-Slingsby Sailplanes Ltd, then reverting to the old name of Slingsby Sailplanes Ltd. Home-grown design capability declined, though the company built versions of other aircraft, both powered and unpowered. Slingsby's last glider, which was also their last original such design, was the GRP Vega. This ceased production in 1982, by which time high-performance sailplane design had moved away from the UK. During the industrial upheavals in the UK's aerospace and marine sector, the company became Slingsby Engineering, part of the public/private holding company British Underwater Engineering (BUE). In July 1982 Slingsby Aviation was set up by, and as part of, Slingsby Engineering. At this time Slingsby Aviation employed around 130 people on its 12,220sq. m site. Slingsby Aviation's SAH 2200 hovercraft has operated in such varied regions as the Arctic and Africa.

Slingsby's venture into powered aircraft had started with motor-gliders, but the first purpose-built, powered trainer aircraft was the Firefly, based on the French Fournier RF-6 design. In 1981, Fournier sold the development rights of their two-seat RF-6B to Slingsby, where it was renamed T67. The earliest examples, the T67A, were virtually identical to the Fournier-built aircraft, but the design was soon revised to replace the wooden structure with one of composite material. Slingsby produced several versions of the Firefly, developing the airframe and adding progressively larger engines. The Slingsby T67M, aimed at the military (hence 'M') training market, was the first to include a constant-speed propeller and inverted fuel and oil systems. Over 100 T67M's were built in three versions.

In 1993 the T67M design was enhanced even further by the installation of a 260hp (190kW) Lycoming AEIO540-D4A5 engine, fitted with a Hoffman three-bladed, variable pitch, constant-speed propeller. The cockpit was redesigned with the student pilot occupying the right-hand seat, so that the centrally positioned throttle would be in his or her left hand. A total of fifty-one T67M-260s were produced for a UK MOD contract to train RAF, Royal Navy, British Army and foreign and Commonwealth pilots through the Joint Elementary Flying Training School. The production line for these T67s was still running and would provide me with much of my flying over the next two years.

But the big breakthrough for the company was in winning a contract to supply 114 T67M-260s to the US Air Force for their Enhanced Flight Screening Program. In USAF service the aircraft was designated the T-3A and was the T67M-260 with the addition of air conditioning. When I went to Kirbymoorside in early 1996 the USAF had lost one T-3A and its two occupants due to the instructor's inability to recover from a spin. This would not be the first T-3A loss over the next few years.

We started our tour by walking through the factory area. There were bits of aeroplanes being formed out of GRP, and the place reeked of plastic and resin. In common with all composite-structure manufacturing facilities, one of the major machines in the factory was the autoclave: effectively a huge oven for 'cooking' the parts to perfection. In one area a long space was taken up with a machine identical to one I had seen on a tour of a rope-maker's factory in the village of Hawes, in the Yorkshire Dales. I had actually driven right past it on my way to Kirbymoorside that very morning. Don was surprised that I knew what it was and how it worked. But this rope-making machine, which took up much of the shop floor, was spinning threads of Kevlar rather than flax or sisal. Nonetheless, I still had no clue as to where this 'rope' might go in the aeroplane.

It was, Don explained, to be wrapped around the single main spar of the wing, which was a moulded and cooked piece of GRP. The rope would increase the spar's strength and help to keep it rigid under g-loads. The use of GRP meant that the Firefly had a unique instrument – a main spar temperature gauge. If this rose above 50°C then the normal g limit of +6 had to be reduced to +5. If it went above 55°C then the machine was grounded – because the effect of the heat might distort the spar under g. I was shown the assembly line; as we walked down the length of the sheds the aircraft took shape until, at the far end, a T67 M260 was ready for its ground testing.

At this point I was invited to inspect the finished product and sit in the cockpit. I was impressed with the modernity of the instrument panels, which were well laid out and furnished with all one needed to fly safely round the flight envelope, in cloud and at night. There were two VHF radios and a navigation suite totally suitable for an aircraft of its class. The field of view seemed good, but I felt that the lack of adjustment in sitting height might be a bit of a disadvantage to vertically challenged folk like me.

It was time for lunch, so we retired off site to a local hostelry. When we returned it was time to get down to the interview. This was not too rigorous;

knowing Don so well undoubtedly helped. One technical question did come up and it was about spinning. Don told me about the loss of the USAF T-3A and said that a spin mode had been discovered whereby at higher density altitudes, in spins to the right, it was possible, after applying reverse recovery actions, for the spin to continue at a higher rate than normal. Don asked me if I had any ideas as to why this might be happening.

'I did notice one thing,' I responded, 'and that is that there is no cut-out on the inside edges of each elevator. That means that when the stick has been moved forward during the attempted recovery it might blank off too much of the airflow going up over the rudder, so it could be receiving less airflow than is required to give the necessary aerodynamic force to break the spin. A lot of trainers have a V-shaped cut-out there that lets the air flow upwards over the rudder more easily.'

That observation was considered but no further comment was made. The MD and Don said that they would be happy to offer me the position of deputy CTP and over a cup of tea they told me about what they were willing to pay me as a daily rate. I asked about how often I might be called upon and their answer seemed a reasonable fit with my lifestyle. Don and I arranged a date for me to return when he could introduce me properly to the Firefly. So the deal was sealed and I drove home to tell Linda.

On Thursday, 28 March 1996, I had my first up close and personal encounter with the Slingsby T67 M260 Firefly. I had driven over via the Yorkshire Dales again, where spring was burgeoning and the lambs were gambolling. I met up with Don and we walked out to the aircraft from the small Flight Test Office; it wasn't big enough to be called a department. This Firefly was the company demonstrator and had the registration G-EFSM. It was painted mainly white, with red under the nose, on the wing outer panels and on the leading edge of the tail. There were also blue and red go-faster stripes running from nose to tail; it looked very attractive. In size it was similar to many primary trainers – about 24ft long – but the wingspan of 35ft showed its parentage from the line of French powered gliders.

After a good look around the outside we donned our backpack parachutes, climbed aboard from the rear of the wing and strapped in; I was sitting in the first pilot's seat on the right. Jon Poole, the chief aircraft engineer, who I had met earlier, was on hand with a fire extinguisher for our start-up. The checklist was fairly simple and we soon had the engine turning at about 1,200rpm to warm up, while we switched on the radios and nav. aids, and checked the operation of the flaps and flying controls.

Then came a unique experience. Between the small aircraft hardstanding and the grass runway there is a stream, over which there is a wooden bridge for access to the airfield. I had never taxied over a bridge in a flying machine before! After completing the engine health and pre-take-off checks I lined up on the south-westerly grass runway, and applied full throttle. A very satisfying growl came from the six-cylindered powerplant up front and we were off quite smartly, if a little bumpily. The admirable power-to-weight ratio of this little plastic trainer made it necessary to use a good push on the rudder bar to offset the torque and yaw. We lifted off after a ground roll of about 1,000ft and at a shallow angle of climb I quickly achieved the climbing speed of 90 knots and a climb rate of about 1,300ft per minute – very acceptable!

However, I found that holding the approximately 30–50lb foot load to keep the aeroplane in directional balance was an annoyance. I remembered the PC-9's throttle-mounted electrical rudder trimmer and thought that something similar would be a good idea for the Firefly. We climbed to 10,000ft and arrived there about nine minutes after take-off. Now remembering my days as a Chipmunk instructor, and the hours I had spent climbing back up for the next event, I thought the climb performance of the T67 M260 would make it a productive primary trainer. Once up there, Don asked me to carry out some stalls, with the flaps up ('clean'), then with half-flap and finally with full flap down. Using the usual checks and techniques, I found that the Firefly stalled just like a trainer should, with no bad habits and was easy to recover. The aircraft stalled at about 62 knots clean and 55 knots with full flap, and the buffeting of the air breaking away from the wing just before the stall gave a discernable natural warning of what was about to happen.

Another note I made to myself was that I found the sturdy flap lever, situated between the two seats, quite a pull to operate and annoyingly close to my right elbow and funny bone when the flaps were fully down. I could see (or feel) that it was obvious to the pilot when flap was selected and thus there was no need for an indicator. But I wondered whether electrical flap operation with a selector switch and miniature indicator would be that much of a weight penalty. I resolved to refine my judgement about it when we got back to the circuit. But next on Don's agenda was to let me throw the aeroplane about with some aerobatics.

'Don't you want me to spin it?' I asked.

'No – not yet. We'll do that this afternoon,' he responded. 'When you've had a good lunch!' he added with his characteristic chuckle.

Before we did any aerobatics Don asked me to accelerate to the Firefly's maximum allowed speed ($V_{ne}$) of 195 knots. This required a dive, as the maximum level speed at 8,000ft with full throttle was about 145 knots. Once in the 15-degree dive the aircraft accelerated well and we soon arrived at 195 knots. I had to pull the throttle back a little to make sure the engine didn't exceed its maximum limit of 2,700rpm. Then Don pointed out that a common problem was that the canopy latch could start to move at these high speeds. Indeed, the canopy could be seen to be trying to lift and the noise was quite impressive; but the mechanical canopy latch, above my head, was still firmly engaged.

I used the speed to fly a loop using +4g, recovering to level flight at 130 knots. Then I did a rate-of-roll test before doing anything further; I suspected that those long wings and conventional ailerons would militate against a sparkling roll rate. And I was right. Using full aileron and no rudder, the best I could get was around 60–80 degrees per second. This meant that a full aileron roll would take five to six seconds, which is a long time compared with many trainers. I flew the aircraft inverted at 130 knots and, keeping an eye on the rate of climb and descent indicator (RCDI), pushed until we were flying level. For my future reference I then noted where the horizon was cutting the windscreen arch. The T67 M260 has fully inverted capable fuel and oil systems so there is, theoretically at least, no limit to the time you can fly around upside down.

I rolled out of the inverted attitude, using rudder and aileron, and continued round to perform a slow roll. That was followed by a barrel roll, a stall turn in each direction and a quarter clover leaf into a final loop. Next on the agenda was to pretend that the engine had failed and fly at the gliding speed of 80 knots. I picked a landing area in the countryside below and we descended gently earthwards, those longer than average wings now working in our favour. After climbing away from the field I decided to make my approach, but there was one final test for me.

'Take us back to Kirbymoorside, old lad,' came from he who must be obeyed.

As I had not flown over this bit of Yorkshire since I was a young lad, I now had a small problem. I climbed to 2,000ft and checked that the compass was correctly aligned, looked around and saw that the North York Moors were to our right, and determined that I was heading west, so we were probably east of our destination. Then I spotted a town to my right with a railway line coming into it from the north. *That must be Pickering, where the North Yorkshire railway ends*, I reasoned silently. I maintained my heading and within minutes I had picked out the town of Kirbymoorside. By dint of scanning to the left of there I picked out the roofs of the factory and then the grass strip.

Don made a call on the radio to announce our arrival. Slingsby did not operate an ATC service, but there was a radio in the design office where one of the FTOs, usually Dave Goddard, would respond. The calls were for information only; everything we did on the airfield was 'at the pilot's discretion'.

Don took over to show me a circuit and, as he put it, 'to keep my hand in'. The circuit was flown at 90 knots until the turn on to finals when he lowered to half flap and the speed reduced progressively to 70 knots at about 300ft. Then full flap was selected and the speed reduced to 65 knots over the airfield boundary, aiming to round out with the throttle closed and touchdown on the main wheels at 55 knots. After that first demonstration I flew another three, one without flap, and then we stayed down. The Firefly's big tyres and rugged undercarriage absorbed the bumpiness of the runway and the brakes worked well; we stopped after a run of about 1,100ft.

Overall I liked the Firefly. The field of view was excellent, the instrumentation and equipment modern without being ostentatious or exotic, and most of the handling and performance was good. I had a few concerns but thought I would hold on to those until I had got to know this little trainer better.

As promised, the postprandial sortie concentrated on the Firefly's spinning characteristics. I wanted to check that it would pass the requirements tests for a trainer. To be honest I didn't expect it not to! After climbing to 8,000ft, Don let me try them for myself. The entry from level flight at 65–70 knots, made with simultaneous application of full aft stick and rudder, gave a pretty standard response: a tight barrel roll in the direction of the applied rudder with discernable yaw and the nose dropping below the horizon after 270 degrees of roll. At the completion of that first roll I put the controls central and the aircraft stopped spinning almost immediately. I tried this in the opposite direction with an identical result. Test number one passed!

Then it was on to the fully developed spins. We agreed on four full turns before recovery action would be applied. Once that first turn was over the spin rate stabilised at about 150 degrees per second, the nose was about 30 degrees below the horizon and the airspeed fluctuated between 50 and 75 knots. It was quite a steady spin with not much variation in roll or yaw rate.

'Four turns,' I called. 'Recovering.'

I applied full rudder to oppose the yaw and then moved the stick centrally forward – the standard spin-recovery actions – and the aircraft came out of the spin in less than two turns. The loss of height per turn was about 250ft. Test number two passed!

The third test was to see whether the aircraft would recover if the student did the spin recovery actions in the wrong order. So this time after four turns I moved the stick forward first and then after a pause of a couple of seconds applied full rudder. The immediate effect was that the spin rate went up by at least double, to over 240 degrees per second. But it still recovered, taking a full two turns to do so. Test number three passed!

We were not going to do inverted spins, but Don wanted to show me a problem that had been uncovered that was not always reproducible.

'Climb to 12,000ft please, Mike.'

I did. After we had levelled off there and we had done our pre-spinning checks Don explained what he was going to do.

'I'm going to enter a spin to the right, let it settle for three turns and then apply reverse recovery actions. OK?'

I confirmed that I was indeed OK. In we went, the spin stabilised nicely and after turn three Don moved the stick forward. The spin speeded up, then he applied rudder, the spin continued, if anything faster than ever. We did another four or five turns – I was losing count – and then Don pulled the stick back. The spin stopped almost immediately. We pulled out of the dive and flew straight and level until our internal gyros had settled down.

'If your lunch is still in place, go ahead and try it for yourself,' Don invited.

Not ever having been affected by airsickness and not being averse to a challenge, I took over and climbed back up to 12,000ft. I did the same as Don had with identical results. The high spin rate made the whole thing very disorientating and I imagined a student having great difficulty. It struck me as something that needed fixing. We returned to the airfield where I tried a glide approach and landing. After a third, solo sortie and a final chat I hit the road to return to Lancashire. It had been a very long but rewarding day.

I wasn't due to return to Kirbymoorside until June. However, a tragedy unfolded in early May that would change things. I had been told very early in my contacts with Don Headley that he had been looking for a qualified test pilot to help him because a talented local pilot called Peter Clark had been pressing Slingsby to hire him as deputy CTP. Pete Clark was a well-known aerobatic display pilot who had been flying the Firefly to a very high level of accomplishment for many years. He was also a protégé of the previous CTP, Norrie Grove. It was the CAA, in the shape of Bob Cole, who had apparently agreed with Don that Peter was not the right man for the job. I could offer no opinion because I didn't know anything about Mr Clark; I had never met him or seen any of his aerobatic displays. However, I did think that if we ever needed the company aircraft to be displayed he might be a good man to keep on board – despite his reported resentment at not getting the job.

On Sunday, 4 May, I was at Old Warden for a flying display, where I would be flying one or more of the Shuttleworth Collection's historic aircraft. I learnt that one of the other display items would be a Slingsby Firefly flown by no less than Pete Clark. I thought I might try to meet up with him and sound him out – or at least find out what his real feelings were. That morning I had to fly my first flight in the collection's Spitfire Vc (someone had to!). The first sortie was planned for me to transit to Duxford, near Cambridge, and after some handling exercises en route practise some landings there. After refuelling at Duxford I was to carry out a couple of practice displays and then return for my first landing at Old Warden – a trickier proposition. As if the pressure was not enough, I had to get back by noon for the pre-display briefing. I just made it!

So my plan of introducing myself to Pete Clark went by the board. *Never mind*, I thought, *I'll try to catch him later*. I went into a very full briefing room on the stroke of noon and stood at the back. I looked at the pilots sitting in front of me and tried to work out which might have been Mr Clark. There was a chap with dark hair and a blue flying suit that I thought might be him. However, at the end of the briefing he left and I had to stay behind to brief with two other collection pilots for a formation slot early in the programme. So another chance missed.

By the scheduled start time of the display I was standing 'air side' with a couple of other collection pilots waiting our turn to go to our aircraft. Then a red Firefly took off from the north-easterly runway, and I realised that must be Pete Clark flying it. Just after lift-off I was amazed to see the aircraft roll inverted at about 30ft and fly away, still upside down, climbing to the north.

'That was a bit unnecessary,' I said. 'Doesn't he know that the CAA is here today?'[3]

'Yes, it was very sporting,' agreed one of my companions. 'He's the first one on, so we'll watch him and then go to our aircraft.'

So we did. The red Firefly arrived from the south-west, diving until it was very low and very fast – I guessed he was going at or close to the maximum speed of 195 knots. He pulled up sharply at the display centre into a vertical climb and carried out a half-roll. As his speed fell to almost zero the aircraft was put into a spin. The effect was a tumbling manoeuvre called a Lomcovak.[4] That evolved into a regular spin. My companion and I watched; I think we were both silently counting the turns.

After five I said, 'He's pushing his luck.' Then the spin stopped. I looked at the height against the background and thought that he *just* might pull out in time. But the next thing he did absolutely shocked and astounded me. He pushed.

'He'll never make it!' I shouted.

The aircraft, still inverted, with its nose rising, disappeared into or behind the copse of trees on the far side of the runway. Then came the noise: a muffled, distant crunch and crackle.

The realisation came quickly to us all. Pete Clark had crashed. We despatched the fire vehicle. I think we all knew the chance of survival from an inverted entry into trees was about zero.

And so it was. The shocked fire crew came back with whispered comments of aircraft and human wreckage. What a tragedy. I was particularly upset because of the Slingsby connection, which no one else had realised.

Don contacted me as soon as I was home. He told me that Pete had been booked to appear at that year's Middle Wallop Air Show in the middle of June. Middle Wallop in Hampshire is the HQ of the Army Air Corps, and

---

3. The Civil Aviation Authority had officials who were well versed in the flying display business who would turn up unannounced to ensure that all the rules and regulations were being followed. This included checks that pilots were sticking to the limitations of their display authorisations.

4. The Lomcovak was invented by a Czech pilot at the 1958 World Aerobatics Championship. It is said to mean headache – probably because doing the manoeuvre gives one a headache!

the two-day show was an important annual event and probably the biggest air show in Europe to take place on and from a grass airfield – albeit one of large dimensions.

'You're a display pilot aren't you?' he asked.

'Yes, Don, but of fragile old aeroplanes and the occasional jet. I'm not in Pete Clark's league – nowhere near it,' I replied.

'You're being too modest. I've seen your aerobatics, mate – surely you could put something together before 14 June, couldn't you?'

'Well, let me think about it and I'll get back to you,' I said.

'Well one thing that the company does want is for you to spin the aircraft publicly – we're getting more bad PR about the Firefly and spinning,' Don urged.

'Yes, I understand, but the classic spin is not really an air-show manoeuvre. Anyway Pete Clark had recovered from the spin; he just did so too low. But I can sense the problem – I'll put something together and then when I'm next over we'll talk about it.'

I left it at that.

By the time the Middle Wallop Air Show came round I had agreed a sequence with the company and practised enough to feel confident that it would work. I still wasn't happy about the spins but I pressed on. Starting at 3,000ft I entered a right-hand spin, did three full turns, recovered at about 1,500ft and entered a left spin recovering at 500ft, so that I could then start what I regarded as my 'normal' aerobatic display. That was a sequence of all the basic aerobatics, but starting with an avalanche,[5] and including a long inverted fly-past and push-up. I flew the sequence twice on the 14th and once on the 15th. I was very sad that it was probably nowhere near as good as the display that would have been given by a man I had never met and had watch die.

Over the next two years I would fly various models of the Firefly, but spent by far the most hours on the M260. Most of my work was in post-production testing, which involved the aircraft's first flight after roll-out from the factory and ground tests. I'd never before flown an aircraft with no hours yet logged

---

5.   The avalanche is a flick roll performed at the top of a loop.

in its servicing record. The test schedule was flown over two sorties, the first solo and the second with a FTO. The aim of the tests was to fly round the full flight envelope, including a thirty-second inverted portion, and check airborne engine performance. Any anomalies would be noted and fixed before delivery to the customer; these were rare. A third sortie was to get the radio compass and nav. aids fully checked out. I did this by visiting a company twenty minutes' flying time away at Leeds-Bradford airport – a pleasant afternoon out!

During the competition for the university air squadron and AEF contract, the MOD, as was their wont, moved the goalposts. A more recent anthropometric survey was brought into play, and doubts were raised about the Firefly's ability to meet the new criteria for maximum sitting height. After clarification it was deemed that 'something must be done'.

As the seat was on top of the wing main spar it couldn't be lowered. So the only other way to go was to raise the canopy height to give more head room. The design office came up with the required shape and the Swiss canopy manufacturer was asked to provide an estimated cost. But there were aerodynamic and performance implications that needed testing before a final commitment was made. Accordingly, a fibreglass shape was produced and fixed over a standard canopy. It wasn't totally transparent so Don ended up flying around with a limited view of the outside world while the numbers were taken and crunched.

The upshot was that the order for the new canopy shape was confirmed and deliveries started. I got involved at this stage, when we could confirm the effects of the new shape and make any changes to the aircraft manual that were necessary. Although the new canopy was noticeably more bulbous, it had only a marginal effect on handling and performance. I suggested that we check it met the new requirement using real bodies. I knew a couple of test pilots at Boscombe Down who had longer than usual backs, and received company clearance to take the demonstrator with its new canopy there and fly with them.

The first guinea pig was my old friend John Thorpe, who was quite impressed with the handling and performance of the Firefly M260. More importantly, his head clearance, wearing a standard RAF helmet, was satisfactory – even with negative-g applied. I flew with four other Boscombe Down aircrews who had longer than average back lengths; all went well with three of them. The other could not prevent his helmet hitting the canopy under negative-g conditions. However, his back length turned out to be exceptional and beyond the stated requirement. I passed the results up the line.

In early 1977 we decided that we should be present at the Paris Air Show at Le Bourget in June. I worked up a display and got out the maps. On 10 June, Jon Poole and I set off for 'Gay Paree', via Lydd airport on the English south coast, where we refuelled and cleared customs. We arrived at Le Bourget, north-east of Paris, in the afternoon. That kicked off two days of negotiating French red tape and getting my display approved. We were staying in a hotel in the centre of the capital and used the Metro to get to and fro every day. It worked surprisingly well.

The show started on 14 June and would run until the 22nd. I started my five-minute display slot after holding over a railway marshalling yard south-east of the airfield. While holding there at 1,500ft I inverted the aeroplane to make sure there was nothing loose in the cockpit with me. On one day, after a heavy rainstorm, I got soaked when several litres of the wet stuff fell on me from the innards of the aircraft!

There was only one day when I could not fly my display due to the cloud base being below my allowed minimum. The F-16 that had preceded me had done his display in a thunderstorm and kept disappearing into the dark, rolling cloud. That had given me the motivation to give it a go. But without the benefit of the F-16's lively handling qualities, sparkling roll rate and HUD, I felt that I just couldn't push my luck. Later the head of the Flying Control Committee commended my decision. Participating in the Paris Air Show was an experience I had never imagined I would get.

One of the limitations of the Firefly was its less than fighter-like rate of roll. Flick rolls, effectively short-term spins, could be used to make it go around quicker, but not during day-to-day training. Moreover, constantly flick rolling the aircraft puts extra loads on the empennage that could not be easily quantified; this would reduce the aircraft's fatigue life. The lateral control system needed a boost. During our time in Paris Jon Poole had inspected the ailerons of several high-performance aerobatic machines, such as the Extra 300 and Sukhoi 26M. He had found that they were all fitted with sealing strips along the hinge line. This prevented leakage of high-pressure air from below the wing to the wing above, so reducing the local lift and thus the roll rate. We agreed that when we returned we should recommend that the company trial such a modification. We did, but nothing came of it.

I flew with Slingsbys until August 1998. I flew several different models of the T67 including the comparatively feather-light, wooden A model with its 90hp engine. But my favourite was the M200 version, which I thought was a better-balanced aircraft – meaning that the airframe and engine were more compatible. The M260 had better performance but at the expense of some of its handling qualities. In my time I did a variety of engineering and development tests but one flight stands out.

The day that CAA test pilot Bob Cole, who had introduced me to Slingsby, came to Kirbymoorside sticks in my mind. He was still interested to see whether the company had done something to remove the rare but significant spin-recovery problem following a reverse recovery input. Don flew with Bob and then we flew together.

I climbed to 12,000ft and put the Firefly M260 demonstrator into a spin to the right. After four turns I did the reverse recovery actions – stick forward first, the rudder fully to the left. Sure enough it stayed spinning. I pulled the stick back and it snapped out. So it was repeatedly recoverable and only happened at higher altitudes in spins to the right. Bob took over and did the same thing except that it didn't come out! He was counting the turns and the spin rate was building up. At 6,000ft or so he moved the stick back and then forward again. This time it stopped quite abruptly. Phew!

'I made that fourteen turns,' said Mr Cool. 'Did you?'

'Bob, I lost count at ten,' I admitted. 'Can we go back now?'

'Certainly old boy, it's all yours – I'm finished.'

I flew over 140 hours in five models of the Firefly. After I had left the employ of Messrs Slingsby, Don Headley told me that the elevator redesign, with the V-shaped cut-out I had suggested on my first day there, had been tested. It solved the spinning problem.

# 27 INTERNATIONAL TEST PILOTS' SCHOOL

The International Test Pilots' School (ITPS) had been founded in 1986 by James Giles, an ex-RAF test pilot and former ETPS fixed-wing tutor. The school was initially based at Cranfield in Bedfordshire, where it operated alongside, but separate from, the aeronautical university. After about eight years, following financial troubles, the school closed. That was the last I had heard of it.

However, in 1996 my erstwhile test-flying colleague Mervyn Evans called me. He said that, as I lived in the north of England, I might be interested in a part-time position with the resurrected ITPS, now based at the airfield at Woodford, in Cheshire. Woodford was the home of BAe's large aircraft manufacturing (once Avro), near Manchester. After Mervyn had left the RAF to become an airline pilot, he had been recruited as a consultant by ITPS – the new kid on the test-flying training block. Because he lived near Cranfield he had taken up the offer but, he told me, now that it had moved to Cheshire he could no longer manage this part-time commitment alongside his work with the airline. Hence he had sought me out to see whether I might be interested in taking up the position.

The founder of ITPS, James Giles, had joined the staff of ETPS when I was beginning my last year there. He had already started talking about the possibility of a UK-based civilian test pilots' school before I left in early 1984. He contacted me a couple of times after he had started ITPS operations, offering me a position there. But I was having a much better time in the RAF! However, a part-time consultancy position now sounded much more attractive.

The new managing director at ITPS was a Flight Test Engineer (FTE) who had worked with James in the school's first incarnation; he was a South African of Italian extraction called Giorgio Clementi. After my affirmative response, Mervyn contacted Giorgio and organised a meeting. The school's offices, classroom and briefing room were on the south side of the airfield at Woodford, adjacent to the hangars used by the BAe Company test-flying department and the local flying club. Close by was the site that, from 1924, Alliott Verdon Roe's aircraft company used to build and flight test its flying machines.

After hearing what the school wanted me to do, which was a mixture of flying and lecturing, we agreed terms of employment and I fixed dates for my first session. ITPS rented houses in nearby towns where consultants could stay overnight. As such, I could offer to attend for periods of several days to suit the progress of the students and the school syllabus – in coordination with the availability of other consultants.

The syllabus used for the long course was very similar to that of the military test-flying schools. There was also a variety of short courses on offer to attract students from international civilian aviation where, in some countries, different levels of test-flying expertise and experience were regulated by their civil aviation regulators.[1] Most students, whether FTOs, engineers or pilots, were civilian and were from many nations. However, a few were military.

I had to refresh my instructional technique, both classroom and flying, as well as update my knowledge of the latest developments in avionics, flight-control technology and aerodynamics. But the basics stayed the same, and the teaching of test techniques, stability and control in the air was still almost second nature. Unlike the military schools, ITPS did not own a fleet of aircraft. Contracts had been drawn up with several providers to allow flight time on several types of aircraft – some of these already being based at Woodford. The school had similarly arranged access to the BAe 146 Regional Jet simulator, which was also on site. Test-engineering lectures and access to engineering test facilities were also available by arrangement with BAe. For more advanced exercises there was a need to search farther afield to buy flight time on higher performance aircraft at affordable rates.

During my time with ITPS, I flew with students from several nations, including Thailand, Canada, Brazil, Indonesia, Germany, Sweden and Singapore, as well as some from the UK. I flew in several aircraft types new to me, mainly of the flying-club genre, such as the ultra-modern, Austrian-built Diamond Katana with its very quiet Rotax engine, long wings and composite construction. I also flew with students in the French Socata TB-10 Tobago – another modern European answer to the US domination of the light aviation arena. With its 180hp engine, the TB-10 was much quicker and slicker than the Katana and it could carry four people. Both aircraft handled nicely and their stalling characteristics spoke well of their design and development, as well as the contemporary drive by regulators for safety.

For multi-engined training we had periodical access to a twin-turboprop Reims-Cessna 406 Caravan II. Although not large, its cabin, which could carry up to twelve passengers, could also be equipped to carry flight-test

---

1.  This way of licensing flight-test personnel was pioneered by Germany but eventually became Europe-wide.

equipment for practical in-flight training of engineers and observers. At around 8 tons, the aircraft presented sufficient challenge and experience for a variety of handling and performance exercises, as well as experience in the handling of turboprop engines. I found that the 406 was pleasant to fly, well equipped and the engine-out handling and performance were representative enough for flight-test training. A twin-piston-engined Beech Duchess was also hired occasionally, but this much lighter twin did not add significantly to the challenge of twin-engine aircraft flight-testing techniques.

As I was also flying for Slingsby Aviation I suggested that I would be willing to approach the company to ascertain whether the school could have the use of, at agreed and contracted rates, a Firefly. This would add another dimension in that aerobatics and spinning could be safely introduced to the syllabus. On a personal level it meant I could sometimes fly a period at Kirbymoorside and then fly down to Woodford for a few days. The Firefly proved popular with the students and it gave us a chance to assess our students a little more rigorously.

It wasn't long before I noticed a distinct difference between the way ITPS and ETPS worked. Because ITPS did not receive its students in large numbers, at a fixed interval, as did ETPS – with its annual graduate courses of eighteen to twenty students – there was more opportunity for concentrated, one-on-one teaching and more flexibility with the application of the syllabus.

Much of the work was modelled on what I had done at ETPS in the early 1980s but the jet training was missing. However, in late 1996, Giorgio announced that he had drawn up a contract with the Russian aeronautical company Sukhoi Aviation for flight time on their SU-27UB dual-control air superiority, twin-jet fighter – an aircraft comparable with the American McDonnell Douglas F-15 Eagle. Five sorties of thirty minutes each would be bought, at $6,000 per hour, payable in cash! This would act as a final exercise for Capt 'Kris' Krisda of the Royal Thai Air Force, and be flown from the flight-test and development centre at Ramenskoye, 40km south of Moscow. I was to escort and supervise Kris for the week set aside for the exercise. I would also be the money man, carrying $25,000 in traveller's cheques and a couple hundred in notes.

'When I was at ETPS, the tutor had one flight during the final exercise so he could better assess the student's final report,' I said to Giorgio, more in hope than expectation.

'Sorry, Mike, we can't run to any more expense. You'll have to pick up as much as you can while you're there,' he replied.

That was a disappointment but I knew how things were. I would try to glean as much as I could about the jet from the Sukhoi engineers and test pilots. It was an exciting prospect to be actually going to Moscow and spending each day at a place I never dreamed I would visit. Ramenskoye airfield (later renamed Zhukovsky) was part of the world-renowned Gromov Flight Research Institute, founded in 1941, and the centre of Russian aeronautical research and development throughout the Cold War. The airfield at Ramenskoye is the equivalent of Edwards Air Force Base in the USA and has the longest runway in Europe; it is over 17,000ft long.

The ITPS secretary made all the arrangements for visas, travel and accommodation. I briefed Kris on what would be expected from him and we flew a few sorties in the Firefly to make sure he had a good grasp of all the test techniques he would use in his assessment of the SU-27 as a fighter/ interceptor. I pointed him in the right direction in the preparation of his test cards.

On the morning of our departure we took a taxi to Manchester airport to catch the lunch-time flight to Moscow. We flew east into the gathering darkness and once past Poland the ground lights became fewer and further apart. An hour or so later out of my window I could see a huge circle of light coming over the horizon. I had once seen a radar image of Moscow that was used in the Vulcan simulator. Now it was the same big round circle of highlights as on the radar screen, but in yellow on black, instead of green on black.

The time was approaching 11 p.m. when we landed at Sheremetyevo airport and endured the unchanging international ritual of locating our baggage, going through immigration and locating the hosts we had been briefed to meet. That proved to be easier than I had imagined. There was a man with a Sukhoi sign in non-Cyrillic script. He guided us to the car and we loaded our bags for the ride to our hotel in the centre of the city. On the journey I was surprised by the amount and nature of the brightly lit advertising hoardings, and even at this hour the traffic was heavy and seemed fairly chaotic. In the past seven years the nation had certainly absorbed capitalism in a big way.

By the time we had checked in we were both famished. I talked to the nice lady at reception about eating, but she said that all the hotel facilities were now closed. As I was about to suggest that we get our warm coats, gloves and hats to go out into the freezing night she said that there was an independent restaurant on the top floor. Result! We took the lift up nine or ten floors to the top and followed the lip-smacking smell and convivial noise. When we arrived at the door I was totally astonished to find that it was a Tex-Mex restaurant, run by Americans. As Kris had taken me to his favourite Thai eatery in Salford the previous evening, I was pleased that I could offer him something new and different.

We had been briefed to eat breakfast in the hotel and meet with our 'minders' in the main foyer at 7.30 p.m. The dining room was vast and had a large buffet of many wondrous but strange items laid out on tables arranged in a hollow square; I avoided the shredded beetroot and black bread. In the centre of the square was a burner upon which a stern Russian *babushka* was frying eggs to order. I became very amused at watching some American tourists passing their plates to her with the multiplicity of orders that those from the USA use for their morning eggs: 'easy over', 'sunny side up', 'scrambled' and so on. The *babushka* ignored all these commands and dropped the eggs on to their plates in whatever state she declared was the order of the day, her dour demeanour remaining unchanged. I mentally christened her Mrs Kruschev and imagined she had been recruited from the canteen in the KGB HQ, not far away in Gorky Street.

At the appointed hour we met up with the man from last night, Yvgeny, and a delightful lady called Ludmilla, who was to be our translator for the visit; we went out into the cold, snowy day and set off for Ramenskoye.

The journey started on a multi-lane road heading out of town; the traffic was horrendous. After about half an hour we crossed the outer Moscow ring road and headed into the monochrome countryside. Forests of silver birch lined the route and we passed through several towns. During our journey we saw numerous small stalls on the sides of the roads with well-wrapped, hardy souls selling all sorts of produce: eggs, vegetables and even wood. Was this the down side of the conversion to capitalism? Were these the folk destined to be left behind?

I spotted an airfield off to the left, but we drove straight past it; this turned out to be Bykovo – a civil–military transport base. Almost immediately after passing the end of Bykovo's runway we entered what appear to be a large industrial town. At first there were many multi-storey blocks of austere and identical apartments and then we entered an area of imposing brick institutional buildings – parts of the Gromov Flight Research Centre. That was followed by another stretch of pine forest, through which the road went straight as an arrow to the gates of the airfield. We stopped there and were asked to present our passports. At this point we picked up a cadaverous-looking individual who glared at me as he boarded our minibus. He would stay with us for most of our time at the base. Later one of the test pilots would confirm my suspicions as to his job.

'He used to be a KGB political officer. Now he is just a nuisance.'

We were driven to Sukhoi's Flight Test Department and introduced to several personnel. It was difficult to pin down their standing in the local rankings, but the test pilots were easy to recognise; one of them was Viktor Pugachyov, who had set world records in the SU-27. He and his two companions were the most relaxed in both dress and demeanour and did speak a little 'Eengleesh'. I explained through Ludmilla what we expected in the way of information and flying, and after a long interchange over coffee we came to an amicable consensus. Kris was taken away for a medical examination – this had been a mandatory pre-flight requirement in all Eastern Bloc air force operations and obviously continued into the present. That was deemed to be valid for twenty-four hours, so would cover any flying this afternoon and the next morning. Being a fit young Thai, he passed.

We spent the rest of the morning together gleaning as much technical information as we could from drawings and manuals translated into English for potential overseas sales. Just before lunch we went out to the big red and white jet. The weather was still cold and overcast, and snow lay on the ground. One thing I had not agreed with was that Kris would not be occupying the front seat; this was in line with Sukhoi policy for flights by 'paying passengers' – pilots or not. However, I did get agreement that Kris could spend time in the front seat on the ground to make his cockpit assessment.

The SU-27 was the Soviet response to the F-15 Eagle and is similar in size, weight and performance: Mach 2+, 700 knots and +9g. However, unlike the F-15 it has a fully active fly-by-wire (FBW) control system.[2] The cockpit was typically Russian in its layout and look. As ever, the background colour for all the panels was duck-egg blue, and most of the instruments were similar to those found in other Russian fighters. Some of them illustrate divergent

---

2.  Sukhoi had significant trouble in the development of their FBW system, leading to the loss of three SU-27s during testing.

design and development, which have enhancing features. For instance, I very much liked the combination on one dial of the rate of climb and descent indicator with the turn-rate needle. This meant that *in extremis* the pilot could concentrate on just one instrument to re-establish straight and level flight. Another parallel feature was a red button on the stick. When pressed this used the FBW system to put the aircraft in straight and level flight hands off. The field of view from the cockpit was not quite as good as that in the F-15, which I had flown in the USA,[3] as the canopy sill was higher. The Soviet philosophy of tight ground control of fighter intercept operations may have influenced this minor difference. However, the SU-27's performance was stated to be very much on a par with the Eagle and, in 1986, the Russian aircraft, flown by Viktor Pugachyov, had beaten the climb-to-height records set by the F-15 a decade earlier.

Kris was briefed, I checked his test cards and explained to the test pilot what he would be trying to achieve. I watched the jet start, taxi out and depart into the overcast sky, which appeared to be at about 500ft. As I stood there, the feeling I had experienced since arriving in Moscow grew stronger. I felt like a child who had managed to get into the Secret Garden: I was not supposed to be here. Would the thin man from the KGB come out and quietly spirit me away to Lubyanka jail for interrogation? The last and only time I had seen this place was back in 1986 looking at 'verticals' (satellite photographs) and trying to help the folks in the MOD's Technical Intelligence Branch identify certain equipment. In fact, the area that held most of the points of interest was visible on the other side of the main runway. I could see the open-sided shelters that they put their most secret kit under to stop, or at least inhibit, that overhead espionage activity!

During the next half-hour, I went back into the warmth and read some more about the aircraft's systems. Another admirable Russian innovation was an oxygen bottle buried in the airframe for the sole use of aiding the relight of an engine should it 'flame out' at high altitude. In most Western military jets the top of the relighting envelope is about 30–35,000ft, because there's not enough oxygen available for the job above that altitude. Granted, it is a weight penalty to carry the bottle, probably against a rare event, but it would mean

---

3.   See Chapter 32 of *Trials and Errors* by this author (The History Press, 2015).

that a descent from higher altitudes would not be necessary – a requirement that, in the wrong circumstances, could be operationally hazardous.

When Kris reappeared he had a big grin on his face and a reasonable amount of data on his cards. It was time to return to town. We stayed in the hotel that evening: Kris working on the plans for day two, whilst I relaxed as best I could. I had brought a good book.

The next morning I had to change sufficient traveller's cheques to pay for the first three sorties, so Yvgeny was to take me to a bank while Kris was driven out to the airfield for flight number two. We set off into the traffic and soon pulled up and parked. We walked to a bank and rang the bell for entry. Access proved to be much more difficult than in the West. Eventually we ended up at a counter and Yvgeny asked the lady for $12,000. This initiated a conversation in Russian, the tone of which clearly communicated to me that this request had been instantly despatched into the 'too difficult' box. A man appeared and more words were exchanged. The upshot was that we could exchange $6,000 worth of cheques. So we did. I stuffed the notes into my pockets and we went back to the car.

'What now?' I asked.

'We go to exchange bureau,' Yvgeny replied.

Soon we were stood outside a kiosk in the street; this was, surprisingly, the exchange bureau. Inside, behind the window, sat a diminutive lady reading a book. We were stood immediately in front of her. She continued reading. I had heard that Russians are a literary lot, but this was taking it too far! Yvgeny spoke. She looked up and then very slowly and deliberately marked her page in the tome, put it down and said, '*Da?*' Yvgeny explained that we needed $6,000, I showed her the cheques, she gave me a pen, I signed, she took them, and then I received the crisp greenbacks. I now had $12,000 in my pockets. And it had been much easier than using a Russian bank!

When we got back to the car I indicated to Yvgeny that I was concerned at carrying so much cash. He smiled and pulled an object from his leather jacket pocket; it was a revolver.

'Is it loaded?' I asked, nervously.

'*Da,*' he said, with a reassuring smile.

I had to do this money-running exercise three more times, each occasion accompanied by my armed outrider – the reassuring smile always in place.

Our time in Russia passed quickly. The five sorties were completed a day before our booked departure so Kris and I had the opportunity to play tourists for a day. We strolled from our hotel the few hundred yards to Red Square. My sense of disbelief heightened again. I remembered watching grainy black and white TV pictures of those impressive, and somewhat scary, Soviet May Day military parades with the worthies of the party standing on the balcony of the Lenin Mausoleum. We went over, but it was closed – perhaps Len was not in? Opposite the Mausoleum was a vast, three-storey building stretching virtually the whole length of the square: an enormous shopping mall still known by its Soviet era abbreviation GUM. This stands for *Glávnyj Universálnyj Magazín* (Main Universal Store) and was the state-run emporium for Muscovites. Entering the place I was immediately struck by two things: its immense glass roof and the plethora of Western goods on sale. Most of the customers seemed to be fur-coated Russian ladies in long leather boots, often carrying expensive handbags. I wondered whether they knew or even cared about those desperate folk we had seen freezing on the roadsides with their pitiable and meagre goods for sale.

As we walked across the vast, cobbled square towards the unlikely colourful construction that is St Basil's Cathedral, I thought of that young and rather foolhardy German aviator Matthias Rust, who had flown his Cessna from the Finland and landed nearby in 1987. As we got closer to the cathedral I could see that some of its gaudy exterior was in need of a little TLC. It was made of bricks and quite a few were missing. However, it was still an outstanding statement of Eastern Orthodox architecture. When we entered I was surprised how small it now seemed, but the interior decoration was as extravagant as the exterior.

We walked on, around the vast red walls of the Kremlin, once the royal palace for the Tsars, but now a palace for those who governed by a different set of rules – but with a similar outcome for the man and woman in the streets and villages of the Motherland. It wasn't long before we came across a street market and I bought the obligatory set of Russian dolls. I chose one with a political theme: senior communist personages fitting inside each other – a veritable communist collective!

We arrived back in Manchester late the following day where it was typically overcast but a good deal warmer. I sent Kris off to write his report and told him that I would be back in two weeks and expect it to be complete by then. It was, and I set about reading and marking it. Giorgio was anxious to know how we had got on.

'To be honest, Giorgio, it was not as good a service as the military guys at the main TP schools get. They are allowed five hours, not two and half, and they get to sit in the front seat and act as first pilot. On top of that, the limitations brought about by the language barrier are usually absent. But, it is good that you can offer a high-performance aircraft experience before the students graduate.'

The report on the SU-27 was acceptable, but not comprehensive, and I advised Giorgio that Kris should not be given a full graduation certificate but rather a certificate of attendance. Moreover, I advised that we should let the Thai Air Force leadership know that he should be closely supervised in the flight-test role for two years. This was done, although I think it called for a certain amount of tactful negotiation.

I was back in Moscow within a year, this time with two Royal Canadian Air Force officers: pilot Capt Eric Volstadt and FTE Capt Earle. This time we were going to be hosted by Mikoyan and the students would be flying the MiG-29 from the company's flight-test centre at Lukhovitsy, 145km south-east of Moscow. The Mikoyan MiG-29 (NATO reporting name: 'Fulcrum') is a twin-engine jet fighter aircraft designed in the Soviet Union. Developed by the Mikoyan design bureau as an air superiority fighter during the 1970s, the MiG-29, along with the larger Sukhoi Su-27, was developed to counter new American fighters such as the McDonnell Douglas F-15 Eagle and the General Dynamics F-16 Fighting Falcon. The MiG-29 entered service with the Soviet Air Force in 1982. It has performance similar to both these Western types and the SU-27, but less combat radius.

While originally orientated towards air combat, many MiG-29s are multi-role fighters capable of performing a number of different operations, and are commonly armed with a range of air-to-surface armaments and precision munitions. The MiG-29 has been manufactured in several major variants, including the multirole MiG-29M and the navalised MiG-29K. Following the dissolution of the Soviet Union, the militaries of a number of former Soviet republics have continued to operate the MiG-29, the largest of which is the Russian Air Force. The MiG-29 has also been a popular export aircraft; more than thirty nations either operate or have operated the aircraft to date, India being one of the largest export customers for the type.

Our arrival at Sheremetyevo airport became interesting, and not a little worrying, when I got to the immigration booth just ahead of the Canadians. The studied, steely glare of the folks who do that job was deployed in my direction. I waited to receive my passport back but it remained behind the desk. The glare was withdrawn as the uniformed man turned and beckoned to a subordinate. The latter then disappeared and audible mutterings started up behind me.

*I wonder whether they've found out that I once had orders to lob nuclear weapons at their allies?* I thought.

After a while another uniformed man pushed his way through the now discontented queue and pulled me back into the no-man's-land of the airport arrivals area.

'Do you speak English?' I said, wishing instantly that I had learnt this question in Russian. 'What is the problem?'

'Yes, a leetle – your visa ees no valid,' he replied.

I looked at it. By now my companions were alongside me. They looked at their visas. The problem was that the start date was tomorrow – two hours away.

'It's only two hours before the date, can't you let us through?' I asked, 'We are here on business and going directly to the Cosmos Hotel.'

The upshot was that we could wait until after midnight or pay a fine of $300.

'Will you take traveller's cheques?' I asked, waving a bunch under his nose.

'Follow me,' was the reply, more of an order than an invitation.

We set off at quite a pace into the gloomy bowels of the terminal building, ending up in front of a window behind which was the inevitable lady reading a book. My authoritative escort was able to get her attention immediately; I silently took my hat off to him. Information was exchanged, pieces of paper were produced, signatures obtained and I handed over a $500 cheque and held my hand out for the change. I was pleasantly surprised when it appeared and pocketed it quickly.

I was returned to the sanctuary of no-man's-land and my travelling companions, from where we were guided through the now empty passage past the immigration desk. It was not long before we met up with our Russian 'minders', who had been passed the message that we were delayed. A similar night-time ride through a quieter Moscow followed and we were dropped at the entrance to the huge curved building of the Cosmos Hotel. By the time we had checked in, located our rooms and then the bar for a nightcap, our visas were valid and it was soon time for bed.

Because the drive to the airfield would take more than two hours, we were up at 6 a.m. for breakfast. The choice of food was not much to our tastes, but we had enough to keep us going. The car arrived at 6.30 a.m. and we set off on a journey through the environs of the Russian capital, across the outer ring road and on into the monotonous countryside, lost in our own thoughts. On the way out of town, while I was musing on the mediocre hotel breakfast, I spotted a McDonald's. It struck me instantly that this American eatery might be a good location for breakfast; I would suggest it to the 'minders'. The students had received some information on the MiG-29 that had some very amusing and mysterious mistranslations, so they were able to use the journey to revise this and their test plans.

Our reception at Lukhovitsy was similar to that I had received at Sukhoi: warm and friendly tempered by the language gap. One of the test pilots was Roman Taskaev, who had been the junior member of the Russian team at the 1986 Farnborough Air Show. He remembered me and we smiled broadly at each other. I asked about Anatoly Kvochur and he told me that he was now flying for Sukhoi. He had not been there during my visit. We got down to business after the welcome coffee and agreed a programme for the week. Two aircraft would be available. Perfunctory medical examinations followed and then the Canadians were fitted out with their flying equipment.

After lunch we were driven out to the flight line, accompanied by the obligatory retired KGB political officer disguised as 'security'. As we drove around I counted ninety-two MiG-29s sitting out on concrete areas under covers.

*Sales not going so well?* I wondered silently.

On the second morning I told the driver and translator lady that we would stop at McDonald's for breakfast. When we did I paid for all our meals and drinks and it cost me barely $10!

The week passed fairly well to plan. The weather was mostly overcast but the MiG pilots flew all the sorties; however, it was impossible for the students to assess the jet in the visual circuit. I would be telling Giorgio that, while not a total loss of time and money, these assessment sorties had their limitations and we should seek a better solution.

As we had completed the test plans with a day to spare I suggested that we have a day's sightseeing. From my seventh floor room I could see an intriguing upswept monument across the dual carriageway. It was the Cosmonauts' Memorial Museum and we found our way across to it. It was a fascinating visit with many interesting space artefacts on show. One particularly bizarre object was the stuffed dog that purported to be Laika, who became one of the first animals in space, and the first animal to orbit the Earth. Laika, a stray dog from the streets of Moscow, was selected to be the occupant of the Soviet spacecraft Sputnik 2, which was launched into outer space on 3 November 1957.

After taking refreshment in the café we then walked to a vast open area that had odd-looking pavilions in it. This turned out to be the Russian National Exhibition Park and, at a distance, looked grand and imposing. However, up close it had an air of decaying grandeur. Large, column-fronted halls stood around the grounds, with titles declaring their purpose – Agriculture, Industry, etc. – or origin – Georgia, Siberia and so on. There was one dedicated to Space and Aeronautics so we stepped inside. It was with shock that we discovered hundreds of what would these days be called pop-up shops down each side of the wide central aisle. All these commercial outlets seemed to be selling electrical goods: TVs, fridges, washing machines and computers. We walked down to the end of these mini-emporia to receive an even bigger shock. There in the gloom and detritus were various spacecraft and rocket bodies; I recognised a Soyuz and a Vostok, both early manned space capsules. They were just lying haphazardly on the dirty ground. I guessed that in its communist heyday these wondrous objects had hung from the ceiling of this vast hall, as proud symbols of Soviet ascendancy in the space race. This decline to the status of leftover rubbish seemed to be a commentary on events since 1989.

That evening we ate in the slowly rotating Seventh Heaven Restaurant in the Ostankino TV Tower – the tallest freestanding structure in the world for nine years, built in 1967.[4] At about 1,200ft above the ground, the view from our table of the lights of Moscow was amazing. The overcast was just above us and we could see the very thick layers of rime ice that had formed on all the small aerials and other protrusions just below the windows. It was a fitting finale to what would be my last visit to Russia.

In October 1997 Giorgio persuaded me to become the chief instructor at ITPS on a full-time basis. I told him that I could accept the position only on a six-month contract and that he should recruit someone to take over in the following April. In addressing the access to jets, Giorgio had found two civilian organisations that were willing to allow us to buy flight time in two-seat Hunters: Beachy Head Aviation[5] in South Africa and Grace Aire Inc. in Texas, USA (more of the latter later).

---

4.  The restaurant closed after the disastrous fire on 27 August 2000, which killed four people.
5.  Beachy Head Aviation would be renamed Thunder City three years later.

However, before we became more involved with these companies Giorgio had told me he had found a Jet Provost (JP) trainer for sale and had bought it. It was at North Weald, north-east of London, not far from Stansted airport. I knew the place well, after my time with the Harvard Team that was based there. He said that we would go to collect it together. On Wednesday, 19 March, we were flown to North Weald in the Cessna 406 and met up with the man who was going to hand over the JP to us. He was an ex-RAF instructor whom I had met several times before – Bob Thompson. It turned out that Giorgio had arranged for Bob to fly with me for about forty-five minutes before the delivery flight to Woodford. The JP was a Mark 5 registered G-VIVM and wearing the very familiar livery of ETPS. It was no less than XS 230, the second prototype JP-5 that I had flown many times at Boscombe Down! Bob and I flew it for forty-five minutes; it was oh so familiar – like an old friend that I hadn't seen for years. Bob sat there and just watched as I stalled it, did some aerobatics and a few circuits and bumps.

'You enjoy your flying, don't you?' he observed, by way of a debrief.

'So I've heard,' I replied with a big grin.

When we got back to Woodford the JP was put in the hangar. I don't remember it coming out again before I left ITPS.

Beachy Head Aviation, based at Capetown's international airport, had been founded by a wealthy South African pilot called Mike Beachy Head. It was Mike's aim to set up a base for his collection of high-performance jet aircraft. He had already purchased all three of the ex-RAE Farnborough Buccaneers – aircraft I had flown for many years as a test pilot. He had also bought several Hawker Hunters, among them a two-seat Hunter T8C, and two Lightnings. In late 1998 two of the Buccaneers and the Hunter T8 were flying from Capetown. The rest of his fleet was still in the UK being refurbished, but the first Lightning was en route by sea.

Giorgio arranged a trip for both of us to visit Beachy Head Aviation, draw up a contract and discover how best we might benefit from the opportunity to use a relatively high-performance jet for our students. Licensing me to operate the jet was another factor that needed to be sorted out.

We flew out from Manchester and arrived at around noon. Giorgio still had family in the area so he dropped me off at a very pleasant hotel called The Vineyard, from whose garden there was a great view of the slopes of Table Mountain. Once in my room I couldn't resist testing the southern hemisphere vortex theory by closely watching the water run down the plughole of my shower: it *did* turn clockwise! As previously arranged, Mike Beachy Head came to the hotel to meet me and invited me to join him for an evening out. During that time, some of it spent in the up-market Waterfront area, I learnt that Mike had started in the ground transportation business and expanded that into an air freight company. He had been a private pilot and then gained his commercial licence before getting into the classic jet business. He had already flown many hours on the Hunter and was progressing well in the Buccaneer.

I spent most of the next day getting my commercial licence ratified by the South African Civil Aviation Authority (SACAA); it was fairly straightforward except that they insisted I take a radio procedures test. I passed. After that I spent time back at the hangar and offices of Beachy Head Aviation looking at their technical set-up and checking the aircraft documentation of the Hunter. It was an ex-RAF T8C, previously XL 598 now registered ZU-ATH, painted, like the two Buccaneers, all-over gloss black. I was pleased to see that the SACAA had allowed the continuation of all the military service documentation and procedures; indeed they had insisted on it. I particularly checked that the ejection seat cartridges were in date and that the pilots' parachutes had been removed, serviced and reinstalled within the previous year. I then sat in the Hunter and found that it was virtually unchanged from all those RAF two-seat Hunters I had flown in the past. It looked smart and I felt good about flying it here.

Giorgio asked me privately if he should go ahead and do a deal; I advised him to do so. He and Mike withdrew to an office and came out accompanied by beaming smiles. I was then told that I would be returning during the first two weeks of September to fly with four Indonesian Air Force students; we would be hoping to fly two sorties per day over five working days. Having said our farewells, Giorgio and I set off to visit the SAAF Flight Test Centre at Overberg near Bredasdoorp, just a little under 200km east of Capetown, where Giorgio had some old colleagues from his test-flying days in South Africa. On the way there we passed fields of ostriches and went down a seaside road where there were penguins on the rocks on one side and baboons on the rocks on the other. We stayed overnight in a delightful small hotel overlooking the beach in a charming seaside village called Arniston. Before dinner Giorgio showed me the best whale-spotting place. It was on a rocky promontory, near where there was a large board with pictures of the species of whales that might be seen as they passed from the Indian Ocean into the South Atlantic. Among them was a variety called Right Whales; we didn't spot any – not even the wrong whales!

On Monday, 31 August 1998, I boarded an Air France Airbus 340 to Capetown, via Johannesburg. It was an overnight flight and arrived, after a short stop at Jo'burg, in the mid morning. The company had arranged accommodation for me and the four students at a guest house north of Capetown, overlooking Robben Island[6] and, across the bay, Table Mountain. I had arrived three days ahead of the students so that I could become fully qualified to fly with them.

I flew the Hunter twice before they arrived, once with Mr Beachy Head and once with the SACAA check pilot, Robby Robinson. During that sortie he had put me through my paces, with the usual raft of manoeuvring, practice emergency drills and a practice flame-out approach at Overberg, followed by a few circuits there. After our return to Capetown, Robby signed me up. I was now legally, physically and mentally prepared for the arrival of the student test pilots and engineers.

Over the following week we flew twelve sorties. Unfortunately I was unable to fly any high-altitude sectors of the planned test schedules. On the first trip, as we climbed above 25,000ft the cabin pressurisation failure warning sounded. I reported the fault after landing, but the only cure would involve grounding the jet for several days – time that we could not afford to lose. Mike Beachy Head was very apologetic, but I assured him that we could achieve most of our planned flying at altitudes below 25,000ft. The weather remained good throughout our stay: it was spring in the southern hemisphere, although the winds did get up on a couple of days, which was normal, apparently, at this time of year. One slightly disorientating thing I took some time to get used to was that the sun at noon was north of the vertical and not south of it. But the good visibility, reliable compass and the excellent radar coverage from Cape ATC ensured that I didn't get lost!

On our daily minibus ride to the airport we passed through neighbourhoods where the rich folks lived, invariably behind razor-wire-topped walls and large gates; further on we passed crowds of coloured men waiting for buses. The driver asked us to lock the doors every time and he tried his best never to

---

6.  Robben Island was the location of the prison where Nelson Mandela had spent twenty-seven years of his life. He was the President of the Republic of South Africa at the time of my visits there.

stop near these crowds. Next we passed huge collections of shacks around the airport boundaries. The contrasts were stark. The Rainbow Nation still had a long way to go to achieve true equality.

At the end of the week I had to enter several technical faults in the Hunter's engineering logbook. These included the pressurisation failure and one electrical generator not working. Because of the good weather I had decided to continue to fly with these technical issues, so that we could get the job done. When I returned I told Giorgio that unless Beachy Head could improve its reliability, or offer another two-seat Hunter as a back-up, we should not use them again.

Before I left the employ of ITPS the erstwhile CTP at Woodford, another 'Robby' Robinson, another ex-ETPS tutor, took over as chief instructor from me. After I moved on I would still have contact with the school, because my next flying job was with the other organisation with a Hunter that Giorgio had approached – Grace Aire Inc.

# 28 TEXAS

In November 1997 I went to Grace Aire at its HQ in Corpus Christi, Texas, to discover what was on offer to ITPS and whether any arrangement would be a workable solution. Before I left the UK I requested information on the aircraft and the legal requirements for flying in the USA as a civilian commercial pilot. It appeared that I would need to offer my UK licence for inspection by the US Federal Aviation Authority (FAA) as well as proof of my flying experience.

On Monday, 1 December, I arrived at Corpus Christi airport after a long journey, located my hire car and went to the nearby Drury Inn hotel. The next day I found the Grace Aire offices at the airport. There I met the part-time Ops Officer, Richard Wessling, an ex-US Marine Corps Harrier pilot; the delightful mature lady secretary, Charlsie; and the founder and CEO Dr Terry Elder. I discussed how I envisaged ITPS could use the Hunter for a variety of test-flying training events. One of the most exciting options was that this Hunter had, like those I had flown at ETPS, been fitted with spin panels. This offered a realistic possibility for our students to experience swept-wing spinning exercises – an activity with which I had some experience.[1]

The Grace Aire Hunter was an ex-RAF T7 (XL 617 now registered as N617NL). It was painted all-over red, with 'No Fear' written on the nose. It was being cherishingly cared for by a British ex-RAF mechanic called Alan Phillips, who had actually worked on XL 617 when it was based at RAF Brawdy. On disposal in 1989 the aircraft was bought by the Northern Lights Company of Canada and it was refurbished and modified for use in test-flying and flight-test training. Terry Elder had bought it from that company when they went out of business.

Before I could fly I had to get clearance from the FAA to operate as a commercial pilot on what was classified as an experimental-class aircraft within the USA. Terry arranged for me to visit their local Flight Standards Officer in Houston. I flew there using a regular local flight and hired a car to get to the FAA offices. There I met a very amenable gentleman who thoroughly examined my CAA licence, and my latest RAF and civilian logbooks; he was a man of few words. However, when I explained what I was aiming to achieve he became much more animated and interested. After some discussion about how I should arrange for use of the south Texas airspace he produced an official document that gave me permission to operate the Hunter in US airspace for one year in accordance with the FAA limitations already placed on the aircraft. As yet I was not sure exactly what those were, but I would find out.

Two days later I was ready to fly. It would be with a FAA-approved check pilot: a man called Tom Delashaw, who I would later learn was a veteran of two tours in Vietnam, holder of the American DFC, and had many hours on the Lockheed F-104 Starfighter. I quickly learnt that Tom was back in his favourite jet because he had become one of a new team that flew two civilian-registered, ex-Canadian AF Lockheed F-104s – unsurprisingly the team was called 'The Starfighters'. Tom was a stocky individual, so strapping into the Hunter together required a bit of coordination to avoid elbows impacting unwanted places. One of the differences between operating in the

---

1.  Three years as a tutor at ETPS. (See *Trials and Errors* by this author. (The History Press, 2015), Chapter 31.)

UK and the USA is the language and terminology used on the radio. I asked Tom to make all the radio calls on this first sortie, which he was happy to do. I would listen and learn.

Although well modernised, with state-of-the-art navigation kit and radios, much of the basic Hunter cockpit was still there. I felt instantly at home and was surprised how much I still remembered. Once cleared for departure I took off, cleaned up and climbed out to the south-west of Corpus. The large US Navy training base at Kingsville, operating T-45 Hawks, was the biggest 'avoid area' and we worked with the Corpus Christi radar controllers to help us keep out of trouble. After climbing to 10,000ft I showed Tom a few of my aerobatics and I went through a couple of emergency drills. He then took over and flew the Hunter while he showed me some of the more recognisable ground features, to help me find my way about without violating too many no-go zones or Mexican airspace, not that far away to the south.

He explained that it was normal procedure to use a small airport south-west of Corpus Christi for visual circuit-pattern training. That municipal airport was near the town of Kleburg; it had a 6,000ft-long runway and a non-directional beacon. However, that was a navigation aid we were not equipped to receive, so I would have to locate Kleburg when I couldn't see it using radials and distances from two local VOR beacons. Tom knew where it was and flew us there, flew one circuit and then handed the jet over to me. The only slight problem I had was that the runway was only half the width of most runways. This gave an optical illusion that made it appear much further away than it really was. However, it was just a case of recalibrating my head. We flew twice that day and then Tom signed me up as FAA approved. The following day I asked Terry to fly in the left seat so that I could refamiliarise myself with flying the Hunter from the right-hand seat.

The aircraft had suffered no unserviceabilities throughout and all the safety equipment was in date. It was clear that Alan Phillips treated the Hunter with a lot of technical TLC. When I got back to the UK I told Giorgio that I was very happy with the prospect of operating with Grace Aire. He said that he would contact the company and make a booking for me and the two RCAF students to fly the Hunter in the following February.

A factor unknown to us beforehand was that Terry Elder also owned a Nanchang CJ-6 two-seat piston-engined trainer. I asked if we might use that for spin work-up exercises and suggested he calculate a rate per flying hour. Terry agreed that we could use it and that he would send the appropriate contract details to ITPS. We decided that he would check me out when I returned with the students.

I flew back to Corpus Christi on 3 February 1998; the two students were due to follow three days later. The first thing I had to do was arrange the procedures for the spinning exercises. The US Navy controllers at Kingsville were very helpful in telling me how to operate from 40,000ft down to 25,000ft in the 'warning areas' over the Gulf of Mexico. I would, they said, need to work with Houston radar controllers and they would coordinate us with any other military manoeuvring traffic in the same area. Effectively it was similar to working with London military radar in the south of the UK.

However, my first flight back at Corpus Christie would be with Terry Elder in the CJ-6. Although the aircraft has a similar appearance to the early Russian Yak trainers, it is an indigenous Chinese design. It has an aluminium semi-monocoque fuselage and wings with an outboard section that have a distinct dihedral. The Grace Aire CJ-6 was powered by a 260hp Zhuzhou Huosai HS-6 radial piston engine. The CJ-6 makes extensive use of pneumatics to control the gear and flap extension/retraction, operate the brakes and start the engine. An engine-driven air pump recharges the system; however, if the air pressure is too low to start the engine then the on-board air tank can be recharged by an external source. If an external source is not available then the engine can be started by hand, by swinging the propeller. The pilots sit in tandem under a full-length transparency, with two sliding canopies for access after climbing via a fixed step on to the wing roots.

Terry showed me round the external checks then we climbed aboard. Alan had already completed the 'pull-through' of the prop to make sure that nothing was pooled in the cylinders that could cause a hydraulic lock and subsequent damage on start. The cockpit was roomy and well laid out; the instruments had all been 'Westernised' and were in familiar units. When I had checked that all the switches and levers were correctly set I gave Alan the wind-up signal and depressed the starter button. There was a pop and hiss as the air passed from the reservoir to the engine starter drive, the propeller turned, I switched the magnetos on and the engine soon fired up. The usual hesitant start of a round motor was soon replaced with a smooth idle at around 1,000rpm. The oil and air pressures were satisfactory and we called for our taxi clearance and waved the chocks away. The tricycle undercarriage made it easy to see ahead, although the 6ft of nose in front meant that I lost sight of the taxiway centreline about 20ft in front of me. The CJ-6 uses a brake handle on the stick, similar to a bike brake handle, with differential braking controlled by the rudder. The brakes worked smoothly and it was easy to turn the aircraft to follow the taxiways towards the runway.

Once we had checked the engine and magneto drops we were ready for departure. When we had got the clearance to go I ran on to the runway and, remembering my days many years earlier on the de Havilland Vampire, also equipped with pneumatic brakes, I did not stop to try to hold power against the brakes – I just upped the power to full throttle. The CJ-6 accelerated readily with very little need to use rudder to offset the power. We lifted off at about 70 knots after a ground roll of around 1,300ft.

At 90 knots the little Chinese trainer climbed at about 1,200ft per minute to 4–5,000ft and then the rate tailed off a bit. Apart from looking around outside, the main thing to watch was the cylinder head temperature (CHT), using the gill shutters to control it; this was done with a knob on the forward instrument panel. We levelled off at 6,000ft to carry out some stalls and aerobatics. The stalls were very normal, with no significant wing drop and a recognisable pre-stall buffet – ideal for a basic trainer. The stall speeds were 65–67 knots clean and about 5 knots slower with the flaps down.

Then we went on to spin. Just as with the stall, the spin did require a concerted effort to achieve using the standard stick back and full rudder entry technique at 70 knots. However, I did find that the aircraft was trying to come out of the spin on its own after approximately two turns. At this point a very nose-low spiral ensued and I had to pull out quickly to avoid excessive speed. I tried another entry at the point of stall with in–spin aileron and that held the CJ in the spin longer. It always recovered as soon as any recovery action was taken. I didn't think that was great for a trainer as it could give a false impression to the students that all aeroplanes would recover easily from a spin. It would be interesting to see what our test-pilot students made of it.

Built as a military trainer, the CJ is no stranger to aerobatics and other more exhilarating forms of flying. The airframe is rated +6g to -3g and will handle all basic aerobatic manoeuvres with ease. I started with a loop from 130 knots using a +3g pull-up. The clear canopy made keeping straight easy and she went round using about 800ft of sky. After that I tried aileron rolls and found the roll rate to be a modest 120 degrees per second. I attempted a slow roll but didn't use enough rudder the first time. The second attempt was better – as always with slow rolls you need to get to know the aeroplane before subjecting it to all that cross-controlling input! Barrel rolls were fine, although I did notice that there was a downward drift in altitude during sequenced aerobatics.

It was now time to go back to the airport. The main concern during the descent, like in all piston-engine aircraft, is maintaining proper CHT, so use of the gill shutters came into play again. Once in the pattern the main thing I had to remember was that if a radial engine is going to quit, it's most likely going to be during a power change. On the way down I had found that the CJ-6 did not glide particularly well, so I planned to fly the circuit patterns fairly close in for safety. Downwind I dropped the landing gear below the limit speed of 120 knots and let the airspeed fall to around 80 knots. I made a continuous turn on to the final approach, initially at 80 knots, then I didn't select the single split flap until I was established on finals at about 300ft. Now it was time to let the speed decay until I had 70 knots over the threshold of the runway. The touchdown at idle power was around 55 knots and the CJ's robust trailing link gear helped achieve fairly passable touchdowns. An unusual type for my logbook, I looked forward to flying the Chinese trainer some more.

By the time the two students arrived I had flown the Hunter three times, including two stall and spin sorties. The procedures and navigation to and from the specified operating areas had proved not to be too demanding and Houston Radar was as helpful as advertised. After flying the students in the CJ-6 we started work in the Hunter, initially doing some lateral and directional stability and control exercises. Those two sorties were followed by four spinning ones during which I managed to successfully initiate three inverted spins. However, in the last of those I heard a thump from somewhere in the aircraft. I was not sure what it was but the engine was operating normally. I told Houston that I was returning to Corpus Christi but did not declare an emergency. The aircraft was handling normally – I just wanted to get back and check if anything had come off the airframe.

Ever since then I have regretted that I did not say on the radio: 'Houston – we have a problem'![2]

---

2. For those who might not recall, these were the words used by US astronaut and commander of Apollo 13 Jim Lovell, when he had to report an on-board explosion in the service module of the spacecraft.

Sure enough a small fairing near the ventrally mounted airbrake was missing and there was a witness mark nearby where it had impacted the tail cone. Nothing terribly serious but that was the end of the ITPS exercise.

The next time I would fly with Grace Aire was at the beginning of my time as the chief pilot (a bit of a grand title as there were only two of us). Before I departed in the spring of 1998 Terry Elder had persuaded me to consider helping him to win a contract with the USAF Test Pilots' School to carry out spinning exercises for their student test pilots. I agreed and that led to a bizarre teleconference call between Texas, California and me in a phone box in Macclesfield. I put the operator's case and assured the school that we could provide at least one sortie per student per course using the facilities at Edwards Air Force Base. A question arose about back-up and Terry was able to tell them that he had a second spin-capable Hunter due to come out of refurbishment later that year. This was news to me!

Later Terry built on the experience and asked if I would be interested in moving to Texas to help on a permanent basis. As my commitment to ITPS was due to end in April I said that I would give it some thought. An important factor now came into play. Terry Elder, who was a medical doctor and committed Christian, was aiming to get income from his Hunters in order to fund medical missions into Central America. He had learned that I was not only an experienced Hunter test-flying instructor but that I also had displayed a Hunter in the UK and Europe. This matched with another income stream he had envisaged: through commercial sponsorship of his aircraft for air shows. This was a huge marketplace for brand exposure in the USA.

As Linda and I were also committed Christians, we felt that we were being led for all the right reasons to take up this job offer. We prayed a lot, as did many of our friends, and in the summer I called Terry and accepted. Despite some difficulties in getting the right sort of visa, everything else fell right into place and we moved into our house, 3102 Seahawk Drive, Corpus Christi, in November 1998.

One tragic thing had occurred between my acceptance and the move. On 18 June 1998 the second two-seat Hunter, which Terry was in the process of buying from the company that had restored it, was written off in a fatal accident. Even more tragic was the fact that this was on its first flight after a twelve-year rebuild to a very high standard by a man I would later meet called Ed Stead. This Hunter (N745WT) had been built by mating the cockpit and forward fuselage of T8 WT 745 with a Swiss Mark 51 Hunter wings, fuselage and tail. On that fatal first flight a sticking fuel gauge had led to the pilot, John Chilvers, a retired USAF lieutenant colonel, running out of fuel only a mile or so from touchdown. He ejected too late. Terry was obviously distraught, but he later acquired an ex-Peruvian Air Force two seat Hunter to give us the back-up we needed.

We worked hard over the following two years to gain US Department of Defense contracts and air show sponsors. We came close on a few occasions: Triumph Motorcycles were very interested, as was another US motorcycle manufacturer. The USAF Test Pilots' School withdrew its tender after the loss of the second jet. We initially maintained a low level of income with more training for ITPS and annual currency and check flights for pilots with FAA licences in the experimental jet category. Tom Delashaw recommended me to become a FAA check pilot, colloquially known as LOA (letter of authorisation). I did practise my air show routine, but on the day that I was scheduled to fly to another airport to gain my US Display Authorisation the Hunter failed me.

During the take-off roll at Corpus Christi, using the shorter 6,000ft southerly runway at about 100 knots, a sudden high-frequency vibration started and I felt that the acceleration had reduced. Initially, suspecting a wheel or tyre problem, I aborted the take-off. Throttle closed, flap fully down, brake parachute deployed and maximum braking applied – all more or less simultaneously. I called, 'Aborting take-off!' on the radio and managed to stop before the end and roll clear of the runway. I shut the engine down and opened the canopy. A fire vehicle arrived and I signalled that I did not need dousing in foam. I put the safety pins back in the seat, clambered out of the cockpit and dropped the 6ft to the ground. By now Alan Phillips had arrived with a tractor. When I looked up the jet pipe there were the white streaks characteristic of partial engine disintegration: the melted metal of compressor blades deposited in the hot exhaust pipe. We later noticed that a small screw in a panel in the nose was missing and Alan found it in the engine. This tiny object had wiped out several compressor blades and the thrust of the engine had been vastly reduced.

During 1999 things went from bad to worse for the business. We decided to sell the Hunters and try to raise money through working up the charitable arm of Grace Aire in the hope of being able to support more medical missions. My staff training now came into play as I wrote papers to be sent to folk like Bill Gates and other notable 'givers to good causes'. But it was all to no avail. Throughout this period our faith was severely tested. We had believed that the blend of our Christian beliefs and my experience as an aviator had been drawn together for this purpose.

Living in Texas was a unique experience and stories from then, outside the flying, could fill another book. But in the end our visa and income both expired; it was time to leave. But where could we go? The price of a reasonably located house in the UK was now out of our reach. It was our eldest son that put us in touch with an estate agent in the UK who had a contact in Normandy, France, who helped folk find houses there.

On 6 June 2000, after two flights from the USA to Paris and then a train journey from there, all with no less than nine pieces of luggage, we arrived at Avranches, Lower Normandy. The American adventure was over; the French one was about to begin. I could not imagine that there would be any more flying in my life. Was it really all over?

# 29 BACK TO SQUARE ONE

Within five weeks of our arrival in *la belle France* we had closed the deal on a house. It was in the centre of a very small village and it needed quite a lot of work – new electrics, central heating, two new bathrooms and decoration. By the end of the year it was warm, cosy and very pleasant to live in.

Over the next year we started to get properly to grips with the language and the notorious French bureaucracy. We found our Norman neighbours very warm and welcoming, and we started making a circle of friends, both French and expat. We also discovered a small group of people who wanted to start an Anglophone church in Manche, the nearest existing church being in north Brittany – a three-hour round trip away. This venture, along with working on the house and garden, and our regular French lessons, kept us busy. But I was missing the flying; 2001 marked forty years since I had first flown solo. The very regular low-level overflights by French military jets such as Étendards, Mirages, Alphajets and Rafales was a double-edged sword for me: exciting to watch but engendering and reinforcing the regret that it was all over!

In the spring of 2001 I received an unexpected phone call from an old friend and colleague, Martin Mayer. He had been OC ETPS when I was Wing Commander Flying at Boscombe Down. We had also run two SETP

European symposia together and, before I had moved to the USA, I had flown as a RAF Volunteer Reserve pilot with Martin's AEF at RAF Woodvale in Lancashire. He was still there and he was ringing me with the news that the Air Cadet organisation were searching for a new boss for the AEF at Boscombe Down. Apparently HQ Air Cadets had not been overwhelmed with applicants.

'Now you're back this side of the pond, old chap, why don't you apply?' Martin asked.

'Don't be silly, Martin, I'm living in France,' I replied, not a little baffled.

'I know that, Mike, but it's not far from the ferry port at Portsmouth to Boscombe. Couldn't you manage to commute weekly and live in the Mess?' he postulated.

'I'm not sure that I'd be left with any money if I did that – the ferry fares from here to there aren't cheap, you know; especially in the summer,' I explained.

'Well, if you get the job you'll be a full-time Reservist at the rank of flight lieutenant. That means that you will receive the maximum salary for the rank, the full rate of flying pay and you'll still get your wing commander's pension. That's quite a pay packet.' He was sounding more and more like an earnest recruiting officer!

'Are you sure, Martin?' I asked. 'I thought there were laws that stopped you getting pay and a pension for the same job at the same time.'

'I'm positive, mate,' he said, 'because that's what I'm getting – pay for this job and my pension every month.'

'OK,' I said, 'I'll talk to Linda about it and look at how it might be achievable. But I've got to get the job first. Who do I call?'

Martin gave me the name and telephone number of the man at HQ Air Cadets, at RAF Cranwell, that I would need to call. Linda and I talked over all the pros and cons that we could think of. Flying until I was 60, or even 65, was a very attractive prospect, but that was me being selfish! In the end I decided to put my name forward for the appointment and then organise the details if I got selected.

After telephone and email exchanges it became clear that their choice was limited to one applicant – me. *I've been here before!* I thought. I went to the UK and Cranwell for two days of interviews, medical examinations and paperwork filling. Everything except one item was fine. My initial blood pressure reading was a bit high. I was told not to worry, go lie down for ten minutes and it would be taken again. If it was then acceptable no more would be said. After the pleasant lie down a friendly and cheerful medic came in and took my blood pressure again. The machine gave a readout on a piece of paper, like a till receipt. It had been hot in the room and the window adjacent to the couch was wide open. The medic put the paper on the windowsill and, as he stowed the blood-pressure machine, away the till receipt disappeared in a gust of wind.

'Take it again,' I said.

'No need – I'll write it in your dossier,' was the reply.

The next morning was the final interview and summary of the medical exams. I expected to be given a suitable aircrew medical category. However, the rather severe-looking senior medical officer looked at my file and said, 'Your blood pressure is too high.'

'Yes, it was initially,' I said, 'but it was fine when it was taken again.'

'Well, there's only one reading down here and that's too high,' came the stern response. My friendly medic must have forgotten to record the second reading.

Now what?

It transpired that the need for me to be in post overrode the medics. The compromise was that I would be provisionally 'hired' subject to wearing a blood-pressure monitor for twenty-four hours. However, there was a considerable waiting time to get my turn to use one – I found it astonishing that the NHS couldn't afford more than two for the whole military section of Peterborough hospital. I offered to source one in France and get the results sent to the doctors there. That was an idea too full of initiative and imagination and, as such, was doomed to failure!

Eventually I got the call to back to the UK and Peterborough Hospital to be fitted with the machine. We stayed with friends overnight and returned the following day for the readouts to be downloaded. Then it was back to France and wait some more. At least HM the Queen had paid for the tickets!

Eventually I received the news that I would be commissioned in January and I was to report to RAF Cranwell on 26 January to undertake No. 164 AEF Commanders' Course with the Central Flying School's Tutor Squadron. The Tutor was the name that had been given by the RAF to the German-built Grob G115. This aircraft was the winner of a competition to provide aircraft for the RAF, university air squadrons and AEFs. The irony for me was that the beaten competitor was the British-built Slingsby T67 M260 Firefly.

During a few days of much déjà vu, taking me back forty years to my first days in the RAF, I was issued with all my service clothing and flying equipment, including an aircrew watch, and measured by the station tailor for a new No. 1 Uniform. It was odd to be walking round the station as a flight lieutenant again, watching out for squadron leaders and wing commanders to salute.

The training unit was a couple of miles from my accommodation in the York House Officers' Mess, so I had to drive there in my little Renault Twingo car. I was often in the company of other CFS students undertaking their long course to become qualified flying instructors (QFIs) with UASs or at the preliminary flying training unit just down the road at RAF Barkston Heath.

The CFS Tutor squadron was a descendant of D Flight of No. 3 Squadron CFS, the unit at RAF Little Rissington on which I had first acquired my own instructional qualification. I had also spent two years back there teaching others to become QFIs.[1] Although in a different location, the atmosphere in the crewroom was nostalgically similar and I was pleasantly surprised to see, after more than thirty years, a couple of my own framed cartoons still decorating the walls. In another link to my past, after I passed through in 2002, the unit assumed the number plate of the first squadron on which I served – No. 16.

The Grob G115 is, like the Firefly, made of composite materials construction with a sprung-steel conventional undercarriage. With its curvaceous shaping, it is a nicer looking aircraft than the Slingsby trainer, but it did not look as sturdy – a quality needed in the role. The seating arrangement is the same side-by-side layout, except that unlike in the Firefly the student sits on the left. Sitting height is adjusted by using cushions. The cockpit is typical for the aircraft's class, with contemporary instrumentation, radios and navigation aids, including a GPS with a rudimentary map. The sliding cockpit canopy allows for a good field of view all round and getting in and out is easy – important when dealing with air cadets. The Grob G115 has a Lycoming 0-360, putting out 180hp and driving a three-bladed propeller.

The Grob was taken into RAF service to operate under Private Finance Initiative (PFI) arrangements with a civilian contractor who maintains ownership of the fleet, as well as providing all the engineering support. In 2002 that company was Babcock Engineering. So, while carrying

---

1.  See *Follow Me Through* by this author (The History Press, 2013).

RAF roundels, the aircraft are all civilian registered, but flown under MOD regulations.

After a couple of days spent learning about the Tutor's technical bits, sitting in the cockpit learning the checks, practising emergency bale-outs, and reading my way into the operating manual, it was time to get airborne. My instructor was to be Sqn Ldr Jim Gardiner, a relaxed and likeable sort of chap who didn't insist on me calling him 'sir'. I did tell him that I had flown the Tutor before. He was surprised and wondered where and when. I teasingly said that it was the aircraft that this modern machine was named after – the 1930s vintage Avro Tutor.[2]

My first flight in the little white plastic aeroplane was on Tuesday, 5 February 2002. I hadn't flown in anything for well over a year, and that was in a civilian Hunter in Arizona! However, once I had stumbled my way through the pre-start checks and got the little motor running I felt more at home. On the move the Tutor was similar to most low-winged light aircraft – easy to steer and control. After the normal engine run-up and magneto checks we were cleared for departure. I lined up on the runway, applied full throttle and we set off down the runway at a respectable pace. Weighing around 2,000lb, it gave a reasonably good power-to-weight ratio for its class. There was a need to offset the torque of the engine with rudder, but not much – nowhere near as much as in the Firefly.

A slight pull on the stick at 55 knots was enough to raise the nose and the aircraft flew off the ground cleanly at about 60 knots and soon accelerated in a shallow climb to the climbing speed of 80 knots. Once settled the Tutor climbed at about 1,000ft per minute and needed a small rudder force to keep it going straight. It was easy to trim in pitch, and it appeared to be nicely stable.

During this first sortie there was a lot to absorb: local radio and airspace procedures, visual and radio navigation cues, general handling, aerobatics and stalling. As we cruised around at 120 knots the Tutor gave me a favourable impression and I continued to compare it with the Slingsby Firefly. It flew much more like the M200 version than the M260 and, as such, was nicely set up as an elementary trainer. The lower powered engine reduced the Tutor's

2.   Avro Tutor G-AHSA belonging to the Shuttleworth Trust.

comparative climb rate by 30 per cent and that would affect its training productivity. The airframe maximum speed limit of 185 knots was 10 knots slower than the Firefly's but the +6 to -3g limits were the same.

The Tutor's stalling speeds were between 50 and 60 knots depending on the flap setting. I did like the fact that the flaps were selected electrically. Most normal aerobatics could be accomplished from 130 knots using 3–4g and slow rolls were their usual tricky selves needing more practice at control coordination. I made a mental note to get lots of practice in on my solo flights. The full aileron roll rate of about 100 degrees per second was much better than the Firefly's 60 degrees per second. Also, like the Firefly, the Tutor's engine was equipped with an oil system that continued to work correctly under negative-g conditions. I did several spins and they proved utterly predictable and easy to recover from.

The Tutor glides at 80 knots giving a descent rate of about 1,000ft per minute. Hence my planning for a practice forced landing from 5,000ft had to be smart enough to allow me to fly to the correct position, pointing in the right direction over my chosen landing area. Another thing I needed to practise more later! Back at Cranwell I soon picked up the correct positioning for flying decent circuit patterns. The half flap limit speed of 125 knots and the full flap limit of 110 knots (incidentally the same as the Jet Provost) gave plenty of latitude for selection. With full flap down and the speed at 80 knots, reducing to 70 knots on the final approach the Tutor was nicely controllable and easy to trim. Touchdowns in the right place after rounding out from 60 knots were also easy to achieve. This was a delightful little aeroplane and I was looking forward to flying it with cadets.

But my job also including teaching the volunteer AEF pilots to fly it and doing regular check flights on them. So, after sixteen sorties, during which I had gained my instrument rating, I had to swap seats and play instructor. A lot of deeply buried instructional technique and verbiage was dragged out from distant brain cells and Jim played the dumb student very well. By the middle of March I had flown my last flight at CFS.

I drove the long road south to Portsmouth to catch the ferry home and wondered how it would be to go back to Boscombe Down for the fourth time – and as a flight lieutenant again. The last time I had been there in that rank had been 1975 – twenty-seven years ago!

I arrived back at what felt like my alma mater to the expected and absolutely normal reception of reams of paperwork to be completed to get a pass, be able to eat in the Mess, drive the car with which I would be issued, and do just about anything other than sleep. I eventually found my way to the unit I was to run, which was styled No. 2 AEF (out of twelve nationally). The AEF was located in the vast Weighbridge Hangar at the north-east end of the acres of concrete that was Boscombe Down's main parking area. The upper floor on the south side of the hangar was the domain of not only the AEF but also Southampton University Air Squadron (SUAS). The offices and the aircraft were shared between the two units.

First I met with the man who had been waiting impatiently for my arrival, Sqn Ldr Sid Adcock. He was welcoming and we started the handover straight away. Sid would be staying on the AEF as a pilot, so I would have his expertise to call on should I need it. The set-up was pretty simple. The only permanent member of staff on the AEF was the boss. The ops support came from the UAS and the servicing was civilian. The twenty-four pilots I had to fulfil the task of flying the cadets from allocated schools and Air Training Corps squadrons were all volunteers. About two-thirds of them were retired, ex-military pilots, mostly now flying for airlines; these guys held RAF Volunteer Reserve (RAFVR) commissions, normally in the rank of flying officer. The other third were serving military pilots on ground tours. The requirements for currency were the same for all and Sid explained that keeping a record of that was paramount. Each pilot had to fly a check flight annually and currency checks if their currency lapsed. Those checks were all my responsibility, as was the conversion to type of all new pilots. The turnover amongst the RAFVR pilots was relatively low, but the serving military, as is normal, often moved on to locations too far away. Sid showed me the lists of applicants still waiting for a place; it was surprisingly long.

There was a lot of administration connected with all this, and with maintaining contact with our many customers. Again the only man in the office to do it all would be me. *Would there be time for flying?* I wondered. While I was doing my training I had met an old friend who had run an AEF for many years; he imparted the following pearl of wisdom: 'The job's easy – it's the interruptions that are difficult!'

But it was only a couple of days before Sid and I had completed the transfer of command and he had left me to meet the first bunch of air cadets. Some things I left as they were, some others I changed. I particularly wanted the young people to get a better understanding of the pilots they might fly with. I made a rogues' gallery of photographs to put on display in the cadets' crewroom. At the daily introductory briefing I would give a quick summary of the flying background of each pilot on the schedule for the day.

When it came to me I used to say, 'I've now been flying for over forty years and I'm starting to get the hang of it – so those of you flying with me should be okay.'

The working week for AEFs has to match the availability of the cadets and their responsible adults. As we served ATC squadrons, whose members went to day schools, and CCF cadets from boarding schools, the best compromise was to work a Wednesday to Sunday week. However, during the major school holidays we would revert to the conventional Monday to Friday.

The normal pattern was that we would fly four or five consecutive twenty-minute trips for the cadets – the number being dictated by how much fuel was left in the tanks. Most cadets would ask to experience aerobatics, whereas a few would request that aerobatics be avoided. We could let them try flying the aircraft and some of the more experienced and senior cadets were good at it. However, we were banned, at least officially, from letting them attempt landings.

The Tutor was just about ideal for the job and the location at Boscombe Down was good for sightseeing, especially at the weekends, which were our busiest times. The mysterious megaliths of Stonehenge and the ancient town and castle of Old Sarum were only a couple of minutes' flying time away. Further to the south-west was a whole series of huge badges, mostly regimental, cut into the white subsoil of the ridge of hills, along the top of which ran part of an ancient road – the Ridgeway – thought to have been in use for 5,000 years, connecting the south-west of England with London and the east.

During the normal working days I had to make sure that all the pilots gave priority to Boscombe Down-based air traffic whenever they could. This could make it difficult to fulfil our target to fly every cadet that had turned up. It was difficult for some of the jets to mix it in the visual circuit pattern with our little 'puddle-jumpers' and their relatively slow speed. After a busy three days trying to fit ourselves in with Tornados, Jaguars, Harriers, Nimrods and all the ETPS jets, the weekends were bliss! We had the total freedom of the skies, although that was when all the local private pilots got airborne – thinking that they too had the freedom of the skies.

Domestically I had discovered that I could leave my Twingo in the car park at HMS *Excellent*, which wasn't a ship, but the Royal Naval shore establishment on Whale Island, a ten-minute walk from the ferry terminal at Portsmouth. Not only was it free but I had to leave my car keys at the guardroom, so relieving me of the nightmare scenario of arriving back in the UK having left the keys at home in France. Well done, navy! But the real bonus was that I could now travel as a foot passenger which, while not being steerage class, was much cheaper than taking the car every week. It just meant that Linda had to do a lot more driving at the other end.

It was a wonderful experience to be able to give back to the youngsters what I had received as an air cadet over forty years earlier. While not all were enthusiastic (and some had tasted their meals twice) the general level of enthusiasm and appreciation made it all worthwhile. It was also great to be back at Boscombe Down and see senior management and leadership positions were now being filled by guys who were students or junior test pilots the last time I was there. One of these was Gp Capt Laurie Hilditch, who was occupying the Chief Test Pilot's Office when I arrived. During my last tour Laurie and his wife Margaret lived in the house opposite ours on the married patch. Laurie was a then a flight lieutenant fighter pilot on a ground tour with the Central Trials and Tactics Organisation (CTTO). One day he asked me about becoming a test pilot.

'What do you think my chances of selection are?' he asked. 'What do I need to know?'

'You need to know a lot of stuff, Laurie. But the really important thing is your sense of curiosity,' I replied. 'You know that annual aviation quiz that appears in *Flight International* magazine, don't you?' He said that he did.

'Well, if you can score above average in that then you're on the right track.'

At first he appeared a bit non-plussed. I told him to think about it: the quiz covers many topics within the wide expanse that is aviation. If a chap has the wide-ranging knowledge to answer at least half of the questions correctly then he probably has the capacity to absorb all he needs to know, not only to get selected but to do well as a test pilot. Laurie was, of course, selected and went to the US Navy Test Pilots' School, where he was a distinguished graduate, and hadn't looked back since. It was a real pleasure to walk into his office and give him my best salute.

Laurie Hilditch's successor was Andy Young, who had been a squadron leader fast-jet test pilot during my previous incarnation at Boscombe Down. There was to be a formal dinner night to celebrate the Scottish eating and drinking festival that they call Burns Night. Andy's Scottish heritage meant that he was going to act as President for the occasion. I received a telephone call from him.

'Hello Mike, are you going to be at the Burns Night revels?' he said, as a perfectly harmless opener I thought. However, he went on, 'When were you commissioned as a flight lieutenant again?'

Wondering why he would want to know, I told him.

'Good. I was looking for the most junior officer attending so that he can be the Vice President [always known as Mr Vice in military parlance]. Congratulations – it's you.'

I laughed and could instantly see the irony, secretly looking forward to it. Mr Vice's duty starts after the meal is over, the table is pretty well cleared and the port has been passed. The President gains everyone's attention with a rap of his gavel, stands and says, 'Mr Vice – the Queen.' Everyone rises and waits until Mr Vice announces the Loyal Toast.

On this occasion Andy, no doubt remembering previous times we had dined formally together in the Boscombe Down Officers' Mess, when I was President of the Mess Committee (PMC) and he was just another diner, he added the words, 'I've been looking forward to this all evening' before 'Mr Vice – the Queen'.

During the 'natural break' after the toast I was, with lots of other chaps, in the gent's loo. Our boyish Senior ATC Officer shouted out, 'How long is it since you've done that, Mike?'

'How old are you?' I asked.

'Thirty-six,' he replied.

'Well, I was last Mr Vice when you were three.' Cue lots of raucous laughter.

In late October 2002, following my six-monthly medical examination, I received some unwelcome news. The doctor announced that she thought I had become diabetic. I was immediately grounded pending further tests and a decision from higher medical authority. The upshot was that I did indeed have mild type 2 diabetes and that I could contain it with medication and diet. So not so much red wine with my meals and cut down on the carbs. I didn't eat sweet stuff, and never had, so that was easy. My father and grandfather had both become type 2 diabetic in their later years and, as I was headed towards 60, I supposed that it was now my turn.

But the worst outcome was that the RAF rules stated that I could no longer fly solo or without a pilot qualified on type with me. That meant no more flying with cadets, no more grabbing an aircraft for a session of aerobatics on my own – would they let me stay in the appointment, I wondered. The answer to that was 'yes' because a large part of the job was flying checks on my twenty-four pilots. I had two other instructional qualified pilots, so I could use them to do the first two sorties with any new pilots and I could take over once they had flown solo and thus 'qualified on type'. So it perhaps was not too bad. However, it did firm up my decision to quit when I reached the age of 60, in April 2004.

My long-distance commuting carried on and the routine of AEF life continued unabated. The interruptions kept coming and I built up a good relationship not only with my own staff, but with the staff and students of the UAS and the officers of the Air Cadet units that were our 'regulars'. The test-flying business went on around us and I mostly kept well out of the way. However, chatting to test pilots old and new at happy hour on Friday evenings was always a pleasure, and it was great to be able to keep in touch with some of the latest developments. I tried hard, but often failed, not to tell them how it was 'in my day' – classic boring old f★★★!

I also became involved with the newly formed ETPS Association and joined the committee that got this social instrument for past graduates going. I took on the role of social secretary and arranged several functions before I left.

As I neared the end of my tour I had a yen to fly one more time in a jet. ETPS had the only Dassault/Dornier Alphajets operating in the UK and I had not flown one before. My old friend and colleague from two previous tours at Boscombe, John Thorpe, had retired from the RAF and was now a civilian tutor on ETPS. So, shamelessly playing on our close friendship, I enquired as to the likelihood of him getting clearance for me to fly with him in an Alphajet.

'Leave it with me, Brookie,' he said. 'I don't see a problem, but I need to get the OK from he who must be obeyed.' He was referring to the aforesaid CTP, Andy Young, who was doing the job that John himself had done about a decade before.

An affirmative answer came within the week and John set up a flight on 17 March. A few days before that John gave me an aide-memoire that the staff and students used when flying the Alphajet. I also was given a reminder of the ejection seat drills and fitted for an anti-g suit.

On the day of the flight we met up and I was surprised to find that John had arranged for us to be photographed, not only on the ground but in the air as well.

'Well, mate, if this is going to be your last ever flight as a fast-jet pilot you might as well have something to remember it by,' John explained. He could obviously still pull a few strings even if he was a civvie!

We walked round the chic, bijou French jet together. It really was an attractive aircraft with lines reminiscent of a dolphin. I climbed into the front cockpit, checked the Martin Baker ejection seat and sat down to strap in. It was all pretty familiar so far. The cockpit was like a small version of the Jaguar office, with many similar-looking gauges. John walked me through the checks and the engine start procedures. Like its big brother, the Jaguar, the Alpha has two engines. They are also bijou – two Turbomeca Larzac turbofans giving just less than 3,000lb of thrust each. At a take-off weight of around 11,000lb, the thrust-to-weight ratio is just less than half.

The engines started as advertised and we checked the moving bits of the wings and the airbrakes, which were left deployed at this stage, before we moved off. With our canopies latched slightly open, we headed down the taxiway, past the AEF, to the marshalling point. John ran through the pre-take-off checks and we were ready to go. I lined up, held the brakes on and advanced the small throttles to the stop. The engines wound up to max, all looked good, I released the brakes and the Alphajet accelerated faster than I had thought it would. John gave me a cue for easing the stick back, and at about 130 knots we were clear of the ground so I retracted the landing gear. At its climbing speed of 280 knots, the Alphajet gained altitude well – at about 10,000ft per minute. We were followed by a Jaguar, with ETPS tutor Justin Paine and a photographer on board.

We levelled off between cloud layers at about 8,000ft and the Jaguar formated[3] on us for a few minutes. I smiled for the camera.

'Right, your turn to formate on him,' said John. He took over just to get us in position and then gave control back to me. 'Off you go, Brookie – enjoy yourself.'

So I tried my best to. I had not flown in formation for years but it's like riding a bike – once you've got it you never lose the knack. After five minutes of mostly gentle manoeuvring John called the Jaguar to tell him that we would carry on alone and Justin broke away.

---

3. The word we used for flying in formation with or on another aircraft.

'Okay. Fill your boots – just ask if you need a reminder of anything, or if you lose control,' he joshed.

I started with full aileron rolls. It certainly went round quickly – almost 270 degrees per second – and it was easy to stop the roll precisely: very nice for the Patrouille de France aerobatic team! A loop from 350 knots with +5g went round very nicely, with a nice precision of control in pitch and a very useful buffet to let me know when I was getting close to the maximum lift angle of attack. Having a free hand, I threw a few aerobatics together, with a barrel roll followed by a half Cuban eight into a slow roll and then a big wingover. In maximum-rate turns at 360 knots there was definitely manoeuvre stability and a comfortable stick force per g; +6.5g was the maximum that I pulled and, although a bit out of practice at g-levels above +3, my anti-g suit did its work and I stayed awake.

I wanted to try a spin but the cloud structure didn't allow it, so John suggested that we descend and fly around at low level for a while. I told him that the navigation was up to him. I descended at 360 knots to 250ft above Somerset and accelerated to 420 knots. The little jet slipped easily along, the view from the cockpit was excellent and the fine French handling qualities made low-level flight a delight. I was, for the final time, back in my all time favourite aviation place – low and fast.

All good things must come to an end. There was still enough fuel for a few circuits back at base so I pulled up, headed east and called Boscombe Approach. John's wife Jenny was a controller at Boscombe and her dulcet tones came back at me. We set up to rejoin the visual pattern by a run-in and break from 420 knots. As we flew alongside the main runway I throttled the engines back and deployed the airbrakes, rolled to about 80 degrees of bank and pulled +5g. The speed soon bled off and as I rolled out downwind I retracted the airbrakes, dropped the gear at 200 knots and selected a few degrees of flap. Turning finals, I flew the angle of attack (AOA) rather than speed at 9 degrees and selected all the flap. The minimum speed was to be 115 knots on finals and I used the power to get myself on the right angle of approach. Over the end of the runway I slowly retarded the throttles and raised the nose, not to exceed 14 degrees AOA, and the Alphajet touched down nicely at about 100 knots. Delightful!

After a few more patterns John said that I ought to end with a flourish.

'What do you mean, JT?' I said.

'Go out to the initial point and run in at any speed and height you like,' he replied. 'You know, the sort of hooligan arrival that we would have not approved in our past.'

So I told the local controller that I was going back to initials and wound the little jet up to 550 knots. Running in towards that oh-so-familiar big runway, I descended to 300ft and kept the speed up. The break took us back up to 1,000ft and I came round the corner on speed and alpha in the Alphajet. Touchdown was passable and as we cleared the runway I thanked my friend John profusely for making my last jet flight so memorable. I silently thanked Monsieur Dassault and his brilliant test pilot, Jean-Marie Saget, for making the aircraft fly so well. I could not avoid comparison with the BAe Hawk and thought that, though it was a close-run thing, the Alphajet had the edge as a trainer for fighter pilots.

A month later I flew my final sortie with No. 2 AEF; the new CO of SUAS, also called Adcock, flew with me to make it legal. There was a nice symmetry in that my first flight had been with a Sqn Ldr Adcock – just a different one. I then spent a few days handing over to my successor, Sqn Ldr (shortly to be Flt Lt) Steve Jarmain, who had been one of my serving volunteer pilots and had now left the RAF. I also went through all the palaver of handing back kit and, yet again, my aircrew watch. The RAF must be the only company in the world that takes a timepiece off you on retirement, rather than giving you one!

I threw a final, final farewell party – now the fourth time I had left Boscombe Down. I held it on a Friday evening, initially in the all-ranks Harvard Club and then moved to the Officers' Mess to catch the remnants of happy hour. The next morning, not too early, I set off out of the gates to return to France and back to Civvie Street. As I did so, I remembered the day in June 1973, thirty-one years earlier, when John Thorpe and I had been through two gruelling days of interviews and exams to hopefully be selected as trainee test pilots.

'I don't know about you, Mike, but I don't think I'll be seeing that place again,' John mused, as I drove us up the hill and over the near horizon. I agreed with him. Sometimes in life you can get it so wrong!

# EPILOGUE

I was truly blessed to spend my life doing something for a living that I would have, if I could have afforded it, paid to do. From learning to fly gliders as a teenager to spending over twenty years as a test pilot, it has been a constantly fascinating working life. Admittedly there were times when I had hoped that things had worked out differently, but as I matured, and especially when I came to a living faith in God, I learnt that changes of plan and direction offer opportunities rather than disappointments.

I have thoroughly enjoyed sharing all these stories and experiences with you, my readers, even if it has taken four volumes to do so. That enjoyment has been vastly increased by the number of folk from my past, some from long ago, who have been in touch to tell me how much they have drawn vicariously from reliving some of their aviation experiences. There are also those wonderfully kind strangers who took the trouble to put good reviews on websites or send them to the publisher for onward transmission to me. Thank you all.

However, I still haven't told the whole story. In parallel with all the tales I've told over the past four years, so well presented by my publisher, has been another string to my aeronautical bow: display flying. I started that activity on my first squadron – those of you who have read *A Bucket of Sunshine* might recall that. Later I became a pilot with the Shuttleworth Collection and flew many of the historic flying machines that the collection keeps flying – from a 1910 Avro Triplane to the Supermarine Spitfire. I also flew in many air shows with the Harvard Team and Jet Heritage – both civilian organisations dedicated to keeping historic aircraft in the public arena, despite the enormous costs of doing so.

I know from much of the correspondence that I have received that these flying activities are also of great interest to many – the size of the crowds at air shows is testament to that. So I do hope that my next, and probably final, book will tell tales from these entries in my flying logbooks and the indelible memories that I still, thank God, have.

# APPENDIX 1

# AIRCRAFT I HAVE FLOWN

*Military Registered*
First Pilot or Captain

| Jet | Mark |
|---|---|
| BAC 1-11 | |
| BAe Jaguar | GR1, GR1A, T2, T2A |
| De Havilland Comet | 4C |
| De Havilland Vampire | T11 |
| English Electric Canberra | B2, PR3, T4, B6, B(I)6, PR7, B(I)8, PR9, SC9, T17, T17A, T19, T22 |
| English Electric Lightning | T4, T5 |
| Folland Gnat | T1 |
| Hawker Hunter | F6, F6A, T7, T8A, T8C, T8M, T12, FGA.9 |
| Hawker Siddeley Buccaneer | S2, S2B, S2C |
| Hawker Siddeley Nimrod | MR1, R1 |
| Hunting Jet Provost | T3, T4, T5, T5A |
| McDonnell Phantom | F4K, RF4C |

| Turboprop | Mark |
|---|---|
| Armstrong Whitworth Argosy | C1 |
| Hawker Siddeley Andover | C2 |
| Pilatus PC-9 | |

| Piston | Mark |
|---|---|
| Beagle Bassett | CC1 |
| DH Devon | C2 |
| DHC Chipmunk | T10 |
| Piper PA-31 Navajo Chieftain | |
| North American Harvard | 2B |
| Scottish Aviation Bulldog | T1 |
| Vickers Varsity | T1 |

| Helicopter | Mark |
|---|---|
| Aerospatiale Gazelle | HT1, HT2 |
| Westland Sea King | HAS 1, HC 4, HAS 5 |
| Westland Wessex | HAS1, 2, 3, 5 |
| Westland Whirlwind | T10 |

## Gliders
Slingsby Cadet Mark 3
Slingsby Sedbergh
Slingsby Prefect


Under Instruction or Second Pilot

| Jet | Mark |
|---|---|
| Aermacchi | MB-339 |
| Boeing | KC-135 |
| Dassault | Alphajet |
| Douglas Skyhawk | TA-4D |
| General Dynamics | F-111D |
| Gloster Meteor | T7, NF11 |
| Hawker Harrier | T4 |
| Hawker Siddeley | 125 |
| Lockheed | F-104 Starfighter |
| McDonnell | F-15 Eagle |
| North American | T2J-1 Buckeye |
| Northrop | T-38 Talon |
| Panavia Tornado | F2A |
| Republic | T-33 |

| Turboprop | Mark |
|---|---|
| Aeritalia | G222 |
| DHC | Buffalo |
| Embraer | EMB-27 Tucano |
| FMA | IA 58 Pucara |
| Lockheed Hercules | C1, W2 |
| Nord | 262 |
| Shorts Tucano | T1 |
| Vickers Viscount | |

| Piston | Mark |
|---|---|
| Avro Shackleton | MR2 |
| DHC Beaver | AL1 |
| DH Sea Devon | |
| Douglas DC-3 Dakota | |
| Hawker Sea Fury | TT20 |
| SIAI Marchetti | SF 260 |

| Helicopter | Mark |
|---|---|
| Aerospatiale/Westland Puma | HC1 |
| Augusta Bell HB 204 | |
| Bell AH1 Huey Cobra | |
| Boeing Chinook | HC1 |
| McDonnell Douglas AH-64A Apache | |
| Sikorsky UH 60A Blackhawk | |
| Westland Lynx | AH 1 |
| Westland Scout | |

## Civil Registered
First Pilot or Captain

## Jet
Hunting Strikemaster

| Piston | Mark |
|---|---|
| Aeronca Champ | |
| Avro Triplane (replica) | |
| Avro Tutor | |
| BA Swallow | |
| Beagle Pup | |
| BN Islander | |
| Boeing Stearman | |
| Bristol FE 2B Fighter | |
| CAP 10 | |
| Cessna 150 | |
| Cessna 152 | |

Cessna 172
Cessna 210T
DH 51
DH 60 Gipsy Moth
DH 60 Cirrus Moth
DH 60 Hermes Moth
DH 82A Tiger Moth
DH 87 Hornet Moth
DH 94 Moth Minor
Diamond Katana DV 20
Glos Airtourer 100
Gloster Gladiator
Grob G109
Grob 115E Tutor
Hawker Hind
Hawker Tomtit
Jodel 1050
Miles ME2 Hawk Speed VI
Miles Magister
Nanchang CJ-6
Parnell Elf
Percival Gull VI
Piper PA28-140 Cherokee
Piper Cub
SE.5a
SE.5 Replica
Slingsby Firefly T-67A, T-67M, T-67M 200, T-67M 260
Supermarine Spitfire Vc

**Helicopter**
Bell 206 Jetranger 2

**Glider**
LET L-13 Blanik
Schneider Grunau Baby 3
Scheibe Spatz B

Under Instruction or Second Pilot

## Jet
VFW 614

## Piston
Auster AOP 9
Auster Aiglet
Beech 19A Musketeer
Beech S-35 Bonanza
Beech 58 Baron
Beech 76 Duchess
Blackburn B2
BN Firecracker
Boeing B17G
CAB GY-20 Minicab
Cessna 406 Caravan II
Dornier Do 228
Embraer EMB 25
Flexwing Microlight
Mooney 20E
Percival Provost T1
Piper PA 23 Apache
Piper PA 28 Tomahawk
Piper PA 30 Twin Comanche
Rutan Varieze
Scottish Aviation Twin Pioneer
Socata TB 10
Trago Mills SAH 1
Zlin Trener

## Turboprop
Cessna 208 Caravan
DHC Dash 7
Dornier 228
SA Jetstream
Shorts SD 330

**Helicopter**
Augusta A 109
Robinson R22

# APPENDIX 2

# GLOSSARY

| | |
|---|---|
| A&AEE | Aircraft and Armament Experimental Establishment |
| AAR | Air-to-Air Refuelling |
| ADC | Aide-de-Camp |
| AEF | Air Experience Flight |
| AEO | Air Electronics Officer |
| AEW | Airborne Early Warning |
| Air Cdre | Air Commodore (RAF one-star rank = brigadier) |
| AOA | Angle of Attack |
| ASI | Airspeed indicator |
| ATC | Air Traffic Control |
| ATF | Air Transport Flight (at RAE Farnborough) |
| AWACS | Airborne Warning and Control System |
| BAC | British Aircraft Corporation |
| BAe | British Aerospace |
| BBMF | Battle of Britain Memorial Flight |
| BMEWS | Ballistic Missile Early Warning System |
| CAA | Civil Aviation Authority |
| CBT | Command Briefing Team |
| CCF | Combined Cadet Force |
| CDE | Chemical Defence Establishment |
| CEO | Chief Executive Officer |
| CFS | Central Flying School |
| CG | Centre of gravity |
| CHT | Cylinder Head Temperature |
| C-in-C | Commander-in-Chief |
| CINCUKAIR | NATO title of the C-in-C of RAF Strike Command |
| COEF | Commanding Officer Experimental Flying (at RAE Farnborough) |
| CPL | Commercial Pilot's Licence |
| CTP | Chief Test Pilot |
| CTTO | Central Tactics and Trials Organisation |
| DH | De Havilland |

| | |
|---|---|
| DHC | De Havilland Canada |
| DS | Directing Staff |
| EAP | (BAe) Experimental Aircraft Programme |
| ECM | Electronic Counter Measures |
| EE | English Electric |
| EFS | Experimental Flying Squadron (at RAE Farnborough) |
| EO | Electro-Optic |
| ERB | Executive Responsibility Budget |
| ETPS | Empire Test Pilots' School |
| FAA | Federal Aviation Authority |
| FADEC | Full Authority Digital Engine Control |
| FAST | Farnborough Air Sciences Trust Museum |
| FCC | Flying Control Committee (for air displays) |
| FI | Farnborough International (Air Show) |
| FLIR | Forward-Looking Infrared |
| Flt Lt | Flight Lieutenant (RAF rank = army captain) |
| ft | feet |
| FTE | Flight Test Engineer |
| FTO | Flight Test Observer |
| g | Force of gravity |
| GAPAN | Guild of Air Pilots and Navigators |
| Gp Capt | Group Captain (RAF rank = colonel) |
| GPS | Global Positioning System |
| GRP | Glass-Reinforced Plastic |
| HARM | High-speed Anti-Radiation Missile |
| HAS | Hardened Aircraft Shelter |
| HATS | Heavy Aircraft Test Squadron |
| HF | High Frequency (radio) |
| HMD | Helmet-Mounted Display |
| HMQ | Her Majesty the Queen |
| hp | horsepower |
| HUD | Head-Up Display |
| IAM | Institute of Aviation Medicine |
| ILS | Instrument Landing System |
| IR | Infrared |
| ITPS | International Test Pilots' School |
| JATE | Joint Air Transport Establishment |
| JP | Jet Provost (basic trainer) |

| | |
|---|---|
| KGB | Soviet Secret Service (*Komitet Gosudarstvennoy Bezopasnosti*) |
| lb | pounds weight/mass |
| LGB | Laser-Guided Bomb |
| LLTV | Low-Light Television |
| LOSSE | Line-of-Sight Stabilisation Equipment |
| m | metres |
| MBWA | Management By Walking About |
| mm | millimetre |
| MOD | Ministry of Defence (UK) |
| MODPE | Ministry of Defence Procurement Executive |
| mph | miles per hour |
| MRF | Meteorological Research Flight |
| NATO | North Atlantic Treaty Organisation |
| nm | mautical miles |
| NVG | Night-Vision Goggles |
| OC | Officer Commanding |
| OCU | Operational Conversion Unit *and* Officers' Christian Union |
| OGL | Open Government Licence |
| OHP | Overhead Projector |
| PA | Personal Assistant |
| psi | pounds per square inch |
| PSO | Personal Staff Officer |
| QCS | Queen's Colour Squadron (of the RAF Regiment) |
| QFI | Qualified Flying Instructor |
| RAE | Royal Aircraft Establishment |
| RAF | Royal Air Force |
| RAFSKTU | Royal Air Force Sea King Training Unit |
| RCAF | Royal Canadian Air Force |
| RFC | Royal Flying Corps |
| RIV | Rapid Intervention Vehicle |
| RNAS | Royal Naval Air Station |
| rpm | revolutions per minute |
| RR | Rolls-Royce (aircraft engine manufacturer) |
| RSAF | Royal Saudi Air Force |
| RWTS | Rotary Wing Test Squadron |
| SACEUR | Supreme Allied Commander in Europe (NATO) |
| SATCO | Senior Air Traffic Control Officer |

| | |
|---|---|
| SBAC | Society of British Aircraft Constructors |
| SETP | Society of Experimental Test Pilots |
| Sqn Ldr | Squadron Leader (RAF rank = major) |
| TACAN | Tactical Air Navigation (equipment) |
| TAP | TIALD Accelerated Programme |
| TIALD | Thermal Imaging and Laser Designation |
| UHF | Ultra-High Frequency (radio) |
| UOR | Urgent Operational Requirement |
| USAF | United States Air Force |
| Wg Cdr | Wing Commander (RAF rank = lieutenant colonel) |
| WO | Warrant Officer (RAF rank = sergeant major) |

# INDEX

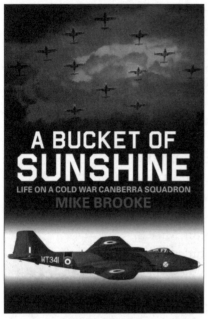
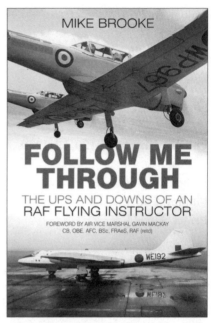
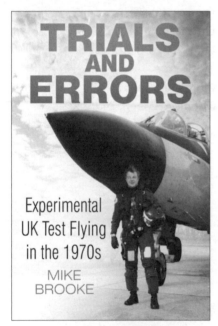
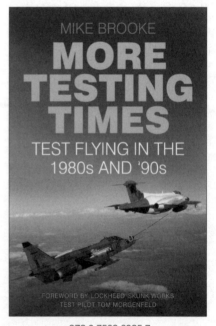